# Gateways™

# Practice Book

## Program Authors

Action Learning Systems, Inc.

**Robin Scarcella, Ph.D., Hector Rivera, Ph.D., and Mabel Rivera, Ph.D.**
English Language Development

**Isabel L. Beck, Ph.D. and Margaret McKeown, Ph.D.**
Vocabulary

**Penny Chiappe-Collins, Ph.D.**
Decoding

Steck Vaughn™

HOUGHTON MIFFLIN HARCOURT
Supplemental Publishers

www.SteckVaughn.com
800-531-5015

Steck-Vaughn *Gateways, Practice Book, Volume 1*

ISBN 10: 1-4190-5659-X
ISBN 13: 978-1-4190-5659-8



If you have received these materials as examination copies free of charge, HMH Supplemental Publishers Inc. retains title to the materials and they may not be resold.  Resale of examination copies is strictly prohibited and is illegal.

Possession of this publication in print format does not entitle users to convert this publication, or any portion of it, into electronic format.

1 2 3 4 5 6 7 8 170 15 14 13 12 11 10 09 08

# Unit 1: How was life for teenagers of the past different from today?



**CHAPTER 1** **Teens in Modern Times**



**CHAPTER 2** **19th Century Living**



**CHAPTER 3** **Growing Up in the 1700s**

## STEP **1** Making Connections

{DONE ✔}

I will connect what I already know to a photograph. I will discuss the essential question, *How was life for teenagers of the past different from today?*

## STEP **2** Developing Vocabulary

I will understand the purpose of the Developing Vocabulary step.
I will learn how to participate in a word chat.

## STEP **3** Practicing Fluency

I will understand the process and structure of the fluency lesson.

## STEP **4** Building Word Study Skills

I will learn five high-frequency words.
I will learn about words with closed syllables.
I will understand the spelling homework assignment.

## STEP **5** Reading for Understanding

I will learn the narrative genre.
I will learn to use the strategy of on-the-surface reading.

## STEP **6** Applying the Conventions of English

I will learn about singular and plural nouns.
I will identify and use simple subjects in my speaking, reading, and writing.

## STEP **7** Writing with Purpose

I will investigate the five stages of the writing process.
I will deconstruct the narrative prompt and scoring guide.

{Summarizing My Learning}

_______________________________________________

_______________________________________________

# Timed Reading

## ROLE OF THE READER

Read the passage to your partner as accurately as possible.

Remember, your reading goal is 80 Words Correct Per Minute (WCPM).

## ROLE OF THE LISTENER

As your partner reads, mark these errors with a strikethrough:

- mispronounced words
- skipped words
- changed words
- added words

Excerpt from
## Looking Up

| | Number of Words |
|---|---|
| It was the first day of school. Students were coming in for the | 13 |
| start of classes. There was so much excitement. People moved | 23 |
| everywhere. Teachers said hello to their students. Friends waved, | 32 |
| talked, and laughed with each other. | 38 |
| Maria was by herself. She was walking slowly down the crowded | 49 |
| hallway on crutches. "Two days before school starts," she thought. | 59 |
| "Just my luck." Maria spent her summer at basketball camp. It was | 71 |
| a great summer, but on the last day Maria broke her leg during a | 85 |
| game. | 86 |
| Now she was back at school and having a hard time getting | 98 |
| used to the crutches. She needed all of her time and energy just | 111 |
| to walk to class. There was no time to catch up with friends or | 125 |
| teammates. | 126 |

Words Per Minute
↓

Errors
↓

Words Correct Per Minute
↓

[ ] − [ ] = [ ]

# Unit 1 High-Frequency Word List

| | | | | |
|---|---|---|---|---|
| books | even | already | eat | park |
| said | where | care | out | yes |
| above | you | here | please | say |
| doing | cannot | idea | pretty | want |
| kept | find | ate | enough | after |
| feel | called | word | ride | story |
| make | see | having | this | fly |
| no | into | without | short | went |
| add | my | told | that | from |
| come | came | have | soon | give |
| boot | away | like | there | her |
| was | two | must | how | when |
| a lot | little | old | with | some |
| saw | one | new | under | think |
| are | down | now | they | giving |
| to | getting | take | well | won't |
| look | funny | of | too | just |
| himself | help | our | need | open |

# Words of the Day

—— —— —— ——   —— —— ——   —— —— —— ——

—— —— —— —— ——

---

# Alphabetical Order

Write the words in alphabetical order.

| books | said | above | doing | kept |

1. ______ ______ ______ ______
2. ______ ______ ______ ______
3. ______ ______ ______ ______
4. ______ ______ ______
5. ______ ______ ______

# Closed Syllable Practice

Read the words in the box. Circle five words that have a closed syllable.

| blue | my | moth | play | sent |
|------|-----|------|------|------|
| ask | clip | too | stand | be |

Identify the closed syllables in the list of words. Say each word and draw a division line between the syllables. Then, underline the ending consonant and circle the vowel sound in the closed syllable.

1. city

2. into

3. happy

4. brittle

5. lesson

# Apply It

Read the paragraph below about an admirable woman. As you read, find words with closed syllables. Circle eight closed syllables.

American Laura Jan Adams (1860–1935) won the Nobel Peace Prize in 1931. When she lost her dad, she was very sad. After a time, Adams knew how she would heal—she would help others. After she visited a home for poor people run by students, she started Hull House in Chicago. She is considered the first social worker in this country.

# Spell It

| **Closed Syllable Spelling Rule** | A closed syllable ends with a consonant sound and only has one vowel sound. The vowel sound is usually short. |
| --- | --- |

1. _______________________________________

2. _______________________________________

3. _______________________________________

4. _______________________________________

5. _______________________________________

# Reading Tree

# Topic Introduction

**Text:** ________________________________________________

**Topic:** ________________________________________________

**Related Terms:**

1. ________________________________

2. ________________________________

3. ________________________________

4. ________________________________

5. ________________________________

6. ________________________________

7. ________________________________

8. ________________________________

9. ________________________________

10. ________________________________

**The term I know most about is:**

________________________________

**What I know:**

________________________________

________________________________

________________________________

________________________________

________________________________

________________________________

________________________________

________________________________

________________________________

________________________________

________________________________

# Summary Tree

**Text:** _______________________________________________

Where

When

Who

What Happened

**Summary**

# Singular and Plural Nouns

| **About Singular and Plural Nouns:** | • A noun is a word that names a person, place, thing, or idea.<br>• The subject of a sentence tells whom or what the sentence is about. A simple subject is the main word or word group that tells whom or what the sentence is about. The simple subject is part of the complete subject.<br>• A singular noun names one person, place, thing, or idea. Examples: *climber, mountain, owl, theory*<br>• A plural noun names more than one person, place, thing, or idea. Many nouns are made plural by adding an *–s.* Examples: *explorers, caves, bats, thoughts* |
| --- | --- |

## Nouns: Singular or Plural?

Read each sentence. Underline each noun and label it with an *S* for singular or *P* for plural above each noun. If the noun is also the simple subject of the sentence, circle it.

1. The book is on the table.

2. Three students won first place.

3. The movie is too long.

4. Students bring pencils on the first day of school.

## Find It in Your Reading

Choose three sentences from your reading that include both singular and plural nouns to write on the lines below. Underline each noun and label it with an *S* for singular or *P* for plural above each noun. If the noun is also the simple subject of the sentence, circle it.

1. ___________________________________________

2. ___________________________________________

3. ___________________________________________

## Put It in Your Writing

Write three sentences about things in your classroom. Underline each noun and label it with an *S* for singular or *P* for plural above each noun. If the noun is also the simple subject of the sentence, circle it. Check to make sure your sentences make sense.

1. ___________________________________________

2. ___________________________________________

3. ___________________________________________

{ DONE ✔ }

**STEP 1 Making Connections**

I will connect what I already know to the narrative "Esperanza Rising" by Pam Muñoz
Ryan and discuss how life for the teenagers in "Esperanza Rising" was different from today.

**STEP 2 Developing Vocabulary**

I will learn three new vocabulary words: *barren, demeanor,* and *disillusioned.*

**STEP 3 Practicing Fluency**

I will read aloud part of "Rounding a Corner" by Joy Nelson with accuracy and pacing.
I will learn how to determine fluency scores.

**STEP 4 Building Word Study Skills**

I will learn five new high-frequency words.
I will learn about words with open syllables.
I will understand the spelling homework assignment.

**STEP 5 Reading for Understanding**

I will review the strategy of on-the-surface reading.
I will learn to use the strategy of under-the-surface reading.

**STEP 6 Applying the Conventions of English**

I will learn about articles.
I will identify and add articles to form a complete subject in my speaking, reading, and writing.

**STEP 7 Writing with Purpose**

I will review the stages of the writing process.
I will review the narrative prompt.
I will begin prewriting using *Topic Toss.*

{ Summarizing My Learning }

# Hidden Clues

Read the clues for each number. Write the correct vocabulary word under each clue. The letters in the boxes will complete the answer to the question at the bottom of the page.

1. Gabriel did not like the movie as much as he thought he would.

___ ___ ___ ___ ___ [1] ___ ___ ___ ___ ___ ___ ___

2. Raquel was always nice to everyone.

___ ___ ___ ___ ___ [2] ___ ___ ___

3. Not much can live in the dry desert.

___ ___ ___ [3] ___ ___

4. The cookie looked very good to Tommy, but it tasted very bad.

[4] ___ ___ ___ ___ ___ ___ ___ [5] ___ ___ ___ ___ ___ ___

5. Our school is empty at night.

___ [6] ___ ___ ___ ___

6. Paul pays attention to how he looks and acts when he meets someone new.

___ ___ ___ [7] ___ ___ ___ ___ ___

## Where did Esperanza and her mother go when they crossed the Mexican border?

The ___ ___ ___ i ___ t ___ ___ ___ ___ t ___ t ___ s ___
    1   2       3   4   5     6    7

| Vocabulary | barren | demeanor | disillusioned |

## Practice Reading Phrases

1. shuffle out of English class

2. brushed past one another

3. a single voice

4. As he walked

5. anything like them

## Practice Reading Sentences

1. Michael was the last student to shuffle out of English class.

2. Kids brushed past one another in the hall.

3. He didn't recognize a single voice.

4. As he walked, Michael reached into his new backpack.

5. No one here had anything like them.

## Timed Reading

{ **ROLE OF THE READER** }

Read the passage to your partner as accurately as possible.

Remember, your reading goal is 80 Words Correct Per Minute (WCPM).

{ **ROLE OF THE LISTENER** }

As your partner reads, mark these errors with a strikethrough:

- mispronounced words
- skipped words
- changed words
- added words

Excerpt from
## Rounding a Corner

| | Number of Words |
|---|---|
| Michael was the last student to shuffle out of English class. | 11 |
| He felt nervous as he looked around the unfamiliar school. His | 22 |
| family had just moved to Los Angeles. It was another new city | 34 |
| and another new school. Kids brushed past one another in the | 45 |
| hall. Their voices and laughter echoed in Michael's ears. He didn't | 56 |
| recognize a single voice. | 60 |
| As he walked, Michael reached into his new backpack. Hoping | 70 |
| to drown out the sounds of the noisy hallway, he clipped his MP3 | 83 |
| player to his belt and turned on his favorite song. "Everything is | 95 |
| new, new, new," he thought. His MP3 player and backpack were | 106 |
| must-have items at his old school. No one here had anything like | 118 |
| them. | 119 |
| Michael was worried. He didn't want to try to be like everyone | 131 |
| else, but he wanted badly to make friends. Starting over at a new | 144 |
| school was hard. He'd had to do so a few times already because | 157 |
| his dad's work sometimes forced his family to move. | 166 |

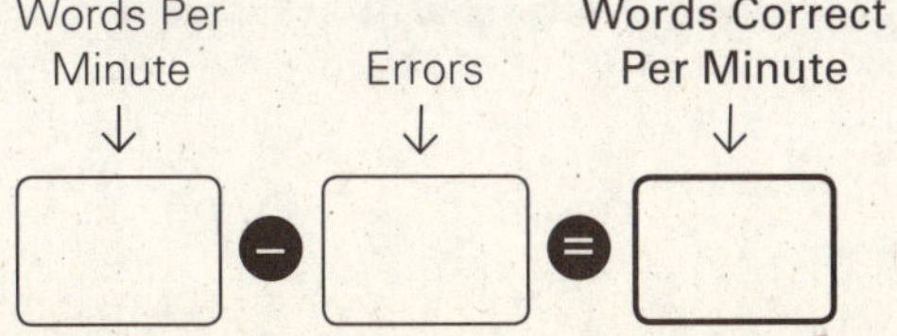

# High-Frequency Words

books    said    above    doing    kept

# Words of the Day

__ __ __ __ __    __ __ __ __    __ __

__ __ __ __    __ __ __ __

# Categorize

Write each word under the correct category.

feel    make    no    add    come

**End in *e***

1. _________________

2. _________________

**One Consonant Sound**

3. _________________

4. _________________

**Action Word**

5. _________________

6. _________________

7. _________________

8. _________________

**Two Letter Word**

9. _________________

# Open Syllable Practice

Read the words in the box. Circle five words that have an open syllable.

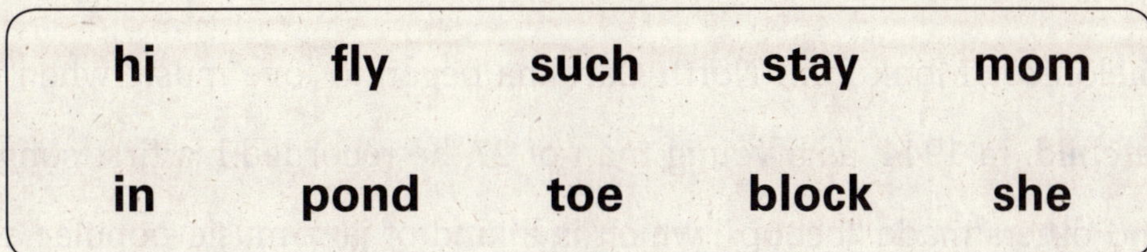


Identify the open syllables in the list of words. Say each word and draw a division line between the syllables. Then, underline the ending vowel sound in the open syllable.

1. **apron**

2. **open**

3. **April**

4. **final**

5. **music**

# Apply It

Read the paragraph below about an admirable musician. As you read, look for words with open syllables. Circle the open syllables.

Thelonious Monk from North Carolina began to love music when he was a child. In 1944, as a young man of 27, he recorded his first song. He and others made "bebop," which is a kind of jazz music popular all over the world.

# Spell It

| Open Syllable Spelling Rule | An open syllable ends in a single vowel sound. The vowel sound is usually long. |
| --- | --- |

1. _______________________________

2. _______________________________

3. _______________________________

4. _______________________________

5. _______________________________

## Rounding a Corner

*— Part 2 of 2*

Michael took the earphones out of his ears so he could talk to the boy. The boy leaned in closer when he heard the music blasting from the earphones of Michael's MP3 player.

"Hey," said the boy, "I love that song." He seemed surprised that Michael actually liked good music.

"Me, too," said Michael. "I saw this band in concert a few months before I moved here."

"I listen to these guys all the time. Did you know they are playing next weekend at the park? We'll all be there," the boy said, pointing to his friends.

"Maybe I'll see you there," said Michael.

### Notes

{ 1. What happened after the boy heard Michael's music? }

_________________________________

_________________________________

_________________________________

_________________________________

_________________________________

_________________________________

{ 2. Would Michael like to go to the park? }

_________________________________

_________________________________

_________________________________

_________________________________

_________________________________

_________________________________

_________________________________

_________________________________

_________________________________

Michael quickly stepped around the boy and walked a few steps before stopping to look at his map again. He asked another student for directions. Michael put his earphones back on and headed down the hall. This time he made a deliberate effort to watch where he was walking.

Later, as his science class let out, someone grabbed Michael's shoulder. Michael tensed up and turned around. It was the same boy from before. "Not again," Michael thought. He tried to think of a way out of the situation.

This time, though, the boy grinned. He reached out to shake Michael's hand. ⏸

## Notes

3. Why does Michael tense up when someone grabs his shoulder?

________________________

________________________

________________________

________________________

________________________

________________________

4. What does the boy do after he grabs Michael's shoulder?

________________________

________________________

________________________

________________________

________________________

________________________

________________________

________________________

________________________

"Hi," he said. "I'm Renaldo."

"My name is Michael. I'm new," Michael replied. "Shocking, right?"

"Well, anyone who likes good music is OK in my book," said Renaldo. "Come find me at lunch. My friends and I will show you around the school."

"Thanks," Michael said. "I will."

Michael breathed a sigh of relief. For the first time all day, he felt great. He stopped worrying what people would think of him, and he felt himself relaxing. "Maybe I'll have a life here after all," he thought. ⏸

{ **What is life like for teenagers of Michael's time?** }

## Notes

{ 5. What does Michael think about his new school at the end? }

___________________________

___________________________

___________________________

___________________________

___________________________

___________________________

___________________________

{ 6. Why does Renaldo offer to show Michael around the school? }

___________________________

___________________________

___________________________

___________________________

___________________________

___________________________

___________________________

___________________________

___________________________

___________________________

# Summary Tree

**Text:** ______________________________________________

1.

2.

3.

1.

2.

3.

Where

When

1.

2.

3.

1.

2.

3.

Who

What Happened

**Summary**

______________________________________________
______________________________________________
______________________________________________
______________________________________________

# Articles

| **About Articles:** | • Articles are the common adjectives *a, an,* and *the.*<br>• Articles modify nouns.<br>• Articles and nouns must agree in number.<br>• We use the singular article *a* before a singular noun that begins with a consonant sound. Example: *a deer*<br>• We use the singular article *an* before a singular noun that begins with a vowel sound.<br>• The article *the* can modify both singular and plural nouns. |
| --- | --- |

## Articles: Singular or Plural?

Read each sentence. Circle the articles and underline the nouns they modify. Write *S* for singular and *P* for plural above each noun.

1. A cat crossed the street.


2. The movie was funny.


3. An army of ants climbed up the walls.


4. The truth will come out soon.

# Find It in Your Reading

Write three sentences from the reading that contain articles. Circle the articles and underline the nouns they modify. Write *S* for singular or *P* for plural above each noun.

1. _________________________________________________

_________________________________________________

2. _________________________________________________

_________________________________________________

3. _________________________________________________

_________________________________________________

# Put It in Your Writing

Write three sentences about things you might see on a teacher's desk. Circle the articles in each sentence.

1. _________________________________________________

_________________________________________________

2. _________________________________________________

_________________________________________________

3. _________________________________________________

_________________________________________________

AGENDA

## STEP **1** Making Connections

{DONE ✔}

I will connect what I already know to the narrative "Esperanza Rising" by Pam Muñoz Ryan and discuss how life for teenagers in "Esperanza Rising" was different from today.

## STEP **2** Developing Vocabulary

I will learn three new vocabulary words: *aroma*, *conform*, and *looming*.

## STEP **3** Practicing Fluency

I will read aloud part of "Rounding a Corner" with a focus on accuracy and pacing.
I will learn how to chart my fluency progress.

## STEP **4** Building Word Study Skills

I will learn five new high-frequency words.
I will review my understanding of words with closed and open syllables.
I will understand the spelling homework assignment.

## STEP **5** Reading for Understanding

I will review the strategies of on-the-surface and under-the-surface reading.
I will learn to use the reading strategy of summarizing.

## STEP **6** Applying the Conventions of English

I will review my understanding of singular and plural nouns.
I will identify action verbs in the present tense in my speaking, reading, and writing.

## STEP **7** Writing with Purpose

I will review the stages of the writing process.
I will write my first draft using a narrative frame.

{Summarizing My Learning}

# Crossword Puzzle

Read the clues for each number. Write the correct vocabulary word on the puzzle.

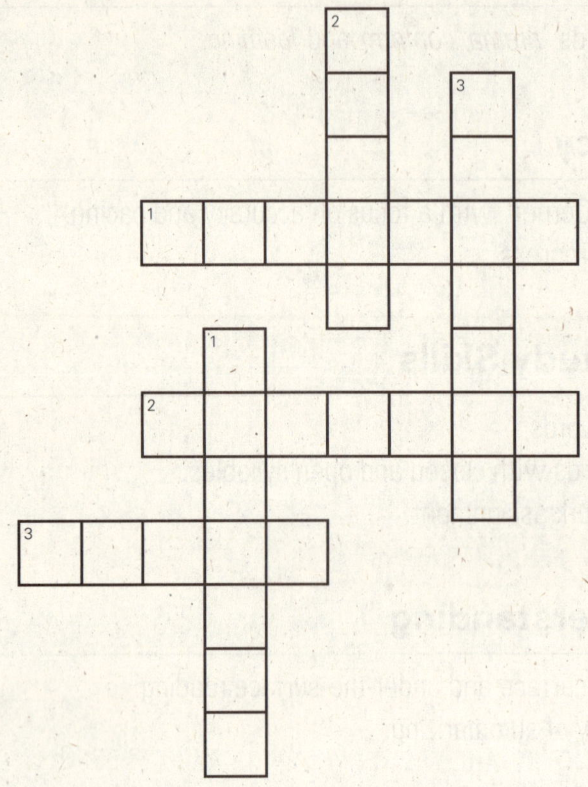

**Across**

1. The fear of losing his lunch money again was _______ over Brian's head all week.
2. Angela did not want to _______ and wear the same clothes as everyone.
3. I can smell an _______ of cookies in the kitchen.

**Down**

1. Tomorrow's game against the hardest team in the state is _______ over Patricia.
2. Juan liked the _______ of Nina's perfume.
3. Mario cut his hair just like other boys his age to _______.

| **Vocabulary** | aroma | conform | looming |

## Practice Reading Phrases

1. took the earphones out

2. He seemed surprised

3. they are playing next weekend

4. I'll see you there

5. put his earphones back on

## Practice Reading Sentences

1. Michael took the earphones out of his ears so he could talk to the boy.

2. He seemed surprised that Michael actually liked good music.

3. "Did you know they are playing next weekend at the park?"

4. "Maybe I'll see you there," said Michael.

5. Michael put his earphones back on and headed down the hall.

## Timed Reading

**{ ROLE OF THE READER }**

Read the passage to your partner as accurately as possible.

Remember, your reading goal is 80 Words Correct Per Minute (WCPM).

**{ ROLE OF THE LISTENER }**

As your partner reads, mark these errors with a strikethrough:

- mispronounced words
- skipped words
- changed words
- added words

Excerpt from

# Rounding a Corner

Number of Words

Michael took the earphones out of his ears so he could talk | 12

to the boy. The boy leaned in closer when he heard the music | 25

blasting from the earphones of Michael's MP3 player. | 33

"Hey," said the boy, "I love that song." He seemed surprised | 44

that Michael actually liked good music. | 50

"Me, too," said Michael. "I saw this band in concert a few | 62

months before I moved here." | 67

"I listen to these guys all the time. Did you know they are | 80

playing next weekend at the park? We'll all be there," the boy said, | 93

pointing to his friends. | 97

"Maybe I'll see you there," said Michael. | 104

Michael quickly stepped around the boy and walked a few | 114

steps before stopping to look at his map again. He asked another | 126

student for directions. Michael put his earphones back on and | 136

headed down the hall. This time he made a deliberate effort to | 148

watch where he was walking. | 153

Later, as his science class let out, someone grabbed Michael's | 163

shoulder. Michael tensed up and turned around. It was the same | 174

boy from before. "Not again," Michael thought. | 181

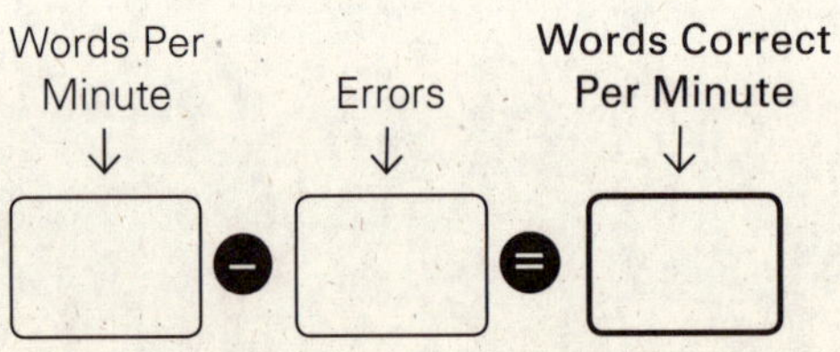

## High-Frequency Words

| | | | | |
|---|---|---|---|---|
| no | feel | come | make | add |
| doing | kept | said | above | books |

## Words of the Day

_______ _______ __ _______

_______ __ _______

## Missing Letters

Write the missing letter for each word. Then, write the complete word.

1. **ar▉** ·····▶ ______ ·····▶ ______________

2. **sa▉** ·····▶ ______ ·····▶ ______________

3. **a ▉ot** ·····▶ ______ ·····▶ ______________

4. **bo▉t** ·····▶ ______ ·····▶ ______________

5. **w▉s** ·····▶ ______ ·····▶ ______________

# Closed and Open Syllable Practice

Read the words in the box. Write a C above three closed syllable words and write an O above three open syllable words.

Identify the closed syllables in the list of words. Say each word and draw a division line between the syllables. Then, underline the ending consonant sound and circle the vowel sound in the closed syllable.

1. **into**

2. **happy**

3. **lesson**

Identify the open syllables in the list of words. Say each word and draw a division line between the syllables. Then, underline the ending vowel sound in the open syllable.

4. **open**

5. **April**

6. **music**

# Apply It

Read the paragraph below about an admirable athlete. As you read, underline at least three closed syllables and write a C above each one. Underline at least three open syllables and write an O above each one. You may mark more than three for each type of syllable.

Katie Hnida made football history. Even as a girl, she wanted to open the door for others. In school, she wrote a story about a girl who put her hair in a ponytail and hid it under her helmet. When the girl helped her team win a big game, she removed her helmet. So, after that, every fan knew she was a girl! Katie hurt her leg playing soccer, so she learned to kick a football. When she was grown, Katie became the first female to score points in a college game when she made her first field goal.

# Spell It

| **Closed Syllable Spelling Rule** | A closed syllable ends with a consonant sound and only has one vowel sound. The vowel sound is usually short. |
| --- | --- |
| **Open Syllable Spelling Rule** | An open syllable ends in a vowel sound. The vowel sound is usually long. |

1. _______________________________________

2. _______________________________________

3. _______________________________________

4. _______________________________________

5. _______________________________________

# Topic Introduction

**Text:** _______________________________________________

**Topic:** _______________________________________________

| Related Terms: | The term I know most about is: |
| --- | --- |
| 1. _____________________ | _____________________ |
| | What I know: |
| 2. _____________________ | _____________________ |
| 3. _____________________ | _____________________ |
| 4. _____________________ | _____________________ |
| 5. _____________________ | _____________________ |
| 6. _____________________ | _____________________ |
| 7. _____________________ | _____________________ |
| 8. _____________________ | _____________________ |
| 9. _____________________ | _____________________ |
| 10. ____________________ | _____________________ |



Practice Book • Unit 1

# Summary Tree

**Text:** _______________________________

1.

2.

3.

1.

2.

3.

Where

When

1.

2.

3.

1.

2.

3.

Who

What Happened

**Summary**

_______________________________________________

_______________________________________________

_______________________________________________

# Action Verbs

<table>
<tr><td>About Action Verbs in Present Tense</td><td>

- A verb expresses an action or a state of being.
- An action verb in the present tense expresses either physical or mental activity that is happening now.
- The predicate is the part of the sentence that tells something about the subject. The predicate of a sentence always contains one or more verbs.
- Knowing that a noun is singular is a clue that the verb must be singular.
- Knowing that a noun is plural is a clue that the verb must be plural.

</td></tr>
</table>

## Find the Action Verbs

Read each sentence. Underline the action verbs that are in the present tense. Write S for singular and P for plural above each verb.

1. Gus rides to school on the bus.

2. The pots boil loudly.

3. Dogs see better than humans.

4. Wise people speak the truth.

# Find It in Your Reading

Choose three sentences from our reading that contain action verbs in the present tense. Underline the action verbs in each sentence. Write S for singular or P for plural above each action verb you underlined.

1. _______________________________________________

_______________________________________________

2. _______________________________________________

_______________________________________________

3. _______________________________________________

_______________________________________________

# Put It in Your Writing

Write three sentences about your daily schedule.

1. _______________________________________________

_______________________________________________

2. _______________________________________________

_______________________________________________

3. _______________________________________________

_______________________________________________

{ DONE ✔ }

## STEP 1 Making Connections

I will connect what I already know to the narrative "The Lion, the Witch and the Wardrobe" by C. S. Lewis and discuss how life for teenagers in "The Lion, the Witch and the Wardrobe" was different from today.

## STEP 2 Developing Vocabulary

I will discuss the six vocabulary words: *barren, demeanor, disillusioned, aroma, conform,* and *looming.*

## STEP 3 Practicing Fluency

I will read aloud part of "Rounding a Corner" with a focus on accuracy, pacing, intonation, and expression and chart my fluency progress.

## STEP 4 Building Word Study Skills

I will learn five new high-frequency words.
I will learn about syllables that follow the vowel-consonant-silent *e* pattern.
I will understand the spelling homework assignment.

## STEP 5 Reading for Understanding

I will review the reading strategy of summarizing.
I will learn to use the reading skill of summarizing for character, setting, plot, and narrator.

## STEP 6 Applying the Conventions of English

I will review my understanding of singular and plural nouns.
I will identify and use *be* verbs in the present tense in my speaking, reading, and writing.

## STEP 7 Writing with Purpose

I will review the stages of the writing process.
I will revise my draft to improve ideas by adding or deleting text.

{ Summarizing My Learning }

# Hidden Clues

Read the clues for each number. Write the correct vocabulary word under each clue. The letters in the boxes will complete the answer to the question at the bottom of the page.

1. Miguel is very worried that his mom might find the bowl that he broke.

___ ___ ___ ___ ___ ___ [1] ___ ___ ___

2. The food smells delicious to Carrie.

___ ___ [2] ___ ___ ___

3. Jamie has the same new shoes as five of her friends.

___ [3] ___ ___ ___ ___ ___

4. The garden is empty and dry because no one waters it.

[4] ___ ___ ___ ___ ___

5. Ben is upset that his new jacket is not as warm as it looks.

___ ___ ___ ___ ___ ___ ___ ___ ___ ___ ___ [5] ___

6. I try to look and act my best.

[6] ___ ___ ___ ___ ___ ___ ___

**Like many young adults, what does Edmund in "The Lion, the Witch and the Wardrobe" NOT want to do?**

t
___ ___ ___ ___ ___ ___
1   2   3   4   5   6

| **Vocabulary** | barren | demeanor | disillusioned |
| --- | --- | --- | --- |
| | aroma | conform | looming |

## Practice Reading Phrases

1. watch where he was walking

2. as his science class let out

3. think of a way out

4. reached out to shake

5. breathed a sigh of relief

## Practice Reading Sentences

1. This time he made an effort to watch where he was walking.

2. Later, as his science class let out, someone grabbed Michael's shoulder.

3. He tried to think of a way out of the situation.

4. He reached out to shake Michael's hand.

5. Michael breathed a sigh of relief.

## Timed Reading

### ROLE OF THE READER

Read the passage to your partner as accurately as possible.

Remember, your reading goal is 80 Words Correct Per Minute(WCPM).

### ROLE OF THE LISTENER

As your partner reads, mark these errors with a strikethrough:

- mispronounced words
- skipped words
- changed words
- added words

Excerpt from
# Rounding a Corner

|  | Number of Words |
|---|---|
| Michael put his earphones back on and headed down the hall. | 11 |
| This time he made an effort to watch where he was walking. | 23 |
| Later, as his science class let out, someone grabbed Michael's | 33 |
| shoulder. Michael tensed up and turned around. It was the same | 44 |
| boy from before. | 47 |
| "Not again," Michael thought. He tried to think of a way out of | 60 |
| the situation. | 62 |
| This time, though, the boy's demeanor was different. He reached | 72 |
| out to shake Michael's hand. | 77 |
| "Hi," he said. "I'm Renaldo." | 82 |
| "My name is Michael. I'm new," Michael replied. "Shocking, | 91 |
| right?" | 92 |
| "Well, anyone who likes good music is OK in my book," said | 104 |
| Renaldo. "Come find me at lunch. My friends and I will show you | 117 |
| around the school." | 120 |
| "Thanks," Michael said. "I will." | 125 |
| Michael breathed a sigh of relief. For the first time all day, he | 138 |
| felt great. He stopped worrying what people would think of him, | 149 |
| and he felt himself relaxing. "Maybe I'll have a life here after all," | 162 |
| he thought. | 164 |

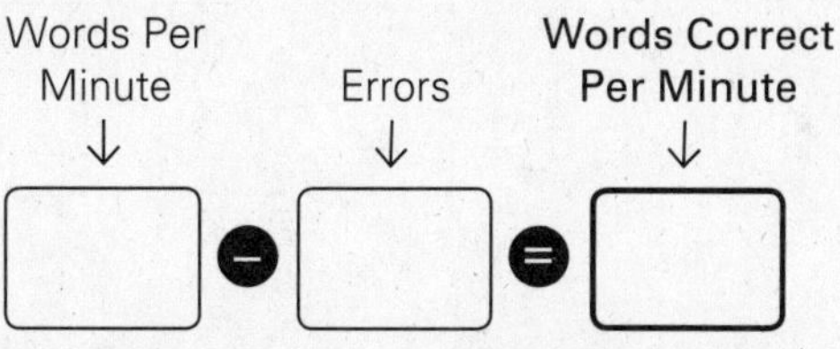

## High-Frequency Words

| | | | | |
|---|---|---|---|---|
| was | are | saw | boot | kept |
| come | no | add | feel | make |
| above | said | books | doing | a lot |

## Words of the Day

__ __     __ __ __ __     __ __ __ __ __ __ __

__ __ __ __     __ __ __ __ __

## Scrambled Letters

Use the scrambled letters below to spell the Words of the Day.

| to | look | himself | even | where |
|---|---|---|---|---|

1. n e e v = __________

2. o t = __________

3. h e w e r = __________

4. l i s h e f m = __________

5. o l k o = __________

# Word Study Skill

Read the words in the box. Circle five words that follow the vowel-consonant-silent *e* pattern.

| | | | | |
|---|---|---|---|---|
| take | seek | smile | tribe | Pete |
| main | true | wave | slow | plan |

## Practice Phonics: Vowel–Consonant–Silent *e* Syllables

Read each word below that contains the vowel-consonant-silent *e* pattern. Write V over the long vowel, C over the consonant, and S over the silent *e*. Some words may contain more than one syllable.

1. airplane

2. fade

3. Pete

4. sunshine

5. time

# Apply It

Read the paragraph below about an admirable pilot. As you read, circle at least six syllables that follow the vowel-consonant-silent *e* pattern and that contain the long vowels *a, e,* and *i*. You may circle more than six vowel-consonant-silent *e* syllables that contain the long vowel sounds of *a, e,* and *i*.

Blanche Stuart Scott of Rochester, New York, really loved her ride!
In her lifetime, Scott learned to skate, ride a bike, drive a car, and fly an
airplane. She drove her first car around so much that she made officials in
her hometown fume. The city council could find no law to make her quit!
Then, Scott learned to fix cars and drove her car across the country. She
was the first woman to do this without a male. Then, Scott found fame
and fortune as a stunt pilot. Her first solo flight was in 1910. She was the
first female test pilot. Once, to escape a crash, she invented a new turn.
Fighter pilots might have found a use for her daring dodge in World War I.
Doing something first always seemed to make Scott feel complete.

# Spell It

| Vowel-Consonant-Silent *e* Spelling Rule | In syllables with a vowel-consonant-silent *e* pattern, the vowel sound is usually long and says its name. |
| --- | --- |

1. _______________________________

2. _______________________________

3. _______________________________

4. _______________________________

5. _______________________________

## Wartime Waiting

*Part 2 of 4*

"Hello, Mr. Pratt," Robert greeted the drugstore owner. He saw his friend Alice sitting at the soda counter. She was waiting for him.

"I'll have a root beer," said Alice, smiling.

"Coming up," answered Robert. He liked his job. He enjoyed the sweet aromas, and he earned enough money to go to the movies and help out at home. He even saved up to buy a war bond. Buying a bond was like loaning money to the government. They used the money to spend on the war and then paid you back later with interest. The one Robert bought cost $18.75. In 10 years, it would be worth $25.

Robert gave Alice her drink. She was taking a break from collecting scrap. The whole city had been donating large amounts of paper and metal. Paper was used to pack things into boxes for shipping. Metal was used to make weapons, bombs, and other equipment. ◐

### Notes

1. Who is sitting at the soda counter when Robert gets to work?

2. Why do you think Robert wanted to buy a war bond?

"How is it going out there today?" Robert asked.

"It is going great! You should see how much metal I am collecting," Alice said. "Some people are even donating the bumpers from their cars!"

Alice had lost her father in the war. She worked hard to help the war effort. She often visited Robert while he was at work. They planned scrap drives and other events together.

After Robert's shift, he rode home on his bicycle. He sped past a poster of a woman rolling up her sleeve to get to work. Robert remembered seeing the same poster the day his mother had decided to find a job. "If she can do it, so can I!" Mrs. Levy had said. "We should both find work while your father is away fighting." ⏸

## Notes

3. What was on the poster that Robert passed on his way home from work?

_______________________________

_______________________________

_______________________________

_______________________________

_______________________________

_______________________________

4. Does Alice enjoy Robert's company?

_______________________________

_______________________________

_______________________________

_______________________________

_______________________________

_______________________________

_______________________________

_______________________________

_______________________________

_______________________________

She'd never thought of getting a job before the war. Now there was so much work to do and few men to do it. Robert and his mother also needed the money.

When Robert got home, he sat next to the radio and turned on the war news. His mother took a seat beside him. They liked listening to the news together. When Robert heard good stories about American troops, he felt like his father was safer. However, tonight was different. The report announced that two fighter planes had been shot down. One of the planes belonged to a special fighter group called the Flying Tigers. Robert's father was part of that group. ❚❚

{ **What do you know about Robert?** }

## Notes

5. What is announced in the report that Robert and his mom hear?

_______________________

_______________________

_______________________

6. How do you think Robert and his mother feel after they hear the report?

_______________________

_______________________

_______________________

_______________________

_______________________

_______________________

_______________________

_______________________

_______________________

_______________________

# Narrative Map: Reading

**Text:** ___________________________________________

## Characters

Main: ___________________________

___________________________

Others: ___________________________

___________________________

___________________________

## Setting

Where: ___________________________

___________________________

___________________________

When: ___________________________

___________________________

## Summary

Part 1: ___________________________

___________________________

___________________________

Part 2: ___________________________

___________________________

___________________________

Part 3: ___________________________

___________________________

___________________________

Part 4: ___________________________

___________________________

___________________________

# Plot

**BEGINNING**

**MIDDLE**

**END**

**Narrator:** _______________________________________________

# *Be* Verbs

<table>
<tr><td>About Present Tense Be Verbs</td><td>

- A verb expresses an action or a state of being.
- A *be* verb in the present tense expresses the state of being that is happening now to the subject of the sentence.
- The forms of the present tense *be* verb are: *am, is,* and *are.*
- A singular *be* verb is used with a singular subject. Examples: *I am; You are; He is; She is; It is.*
- A plural *be* verb is used with a plural subject. Examples: *We are; You are; They are.*

</td></tr>
</table>

## Present Tense: Find the *Be* Verbs

Read each sentence. Circle the correct present tense *be* verb that completes each sentence. Write S above singular verbs and P above plural verbs.

1. The waves (is, are) high.

2. The clock (is, are) broken.

3. The enchiladas (is, are) delicious.

4. She (is, are) sure that I (am, is) ready for this test.

5. They (is, are) proud of their hometown.

## Find It in Your Reading

Read the passage below. Find sentences that contain present tense *be* verbs. Underline the *be* verbs in each sentence. Write S for singular or P for plural above each *be* verb.

Today is a great day. I am happy because our school vacation begins today. Some of my friends are upset because they think that we will have to take work home with us over the break. I am sure that they are wrong. I heard Mr. Fuentes say that once we are done with this science project, we are free! I appreciate Mr. Fuentes because he is always fair to us.

## Put It in Your Writing

Write three sentences about how you feel right now. Check to make sure your sentences contain present tense *be* verbs.

1. _______________________________________________________________

   _______________________________________________________________

2. _______________________________________________________________

   _______________________________________________________________

3. _______________________________________________________________

   _______________________________________________________________

{ DONE ✔ }

## STEP 1 Making Connections

I will connect what I already know to the narrative "The Lion, the Witch and the Wardrobe" by C. S. Lewis and discuss how life for the teenagers in "The Lion, the Witch and the Wardrobe" was different from today.

## STEP 2 Developing Vocabulary

I will discuss the six vocabulary words: *barren, demeanor, disillusioned, aroma, conform,* and *looming*.

## STEP 3 Practicing Fluency

I will read aloud part of "Wartime Waiting" with a focus on accuracy, pacing, intonation, and expression and chart my fluency progress.

## STEP 4 Building Word Study Skills

I will learn five new high-frequency words.
I will learn about syllables that follow the vowel-consonant-silent *e* pattern.
I will understand the spelling homework assignment.

## STEP 5 Reading for Understanding

I will review the reading skill of summarizing for character, setting, plot, and narrator.
I will review the reading strategy of summarizing.

## STEP 6 Applying the Conventions of English

I will review my understanding of subjects and verbs.
I will identify and use subject-verb agreement in my speaking, reading, and writing.

## STEP 7 Writing with Purpose

I will review the stages of the writing process.
I will review the narrative prompt and edit my draft for correct subject-verb agreement.

{ Summarizing My Learning }

# Crossword Puzzle

Read the clues for each number. Write the correct vocabulary word on the puzzle.

**Across**

1. Meeting the bully on his street was __________ over Rick for weeks.
2. Chandra's unfriendly __________ is not how I want to act.
3. The empty lot was dry and __________.

**Down**

1. Sean wanted to __________ by buying the same brand hat as his friends.
2. I love the __________ of fresh popcorn.
3. Pablo felt __________ at the concert when his favorite band played only one song he knew.

| **Vocabulary** | barren | disillusioned | conform |
|---|---|---|---|
| | demeanor | aroma | looming |

## Practice Reading Phrases

1. rushed home from school

2. from his cousin, Hannah

3. since 1939

4. thought back to a letter

5. in the street every day

## Practice Reading Sentences

1. Robert Levy rushed home from school.

2. There was a letter from his cousin, Hannah.

3. Hannah had been living in England since 1939—four years now.

4. Robert thought back to a letter she wrote right before leaving for England.

5. "There are more Nazi soldiers in the street every day."

# Timed Reading

| { ROLE OF THE READER } | { ROLE OF THE LISTENER } |
|---|---|
| Read the passage to your partner as accurately as possible.<br><br>Remember, your reading goal is 80 Words Correct Per Minute (WCPM). | As your partner reads, mark these errors with a strikethrough:<br><br>• mispronounced words<br>• skipped words<br>• changed words<br>• added words |

Excerpt from
# Wartime Waiting

| | Number of Words |
|---|---|
| Robert Levy rushed home from school. He was expecting a | 10 |
| letter from his father, who was a pilot in the Air Force. His father | 24 |
| was fighting overseas in World War II. | 31 |
| Robert checked the mailbox. There was a letter from his | 41 |
| cousin, Hannah. She lived with foster parents in England. At the | 52 |
| start of the war, Hannah had been one of thousands of Jewish | 64 |
| children able to escape Germany. Many Jewish children and | 73 |
| families, including Hannah's parents, were not so lucky. | 81 |
| Hannah had been living in England since 1939—four years | 91 |
| now. She'd written Robert many letters about how awful life was | 102 |
| for Jews living in Germany. Robert thought back to a letter she | 114 |
| wrote right before leaving for England. | 120 |
| "The government is making it illegal for people to shop at | 131 |
| Jewish businesses," she wrote. "My dad says he will have to close | 143 |
| our bakery. I don't know what we will do. There are more Nazi | 156 |
| soldiers in the street every day." | 162 |

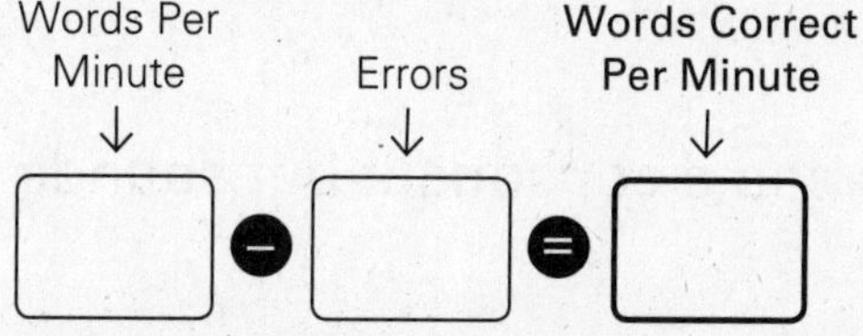

# High-Frequency Words

| | | | | |
|---|---|---|---|---|
| himself | doing | a lot | above | books |
| saw | where | to | even | look |
| make | kept | was | are | boot |
| feel | come | no | add | said |

# Words of the Day

_____ _________ _______

____________

# Word Riddles

Answer the riddles below with the Words of the Day.

| you | cannot | find | called | see |
|---|---|---|---|---|

1. Which word has 3 letters and is something you do?  __________

2. Which word has 4 letters and can also mean "catch" or "discover"?  __________

3. Which word has 6 letters and rhymes with "bald"?  __________

4. Which word has 6 letters and is similar to the words "was not," "do not," and "will not"?  __________

5. Which word has 2 vowels and a consonant but sounds like one vowel?  __________

# Phonics Skill

Read the words in the box. Circle five words that follow the vowel-consonant-silent *e* pattern.

| | | | | |
|---|---|---|---|---|
| **bake** | **brag** | **sent** | **went** | **make** |
| **cat** | **dime** | **globe** | **rode** | **lime** |

## Practice Phonics: Vowel-Consonant-Silent *e* Syllables

Read the words below that have syllables that follow the vowel-consonant-silent *e* pattern and contain the long vowels *o* or *u*. Write V over the long vowel, C over the consonant, and S over the silent *e*. Some words may contain more than one syllable. All words contain a silent *e*.

1. alone

2. cone

3. June

4. those

5. cute

# Apply It

Read the paragraph below about an admirable pilot. As you read, circle at least three syllables that follow the vowel-consonant-silent *e* pattern. You may circle more than three vowel-consonant-silent *e* patterns that contain the long vowel sounds of *o* and *u*.

Blanche Stuart Scott of Rochester, New York, really loved her ride! She learned to skate, ride a bike, drive a car, and fly an airplane in her lifetime. She drove her first car around so much that she made officials in her hometown fume. The city council could find no law to make her quit! Then, Scott learned to fix cars and rode across the country, the first woman to do this without a male. Scott found fame and fortune as a stunt pilot. Her first solo flight was in 1910. She was the first female test pilot. Once, to escape a crash, she invented a new turn. Fighter pilots might have found a use for her daring dodge in World War I. For Scott, life felt complete when she was first.

# Spell It

| **Vowel-Consonant-Silent *e* Spelling Rule** | In syllables with a vowel-consonant-silent *e* pattern, the vowel sound is usually long and says its name. |
| --- | --- |

1. _______________________

2. _______________________

3. _______________________

4. _______________________

5. _______________________

# Quick Write

What do you know about Robert?

# Summary Tree

**Text:** ______________________________

**Where**

**When**

**Who**

**What Happened**

**Summary**

# Subject-Verb Agreement

| **About Subject-Verb Agreement** | • A subject and verb must agree in number.<br>• Use the singular form of a verb with a singular subject.<br>• Use the plural form of a verb with a plural subject.<br>• The subject *you* can be singular or plural. However, *you* is always used with the plural form of the verb. |
|---|---|

## Make Subjects and Verbs Agree in Number

Read each sentence. Circle the verb that agrees with the subject in each sentence.

1. Jake (walk, walks) to the library each day.

2. A good diet (make, makes) a person strong.

3. The rules (say, says) what we must do.

4. The dog (bark, barks) when it thunders outside.

5. You (study, studies) hard for exams.

# Find It in Your Reading

Write three sentences from your reading that include subject-verb agreement. Underline the subject and circle the verb in each sentence. Write S or P next to each sentence to indicate number.

1. _______________________________________________

_______________________________________________

2. _______________________________________________

_______________________________________________

3. _______________________________________________

_______________________________________________

# Put It in Your Writing

Write as many sentences as you can about friends you admire. Check to make sure the subjects and verbs in your sentences agree.

1. _______________________________________________

_______________________________________________

2. _______________________________________________

_______________________________________________

3. _______________________________________________

_______________________________________________

{ DONE ✔ }

AGENDA

## STEP 1 Making Connections

I will connect what I already know to a photograph and discuss the essential question, *How was life for teenagers of the past different from today?*

## STEP 2 Developing Vocabulary

I will review and complete an assessment of six vocabulary words.

## STEP 3 Practicing Fluency

I will read aloud part of "Wartime Waiting" by Ann Weil with a focus on accuracy, pacing, intonation, and expression and chart my fluency progress.

## STEP 4 Building Word Study Skills

I will learn five new high-frequency words.
I will then review syllables that follow the vowel-consonant-silent *e* pattern.
I will take a spelling test.

## STEP 5 Reading for Understanding

I will review the reading strategy of summarizing.
I will review the reading skill of summarizing for characters, setting, plot, and narrator.

## STEP 6 Applying the Conventions of English

I will review my understanding of nouns, present tense verbs, *be* verbs, and subject-verb agreement.
I will write declarative sentences using the conventions learned in this chapter.

## STEP 7 Writing with Purpose

I will review the stages of the writing process.
I will edit my draft for word choice, spelling, and punctuation.

{ Summarizing My Learning }

# Show What You Know

## Read each question. Check the box beside the best answer.

1. If you **conform**, you make yourself
   _________ other people.

   ☐ shorter than
   ☐ the same as
   ☐ different than
   ☐ taller than

2. If you are **disillusioned,** you feel:

   ☐ better than you thought
   you would.
   ☐ sillier than you thought
   you would.
   ☐ worse than you thought
   you would.
   ☐ meaner than you thought
   you would.

3. Which of these might be **looming**
   over you?

   ☐ the great movie you saw last
   night
   ☐ the cake that you get to eat
   after school
   ☐ your new haircut that you don't
   want anyone to see
   ☐ your favorite shirt

4. Which of these things might
   be **barren?**

   ☐ a desert
   ☐ a TV show
   ☐ a crowded party
   ☐ a new movie

5. Something that _________ might have
   a nice **aroma.**

   ☐ talks a lot
   ☐ hears well
   ☐ feels good
   ☐ smells good

6. Your **demeanor** is:

   ☐ how you act.
   ☐ how you play the drums.
   ☐ how much you eat.
   ☐ how you write.

## Practice Reading Phrases

1. sitting at the counter

2. help out at home

3. In 10 years

4. The whole city

5. weapons, bombs, and other equipment

## Practice Reading Sentences

1. He saw his friend Alice sitting at the counter.

2. He enjoyed the sweet aromas, and he earned enough money to go to the movies and help out at home.

3. In 10 years, it would be worth $25.

4. The whole city had been donating large amounts of paper and metal.

5. Metal was used to make weapons, bombs, and other equipment.

## Timed Reading

**{ ROLE OF THE READER }**

Read the passage to your partner as accurately as possible.

Remember, your reading goal is 80 Words Correct Per Minute (WCPM).

**{ ROLE OF THE LISTENER }**

As your partner reads, mark these errors with a strikethrough:

- mispronounced words
- skipped words
- changed words
- added words

Excerpt from
# Wartime Waiting

| | Number of Words |
|---|---|
| "Hello, Mr. Pratt," Robert greeted the drugstore owner. He saw | 10 |
| his friend Alice sitting at the soda counter. She was waiting for him. | 23 |
| "I'll have a root beer," said Alice, smiling. | 31 |
| "Coming up," answered Robert. He liked his job. He enjoyed | 41 |
| the sweet aromas, and he earned enough money to go to the | 53 |
| movies and help out at home. He even saved up to buy a war | 67 |
| bond. Buying a bond was like loaning money to the government. | 78 |
| They used the money to spend on the war and then paid you back | 92 |
| later with interest. The one Robert bought cost $18.75. In 10 years, | 104 |
| it would be worth $25. | 109 |
| Robert gave Alice her drink. She was taking a break from | 120 |
| collecting scrap. The whole city had been donating large amounts | 130 |
| of paper and metal. Paper was used to pack things into boxes for | 143 |
| shipping. Metal was used to make weapons, bombs, and other | 153 |
| equipment. | 154 |
| "How is it going out there today?" Robert asked. | 163 |
| "It is going great! You should see how much metal I am | 175 |
| collecting," Alice said. "Some people are even donating the bumpers | 185 |
| from their cars!" | 188 |

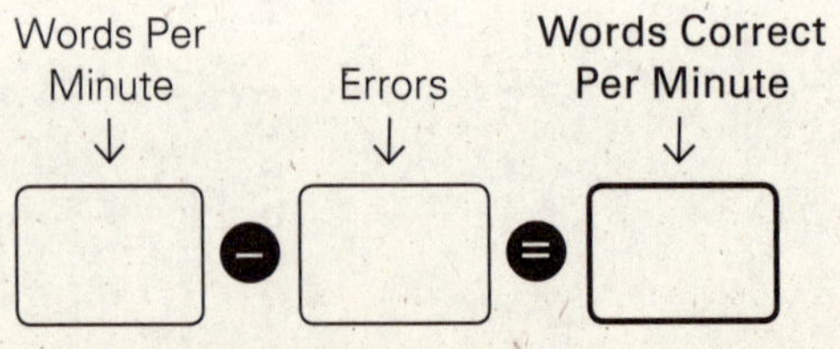

# High-Frequency Words

| | | | | | | |
|---|---|---|---|---|---|---|
| called | a lot | make | was | himself | find | doing |
| to | see | books | come | saw | where | |
| are | look | cannot | above | no | kept | |
| add | boot | even | you | said | feel | |

# Words of the Day

_____ ____ __ ______

_____ ____ ____

# Alphabetical Order

Place the Words of the Day in alphabetical order.

| into | my | came | away | two |
|---|---|---|---|---|

1. ____ ____ ____ ____
2. ____ ____ ____
3. ____ ____ ____ ____
4. ____ ____
5. ____ ____ ____

# Word Study Skill

Read the words in the box. Circle five words that follow the vowel-consonant-silent *e* pattern.

| | | | | |
|---|---|---|---|---|
| plane | time | meet | fade | home |
| peak | gruff | enough | shine | seeker |

## Phonics Practice: Vowel-Consonant-Silent *e* Syllables

Read the words that have syllables that follow the vowel-consonant-silent *e* pattern in the words below. The words on this list are from the reading "Wartime Waiting" in your Anthology. Write an L above each letter that makes the long vowel sound.

1. make

2. like

3. wore

4. life

5. sure

# Apply It

Read the paragraph below about an admirable athlete. As you read, circle at least six syllables that follow the vowel–consonant-silent *e* pattern. You may circle more than six syllables.

Katie Hnida is an athlete to admire. She made football history. Even as a girl, she wanted to open the door for others.  In school, she wrote a story about a girl who decided to hide her hair in a ponytail. When she helped her team win a game, she removed her helmet. So, after that, every fan knew she was a girl! Katie hurt her leg playing soccer, so she learned to kick a football. When she was grown, Katie became the first female to score points in a college game when she made her first field goal.

# Spell It

| **Vowel-Consonant-Silent *e* Spelling Rule** | In syllables with a vowel-consonant-silent *e* pattern, the vowel sound is usually long and says its name. |
|---|---|

1. _________________________________

2. _________________________________

3. _________________________________

4. _________________________________

5. _________________________________

## Wartime Waiting

*Part 4 of 4*

On his way home from school, Robert rode his bicycle through the streets of his neighborhood. He counted the blue and gold stars in the windows of the houses. A blue star meant that someone from that family was a soldier away at war. A gold star meant that the soldier had been killed. Nearly every house had a star. Robert thought of the blue star in his window at home. He hoped it would never be replaced with a gold one.

When Robert got home, the mailbox was empty. As he walked through the front door to his house, he was startled when a man behind him shouted, "Telegram!" The note the man held was addressed to Robert's mother.

### Notes

1. What does it mean if a family has a blue star in their window?

_______________________

_______________________

_______________________

_______________________

_______________________

_______________________

2. Why do you think Robert counts the blue and gold stars in the windows?

_______________________

_______________________

_______________________

_______________________

_______________________

_______________________

_______________________

_______________________

_______________________

Robert felt as if he had been punched in the stomach. The military usually sent a telegram when a soldier died in combat. Robert didn't want to look, and he decided he would wait for his mother. He sat alone with the telegram for over two hours.

"Would you read it for me, please?" Robert's mother asked in a weak voice when she returned home.

Robert opened the telegram. It wasn't what he expected. "Dad is alive!" he shouted.

The telegram explained that his father had jumped from his plane and opened his parachute at a low **altitude.** He'd broken his leg and was blinded in one eye, but he was alive. He was at an army hospital. He would be sent home in a month. Robert hugged his mother. She was crying and smiling at the same time. ⏸

**altitude**  height from the ground

## Notes

3. Where is Robert's father being kept?

4. Why do you think Robert's mother wants him to read the letter to her?

During dinner, Robert talked with his mother about inviting Hannah to live with them. They agreed it was a good plan.

Instead of listening to the war news that evening, they worked on a letter for Hannah. They wrote about their home in Brooklyn, New York. Robert wrote about his school and how he'd help Hannah conform to life in America until her parents returned. They also wrote about Robert's father. They hoped that once he was released from the hospital, he could meet Hannah in London. That way the two could return to America together. Robert and his mother sent the letter the next morning, and they started marking days on a calendar. Every day brought them closer to when their family would again be whole. ❿

{ **What is life like for Robert and Hannah living in this time in American history?** }

## Notes

{ 5. What do Robert and his mother do instead of listening to the war news? }

_______________________________

_______________________________

_______________________________

_______________________________

_______________________________

_______________________________

{ 6. Why do you think Robert wants to help Hannah conform to life in America? }

_______________________________

_______________________________

_______________________________

_______________________________

_______________________________

_______________________________

_______________________________

_______________________________

_______________________________

_______________________________

# Conventions Review

## Review Nouns as Simple Subjects

Read each sentence. Underline the simple subject in each sentence.

1. The test was easy.

2. A fire alarm rang during lunch.

3. The soccer fans enjoyed the game.

## Review Articles

Read each sentence. Circle the correct article that goes with each noun in the sentence.

1. We will create (a/an) mural for (an/the) fair.

2. I bought (a/an) table at (a/an) outdoor market.

3. Do not vacuum (an/the) floor before you wash (a/the) windows.

## Review Action Verbs in the Present Tense

Read each sentence. Underline action verbs used in the present tense. Write S for singular or P for plural above each verb.

1. Leaves turn red and gold in autumn.

2. The wind blows hard over the waves.

3. The thought crosses my mind that we should have lunch.

# Review *Be* Verbs in the Present Tense

Read each sentence. Underline the *be* verbs used in the present tense. Write S for singular or P for plural above each verb.

1. She is strong and smart.

2. You are my closest friends.

3. I am proud of my brother.

# Review Subject-Verb Agreement

Read each sentence. Circle the correct verb to complete each sentence.

1. She (play/plays) trumpet in the band.

2. Do you (want/wants) to watch a movie?

3. The doves (sing/sings) early in the morning.

# Put It in Your Writing

Write three sentences about your favorite kind of weather. Include as many conventions as possible.

_______________________________________________

_______________________________________________

_______________________________________________

AGENDA

{DONE ✔}

## STEP 1 Developing Test-Taking Strategies

I will read a test-taking manual.
I will learn strategies for taking multiple-choice tests.

## STEP 2 Assessing My Learning

I will take a multiple-choice test on skills I learned in this chapter.

## STEP 3 Writing With Purpose

I will publish the final draft of my narrative.

## STEP 4 Analyzing My Results

I will identify which questions I answered correctly and which questions I answered incorrectly.

## STEP 5 Reinforcing My Learning

I will reinforce my understanding of verbs.
I will reinforce my understanding of vowel-consonant-silent *e* syllables.

## STEP 6 Speaking With Purpose

I will watch a video of a speech and summarize its meaning.

{Summarizing My Learning}

# Test-Taking Manual
## Before the Test

### Be Prepared

- Know what you will be tested on and study.
- Get a full night's rest.
- Have all your materials (pencil, eraser, calculator, dictionary) at your desk.

### Be Comfortable but Alert

- Make sure you have enough room to work.
- Do not slouch in your chair.

### Stay Relaxed and Confident

- Remember that you are well prepared and can do well.
- Take deep breaths if you feel anxious.
- Do not talk about the test with the other students.

## During the Test

Follow these five steps for each question on the test.

**Step 1:** Determine what the question is asking you to do.

**Step 2:** Try to answer the question in your own words.

**Step 3:** Eliminate any answers you know are incorrect.

**Step 4:** Choose the best answer.

**Step 5:** If time allows, review your answers to each question.

### Example Question

**1. Which underlined word is NOT spelled correctly?**

> We <u>can</u> go swimming in the <u>lak</u> after we <u>ride</u> our bikes all <u>day</u>.

**A.** can

**B.** lak

**C.** ride

**D.** day

# Skills Assessment 1

**Directions: Read and answer each of the following questions.**

1. **Which choice correctly fills the blank?**

   > Henry _________ the telephone.

   A. is answered
   B. answers
   C. answering
   D. is answer

2. **Which choice correctly fills the blank?**

   > The boy _________ in the swimming pool.

   A. is
   B. are
   C. am
   D. be

3. **Which choice correctly fills the blank?**

   > Shelby _________ magic tricks.

   A. do
   B doing
   C. does
   D. done

4. **Which choice correctly fills the blank?**

   > The tall tree _________ down last night.

   A. was blown
   B. is blown
   C. are blown
   D. be blown

5. **Which sentence is written correctly?**

   A. My dad walk to the store.
   B. The teacher give us new pencils.
   C. The old dog chase the cats.
   D. The baby likes the little toy.

6. **Which sentence is written correctly?**

   A. The fire engine hurrying to the large fire.
   B. My oldest sister is still sick at home.
   C. We walks home from school on Fridays.
   D. My favorite school lunch being pizza.

*Go on to the next page* →

# Skills Assessment 1, continued

**7. Which underlined word is NOT spelled correctly?**

We <u>can</u> see the <u>city</u> below when we <u>hik</u> up the <u>hill</u>.

- A. can
- B. city
- C. hik
- D. hill

**8. Which underlined word is NOT spelled correctly?**

He <u>will</u> <u>tell</u> us <u>about</u> the soccer <u>gam</u>.

- A. will
- B. tell
- C. about
- D. gam

**9. Which underlined word is NOT spelled correctly?**

Manuel <u>gave</u> a <u>blue</u> <u>bik</u> to his <u>sister</u>.

- A. gave
- B. blue
- C. bik
- D. sister

**10. Which underlined word is NOT spelled correctly?**

My <u>white</u> cat <u>wok</u> up <u>under</u> a <u>pile</u> of dirty clothes.

- A. white
- B. wok
- C. under
- D. pile

**11. Which underlined word is NOT spelled correctly?**

It was <u>very</u> hot, so the <u>girls</u> decided to <u>rest</u> in the <u>shad</u> of the tree.

- A. very
- B. girls
- C. rest
- D. shad

**12. Which underlined word is NOT spelled correctly?**

The <u>alarm</u> <u>clock</u> will <u>wak</u> the <u>farmer</u> in the morning.

- A. alarm
- B. clock
- C. wak
- D. farmer

**End of test** ■

# Subject-Verb Agreement

**Reminder:
About Subject-
Verb Agreement**

- Subjects and verbs must agree in number.
- Use the singular form of a verb with a singular subject.
- Use the plural form of a verb with a plural subject.
- The subject *you* can be singular or plural. However, *you* is always used with the plural form of the verb.

## Make Subjects and Verbs Agree in Number

Read each sentence. Circle the verb that agrees with the subject in each sentence.

1. Vivian (read, reads) two books each week.

2. The radio station (play, plays) country music.

3. You (look, looks) tall in those shoes.

4. The plants (need, needs) water.

5. The car wash (open, opens) at 10 A.M.

## Find It in Your Reading

Read each sentence. Underline the subject and circle the verb in each sentence. Write S or P next to each sentence to indicate singular or plural.

1. My cousins left yesterday for a trip to the mountains.

2. The car overflowed with camping gear.

3. Unfortunately, I missed the trip this year.

# Verbs That Agree

Which choice correctly fills the blank?

1.  **Margot _______ her room.**
    A. clean
    B. cleaning
    C. cleans

2.  **The baseball players _______ for exercise.**
    A. run
    B. runs
    C. is run

3.  **You _______ the spelling bee every year.**
    A. winning
    B. win
    C. wins

4. **The sky _______ cloudy today.**
    A. is
    B. are
    C. be

# Write Sentences with Subject-Verb Agreement

______________________________________________

______________________________________________

______________________________________________

## Choices & Challenges
On your own piece of paper…

**A.** Use four of the verbs in the answer choices on this page to write four new sentences. Be sure that the verb in each sentence agrees with the subject.

**B.** Write four sentences from your Anthology, pages 6-9. Circle the subject and underline the verb in each sentence. Explain how you know that the verb agrees with the subject.

**C.** Create four new test questions like the ones on this page.

# Vowel-Consonant-Silent *e* Syllables

| **Reminder: Vowel-Consonant-Silent *e* Syllables** | • In the type of syllable that follows the vowel-consonant-silent *e* pattern, the vowel sound is usually long and says its name.<br>• When reading syllables that have the vowel-consonant-silent *e* pattern, say the long vowel sound. Remember, the ending vowel *e* is always silent.<br>• When readers know about syllables that follow the vowel-consonant-silent *e* pattern, they can sometimes figure out how to say and spell new words. |
|---|---|

## Practice Phonics: Vowel-Consonant-Silent *e* Syllables

Read each word below that contains the vowel-consonant-silent *e* pattern. Write V over the long vowel, C over the consonant, and S over the silent *e*. Some words may contain more than one syllable.

| | | | |
|---|---|---|---|
| 1. code | 3. combine | 5. rake | 7. recede |
| 2. white | 4. Nate | 6. flume | 8. lemonade |

## Apply It

Read the sentences below. As you read, circle at least four syllables that follow the vowel-consonant-silent *e* pattern and that contain the long vowel sounds of *a, e,* and *i.* You may circle more than four vowel-consonant-silent *e* syllables that contain the long vowel sounds of *a, e,* and *i.*

My school is having a bake sale. We are raising money for the debate team. Jevon and I will make our special cake. We use these strange ingredients: peanut butter and rice flour. We let the cake rise twice. If the students like it, we will strike it rich for the team.

# Find the Misspelled Word

Which underlined word is NOT spelled correctly?

1. I **woke** up **lat**, and I **missed** the bus to school.
   - **A.** woke
   - **B.** lat
   - **C.** missed

2. Jen wants to **skate** after we **finish** the **hik**.
   - **A.** skate
   - **B.** finish
   - **C.** hik

3. Chris needs a **ride** **hom** from the store.
   - **A.** ride
   - **B.** hom
   - **C.** store

4. The gift **cam** with a **free** **tote** bag.
   - **A.** cam
   - **B.** free
   - **C.** tote

---

## Choices & Challenges

On your own piece of paper…

**A.** Rewrite the four sentences on this page so that every word is spelled correctly.

**B.** Write five sentences from your Anthology, pages 10-13, that contain at least one word with the vowel-consonant-silent *e* pattern. Underline each word. Write V over the long vowel, C over the consonant, and S over the silent *e*.

**C.** Create four new test questions like the ones on this page.

## STEP **1** Making Connections

{DONE ✔}



I will connect what I already know to a photograph and discuss the essential question,
*How was life for teenagers of the past different from today?*

## STEP **2** Developing Vocabulary

I will discuss vocabulary words in a cumulative review.

## STEP **3** Practicing Fluency

I will read aloud part of "Wartime Waiting" with fluency by practicing phrasing and using
punctuation to inform meaning, and I will chart my fluency progress.

## STEP **4** Building Word Study Skills

I will learn, practice, and spell five new high-frequency words.
I will practice recognizing and using words with the long *a* sound *(ai, ay)* and long *e* sound
*(ea, y)*.
I will understand the spelling homework assignment.

## STEP **5** Reading for Understanding

I will review my understanding of narratives.
I will learn to use the reading strategy of clarifying.

## STEP **6** Applying the Conventions of English

I will review my understanding of nouns.
I will identify and use plural nouns ending in *-y* in my speaking, reading, and writing.

## STEP **7** Writing with Purpose

I will review the stages of the writing process.
I will deconstruct the narrative prompt and scoring guide and begin prewriting.

{Summarizing My Learning}

# Practice Reading Phrases

1. is just fine

2. called them *yanks*

3. wondered if his father

4. checked the mail

5. even if they made it

# Practice Reading Sentences

1. "I'm sure your father is just fine."

2. People called them *yanks*.

3. Robert wondered if his father gave gum to children, too.

4. Like Robert, she checked the mail every day.

5. She worried that even if they made it to England, things might never be safe for her family.

# Timed Reading

**{ ROLE OF THE READER }**

Read the passage to your partner as accurately as possible.

Remember, your reading goal is 80 Words Correct Per Minute (WCPM).

**{ ROLE OF THE LISTENER }**

As your partner reads, mark these errors with a strikethrough:

- mispronounced words
- skipped words
- changed words
- added words

Excerpt from
# Wartime Waiting

|  | Number of Words |
|---|---|
| "You're up early," said Mrs. Levy the next morning. She was | 11 |
| already dressed for work. | 15 |
| "I couldn't sleep," said Robert. "I also wanted to read Hannah's | 27 |
| letter before school." | 29 |
| "I couldn't sleep, either," Mrs. Levy replied. "Try not to worry. I'm | 41 |
| sure your father is just fine." | 47 |
| Robert sat down and opened Hannah's letter. "My dear cousin," | 57 |
| it began. Robert tried to forget about his own worries as he read. | 70 |
| Hannah wrote about American soldiers in England. People called | 79 |
| them *yanks*. They had pockets full of gum to give to children. | 91 |
| Robert's father was in China. Robert wondered if his father gave gum | 103 |
| to children, too. | 106 |
| Hannah also wrote about her parents. Like Robert, she checked | 116 |
| the mail every day. She wished for a letter or a telegram that would | 130 |
| tell her where her parents were. She wished she knew if they were | 143 |
| okay. She worried that even if they made it to England, things might | 156 |
| never be safe for her family. | 162 |

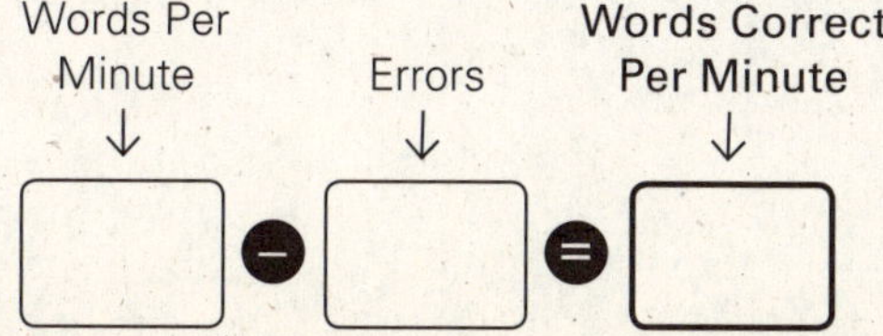

# Words of the Day

_ _ _ _ _ _ _ _ _ _ _ _ _

_ _ _ _ _ _ _ _ _

# Alphabetical Order

List the Words of the Day in alphabetical order.

| little | down | one | funny | getting |
|--------|------|-----|-------|---------|

1. ____________

2. ____________

3. ____________

4. ____________

5. ____________

# Word Study Skill

Read the words in the box. Circle five words that have a long *a* or long *e* sound.

| | | | | |
|---|---|---|---|---|
| pain | ever | gray | ripe | play |
| wait | there | pie | nail | |

# Phonics Practice

Circle the word in each pair with the long *a* sound. For each word, underline the letters that make the long vowel sound.

1. bully     rain
2. wait      heat
3. flea      play
4. furry     nail

# Apply It

Read the paragraph below. Circle words with the long *a* sound spelled with *ai* or *ay*. Also circle words with the long *e* sound spelled with *ea* or *y*.

Sally walked to the railroad tracks. She couldn't wait for the train to come. All the townspeople stood in the summer heat to see it. None of them had ever seen one before! Sally's teacher had posted a picture of a train in their tiny school. But she could not imagine what one would look like coming into town. Suddenly, a horn blew far away. Sally grabbed her father's hand.

# Spell It

| **Spelling Tip** | Many words with the long *a* sound are spelled with *ai* or *ay*. Many words with the long *e* sound are spelled with *ea* or *y*. |
| --- | --- |

1. _______________________________________________

2. _______________________________________________

3. _______________________________________________

4. _______________________________________________

5. _______________________________________________

# Topic Introduction

**Text:** _______________________________

**Topic:** _______________________________

**Related Terms:**

1. _______________________________

2. _______________________________

3. _______________________________

4. _______________________________

5. _______________________________

6. _______________________________

7. _______________________________

8. _______________________________

9. _______________________________

10. _______________________________

The term I know most about is:

_______________________________

What I know:

_______________________________

_______________________________

_______________________________

_______________________________

_______________________________

_______________________________

_______________________________

_______________________________

_______________________________

_______________________________

_______________________________

_______________________________

_______________________________

# Clarifying Log

**Text:** ___________________________________________

| Words to Clarify → | | | |
| --- | --- | --- | --- |
| 1. Make a quick prediction. | | | |
| 2. Look for a prefix, suffix, or root word. | | | |
| 3. Identify the part of speech. | | | |
| 4. Look for clues in pictures or other words. | | | |
| 5. Make a more informed prediction. | | | |
| 6. Confirm the meaning of the word. | | | |

Summary: ___________________________________________

___________________________________________

___________________________________________

___________________________________________

# Review Plural Nouns

**About Plural Nouns**

- A plural noun is a word that names more than one person, place, thing, or idea. You can form most plural nouns by adding -s to the singular form. Examples: *dog, dogs; hat, hats.*
- If a singular noun ends in a consonant and then -y, change the y to i and add -es to form the plural. Examples: *party, parties; duty, duties.*

## Search for Plural Nouns

Fill in each line with the correct plural noun.

In the 19th century, _________________ (settler) moved across the West. Sometimes they traveled under clear _________________ (sky). Sometimes they had to travel through rain, snow, and wind _________________ (storm) with only their covered _________________ (wagon) to protect them. They built _________________ (home), _________________ (farm), and _________________ (city). Life was not always easy for these _________________ (traveler). In many _________________ (place) there were no _________________ (road). Sometimes there were _________________ (conflict) with Native _________________ (American) who had lived on the land for _________________ (century). _________________ (Settler) lived under rough _________________ (condition).

# Find It in Your Reading

Write three sentences from your reading. Underline all the nouns. At the end of each sentence, write the plural form of each singular noun you found.

1. _________________________________________________

_________________________________________________

2. _________________________________________________

_________________________________________________

3. _________________________________________________

_________________________________________________

# Put It in Your Writing

Write three sentences to tell about a time you stood up for something you believe in. Include a variety of plural nouns in your sentences.

1. _________________________________________________

_________________________________________________

2. _________________________________________________

_________________________________________________

3. _________________________________________________

_________________________________________________

## STEP **1** Making Connections

{ DONE ✔ }



I will connect what I already know to the narrative "Old Yeller" by Fred Gipson and discuss how life for the teenager in "Old Yeller" was different from today.

## STEP **2** Developing Vocabulary

I will learn three new vocabulary words: *dingy, hesitate,* and *entice.*

## STEP **3** Practicing Fluency

I will read aloud part of "Wartime Waiting" with fluency by practicing phrasing and conveying emotion and meaning, and I will chart my fluency progress.

## STEP **4** Building Word Study Skills

I will learn, practice, and spell five new high-frequency words.
I will practice recognizing and using words with the long *i* sound *(y)*, the long *o* sound *(oa, ow)*, and the long *u* sound *(ue, ew)*.
I will understand the spelling homework assignment.

## STEP **5** Reading for Understanding

I will review the reading strategy of clarifying.
I will learn to use the reading skill of clarifying for character, setting, plot, narrator, and problem/solution.

## STEP **6** Applying the Conventions of English

I will review my understanding of nouns and subjects.
I will identify and use subject pronouns in my speaking, reading, and writing.

## STEP **7** Writing with Purpose

I will review the stages of the writing process, the narrative prompt, and the scoring guide.
I will choose a topic and complete the prewriting stage.

{ Summarizing My Learning }

# Hidden Clues

Read the clues for each number. Write the correct vocabulary word under each clue. The letters in the boxes will complete the answer to the question at the bottom of the page.

1. The cake looks so good that I have to eat a piece.

___ ___ ___ ___ [1] ___ ___

2. Julio will not buy the expensive CD player right away.

___ ___ ___ ___ ___ [2] ___ ___

3. Sam will wait a few months before moving to Maine.

[4] ___ [3] ___ ___ ___ ___ ___ ___

4. My dog's coat is dull and dirty, so I give her a bath.

___ ___ [5] ___ ___ ___

5. The store manager hopes that a sale will bring in new customers.

[6] ___ ___ ___ ___ ___

6. The old carpet looks bad and needs to be replaced.

___ ___ ___ [7] ___ ___

## What does Papa want to get from taking the cattle to Abilene?

___ ___ ___ ___ m o ___ ___ ___
 1   2   3   4        5   6   7

| Vocabulary | dingy | hesitate | entice |
| --- | --- | --- | --- |



Practice Book • Unit 1

## Practice Reading Phrases

1. just as the bell rang

2. invaded parts of Europe and Africa

3. felt a rush of fear

4. hoped it was a drill

5. in the windows of the houses

## Practice Reading Sentences

1. He got to school just as the bell rang.

2. American troops had invaded parts of Europe and Africa.

3. Robert felt a rush of fear as his teacher pointed to China on the world map.

4. At least Robert hoped it was a drill.

5. He counted the blue and gold stars in the windows of the houses.

## Timed Reading

**{ ROLE OF THE READER }**

Read the passage to your partner as accurately as possible.

Remember, your reading goal is 80 Words Correct Per Minute (WCPM).

**{ ROLE OF THE LISTENER }**

As your partner reads, mark these errors with a strikethrough:

- mispronounced words
- skipped words
- changed words
- added words

Excerpt from
# Wartime Waiting

| | Number of Words |
|---|---|
| Robert sealed his letter and dropped it in the mail. He got | 12 |
| to school just as the bell rang. The teacher began each day by | 25 |
| discussing the war. American troops had invaded parts of Europe and | 36 |
| Africa. They were fighting against Germany and Italy. They were also | 47 |
| fighting Japan on islands in the South Pacific. Robert felt a rush of | 60 |
| fear as his teacher pointed to China on the world map. | 71 |
| An alarm suddenly sounded and stopped the class. It was an | 82 |
| air-raid drill. At least Robert hoped it was a drill. Some of Hannah's | 95 |
| first letters from England described real air raids. Planes dropped | 105 |
| bombs on cities. People gathered together in basements. Houses blew | 115 |
| up around them. Robert thought about Hannah running for safety. | 125 |
| The worries and fears of her life replaced his own. | 135 |
| On his way home from school, Robert rode his bicycle through | 146 |
| the streets of his neighborhood. He counted the blue and gold stars in | 159 |
| the windows of the houses. A blue star meant that a man from that | 173 |
| family was a soldier away at war. | 180 |

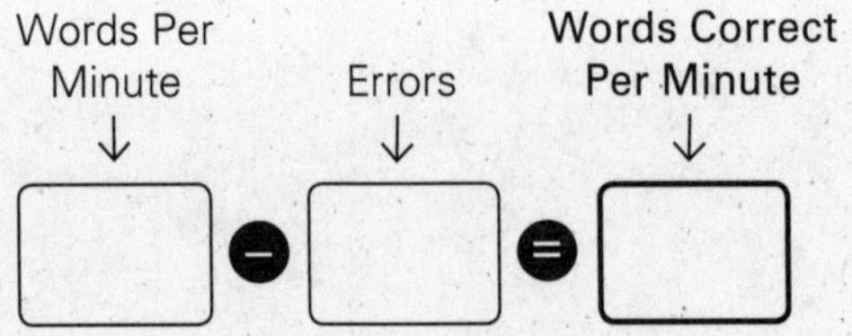

# High-Frequency Words

| little | one | down | getting | funny |

# Words of the Day

__ __ __ __ __     __ __ __ __ __ __ __     __ __ __ __

__ __ __ __ __ __ __

# Categorize

Write each Word of the Day under the correct category.

| help | already | care | here | idea |

**Words with two or more syllables**

1. __________

2. __________

**Words with vowel + silent _e_**

3. __________

4. __________

**Action words**

5. __________

6. __________

**Words for people, places, or things**

7. __________

8. __________

# Word Study Skill

Read the words in the box. Circle five words that have a long *i*, long *o* or long *u* sound.

| | | | | |
|---|---|---|---|---|
| **why** | **thaw** | **my** | **that** | **someone** |
| **goat** | **soap** | **watt** | **grew** | **eat** |

# Phonics Practice

Circle the word in each group with the long *i* sound. Underline the long *o* word. For each word, draw a box around the letters that make the long vowel sound.

1. g r e w     w h y     b o w
2. l o a n     t h r e w     s h y
3. g l u e     f l y     g o a l
4. s k y     c h e w e d     f l o w i n g

# Apply It

Read the paragraph below. Circle words with the long *i* sound spelled with *y*. Circle words with the long *o* sound spelled with *oa* or *ow*. Also circle words with the long *u* sound spelled with *ue* or *ew*.

Long ago, children worked tough jobs for little pay. Many worked long hours in factories, farms, and even coal mines. Why? Some needed money for their families. Others were forced. In the 1800s the United States had few laws to help them. These children often could not go to school. Then, concern for them began to grow. People saw the true cost of child labor.

# Spell It

| **Spelling Tip** | Many long *i* words are spelled with *y*. Many long *o* words are spelled with *oa* or *ow*. Many long *u* words are spelled with *ue* or *ew*. |
| --- | --- |

1. _______________________

2. _______________________

3. _______________________

4. _______________________

5. _______________________

## World's Fair, 1893

*Part 2 of 2*

Then we walked into the Women's Building,
Which featured female talent and fine art.
We saw Cassatt's **murals** and Bronte's writing—
Beauty that set these two women apart.

The next stop for us was Machinery Hall.
The place basically ran the whole show.
Over forty steam engines pumped in all,
Giving each of the bulbs its bright glow.

We then took a long, slow **gondola** ride,
And rode fast electric boats to get back.
We cruised on a steamship for ten cents a ride
And rode trains on an elevated track.

It was time to go meet our parents then,
As the sun was beginning to set.
I couldn't believe this sweet dream was to end.
We hadn't seen everything yet!

**murals** large paintings that cover walls or ceilings
**gondola** a long, narrow boat

---

## Notes

1. Circle the words that rhyme in each stanza. What is the rhyme pattern in this poem?

2. How do you think the narrator feels about seeing all these sights?

---

We met our folks beside a giant pool's edge.
It reflected a dark sky gleaming bright.
White bulbs outlined each building's ledge.
Water in fountains danced left and right.

We walked the **pavilion** together
And described all the sights we had seen.
My mother wanted an automobile.
My father wanted a washing machine.

We returned to the Midway that night
And saw exciting performers galore.
We turned our heads up and looked to the sky
Enticed by flashes and a thunderous roar.

Exploding above in a dazzling rainbow
Were brilliant reds, greens, yellows, and blues.
Someone had launched a great fireworks show.
We all marveled at the wonderful views. ⏸

**Notes**

3. What happens in this section?

_______________________________

_______________________________

_______________________________

_______________________________

_______________________________

_______________________________

_______________________________

_______________________________

4. Why would the narrator describe the water in fountains as dancing?

_______________________________

_______________________________

_______________________________

_______________________________

_______________________________

_______________________________

_______________________________

_______________________________

_______________________________

---

**pavilion**  large tent-like structure

The next day we sadly returned to our farm—
To dim candles, wood, and old gaslights.
We took with us very fond memories,
And our future was more than just bright.

Years later I told my young children
Of the fair and how its sights were so grand.
They rolled their eyes, and they shook their heads,
Each too young to understand.

They said I was old-fashioned,
That I had grown up with the dinosaurs.
The amazing things I saw at the fair
Were now available in all the stores.

I told them that times continue to change
With new inventions and technology.
What will your children think is old-fashioned?
One day you will see. ⏸

{ **What inventions are you familiar with that the narrator saw for the first time at the fair?** }

## Notes

{ 5. Use context clues to clarify the meaning of the word *memories* in the third line. What does *memories* mean? }

{ 6. What did the narrator's children say the narrator was? }

# Narrative Map: Reading

**Text:** ________________________________________________

| **Characters** | **Setting** |
|---|---|
| **Main:** ________________ | **Where:** ________________ |
| ________________ | ________________ |
| | ________________ |
| **Others:** ________________ | **When:** ________________ |
| ________________ | ________________ |
| ________________ | ________________ |

## Summary

**Part 1:** ________________________________________________

________________________________________________

________________________________________________

________________________________________________

________________________________________________

________________________________________________

**Part 2:** ________________________________________________

________________________________________________

________________________________________________

________________________________________________

________________________________________________

________________________________________________

# Plot

BEGINNING

MIDDLE

END

Narrator: ______________________________________

______________________________________

# Problem and Solution

Problem: ____________________

____________________

____________________

Solution: ____________________

____________________

____________________

# Subject Pronouns

| **About Subject Pronouns** | • A subject pronoun is used as the subject of the sentence. Subject pronouns are: *I, you, he, she, it, we, they.*<br>• A subject pronoun tells who or what does something in the sentence.<br>• A pronoun takes the place of one or more nouns or pronouns. However, a subject pronoun replaces the complete subject of a sentence, not just the noun. |
| --- | --- |

## Choose the Subject Pronouns

Circle the correct subject pronoun to replace the complete subject underlined in each sentence.

1. The funny man with the puppet (He, They) tells lots of stories.

2. Your friend Lisa (you, she) knows a lot about the Civil War.

3. Carl and I (I, We) work after school.

4. All of my relatives (They, It) live in Mexico.

5. The Hendersons' house (It, He) is 100 years old.

# Find It in Your Reading

Write three sentences from your reading that include subject pronouns. Circle the
subject pronouns.

1. ___________________________________________________________

___________________________________________________________

2. ___________________________________________________________

___________________________________________________________

3. ___________________________________________________________

___________________________________________________________

# Put It in Your Writing

Write at least three sentences about a time you experienced something new. Be
sure to include at least one subject pronoun in each sentence.

1. ___________________________________________________________

___________________________________________________________

2. ___________________________________________________________

___________________________________________________________

3. ___________________________________________________________

___________________________________________________________

{ DONE ✔ }

## STEP **1** Making Connections

I will connect what I already know to the narrative "Old Yeller" by Fred Gipson and discuss how life for the teenager in "Old Yeller" was different from today.



## STEP **2** Developing Vocabulary

I will learn three new vocabulary words: *motion*, *solemnly*, and *appalling*.

## STEP **3** Practicing Fluency

I will read aloud part of "Wartime Waiting" with fluency by practicing phrasing and by changing voice to reflect characters, and I will chart my fluency progress.

## STEP **4** Building Word Study Skills

I will learn, practice, and spell five new high-frequency words.
I will practice recognizing and using words with the long *a* sound *(ai, ay)*, the long *e* sound *(ea, y)*, the long *i* sound *(y)*, the long *o* sound *(oa, ow)*, and the long *u* sound *(ue, ew)*.
I will understand the spelling homework assignment.

## STEP **5** Reading for Understanding

I will review the reading skill of clarifying for character, setting, plot, narrator, and problem/solution.
I will learn to use the reading strategy of predicting.

## STEP **6** Applying the Conventions of English

I will review my understanding of nouns and pronouns.
I will identify and use object pronouns in my speaking, reading, and writing.

## STEP **7** Writing with Purpose

I will review the stages of the writing process.
I will use a narrative frame to complete a first draft of my narrative.

{ Summarizing My Learning }

_______________________________________________

_______________________________________________

# Crossword Puzzle

Read the clues for each number. Write the correct vocabulary word on the puzzle.

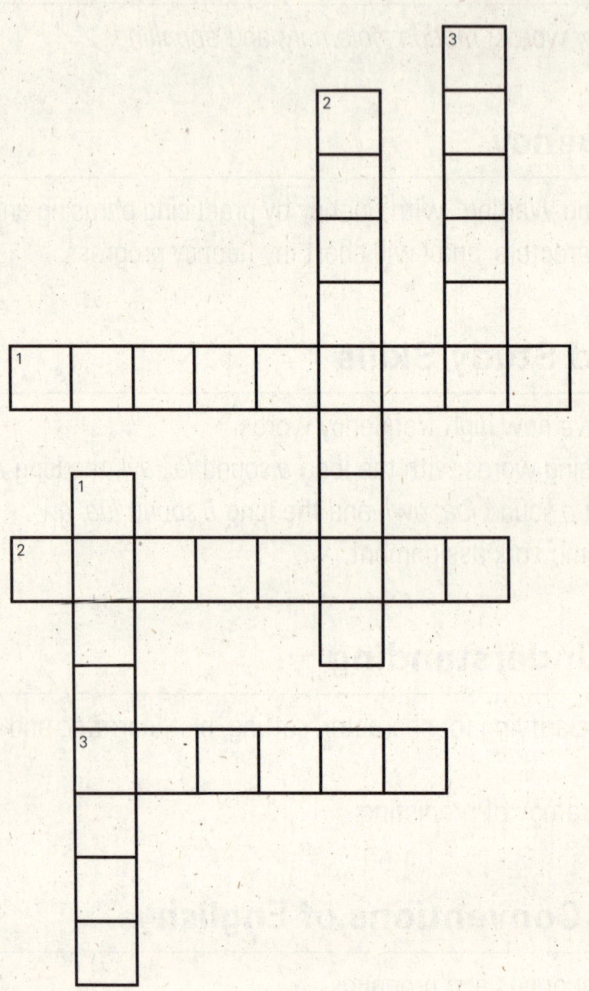

## Across

1. Tariq thought the violent news story was _________ .
2. Hannah _________ told her sister that the dog had died.
3. The usher will _________ to Katlin to show where our group will sit.

## Down

1. Pat's mom _________ walked into Mr. Garza's office so she would not disturb other people in the meeting.
2. Most reviewers called the _________ book scary and upsetting.
3. The judge will _________ her head up and down to show if the answer is right.

| Vocabulary | motion | appalling | solemnly |

## Practice Reading Phrases

1. stars in the windows

2. never be replaced

3. mailbox was empty

4. As he walked through the front door

5. sat alone with the telegram

## Practice Reading Sentences

1. He counted the blue and gold stars in the windows of the houses.

2. He hoped it would never be replaced with a gold one.

3. When Robert got home, the mailbox was empty.

4. As he walked through the front door to his house, he was startled when a man behind him shouted, "Telegram!"

5. He sat alone with the telegram for over two hours.

## Timed Reading

**{ ROLE OF THE READER }**

Read the passage to your partner as accurately as possible.

Remember, your reading goal is 80 Words Correct Per Minute (WCPM).

**{ ROLE OF THE LISTENER }**

As your partner reads, mark these errors with a strikethrough:

- mispronounced words
- skipped words
- changed words
- added words

Excerpt from
# Wartime Waiting

| | Number of Words |
|---|---|
| On his way home from school, Robert rode his bicycle through | 11 |
| the streets of his neighborhood. He counted the blue and gold stars in | 24 |
| the windows of the houses. A blue star meant that a man from that | 38 |
| family was a soldier away at war. A gold star meant that the soldier | 52 |
| had been killed. Nearly every house had a star. Robert thought of | 64 |
| the blue star in his window at home. He hoped it would never be | 78 |
| replaced with a gold one. | 83 |
| When Robert got home, the mailbox was empty. As he walked | 94 |
| through the front door to his house, he was startled when a man | 107 |
| behind him shouted, "Telegram!" The note the man held was | 117 |
| addressed to Robert's mother. | 121 |
| Robert felt as if he had been punched in the stomach. The military | 134 |
| usually sent a telegram when a soldier died in combat. Robert didn't | 146 |
| want to look, and he decided he would wait for his mother. He sat | 160 |
| alone with the telegram for over two hours. | 168 |

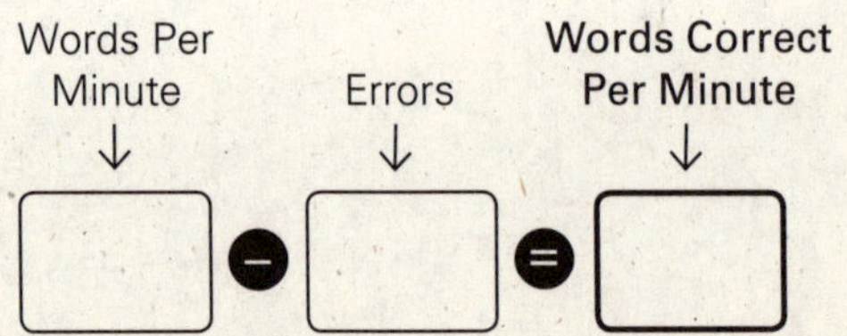

# High-Frequency Words

| help | already | care | here | idea |
|------|---------|------|------|------|
| little | one | down | getting | funny |

# Words of the Day

_________    _________    _________

_________    _________    _________

# Missing Letters

Write the missing letter or letters for each Word of the Day. Then write the complete word.

1. ha█ing    ····▶ _____    ····▶ _____________

2. to█d    ····▶ _____    ····▶ _____________

3. w██d    ····▶ _____    ····▶ _____________

4. ██hout    ····▶ _____    ····▶ _____________

5. █te    ····▶ _____    ····▶ _____________

# Word Study Skill

Read the words in the box. Circle five words that have a long *a, e, i, o,* or *u* sound.

| | | | | |
|---|---|---|---|---|
| fail | bit | moat | blue | apple |
| pry | speak | raw | crash | blood |

# Phonics Practice

Read the words in the boxes. Write each word in the correct column on the chart.

| wean | known | hue | drew | wailing | stray | dry | goal |

| long *a* (ai, ay) | long *e* (ea, y) | long *i* (y) | long *o* (oa, ow) | long *u* (ue, ew) |
|---|---|---|---|---|
| | | | | |

# Apply It

Read the sentences below. For each one, circle the words with the correct long vowel sound.

1. long *a* (spelled *ay, ai*)    Rain fell all day on the town.

2. long *e* (spelled *ea, y*)    Billy was stuck inside with nothing to do but read.

3. long *i* (spelled *y*)    He decided to try writing a story by himself.

4. long *u* (spelled *ue, ew*)    As wind blew outside, Billy wrote his true story.

5. long *o* (spelled *oa, ow*)    When he was done, he decided to show his friend Joan.

---

# Spell It

| Spelling Tip | Many long *e* words are spelled with *ea* or *y*. Many long *a* words are spelled with *ai* or *ay*. Many long *i* words are spelled with *y*. Many long *o* words are spelled with *oa* or *ow*. Many long *u* words are spelled with *ue* or *ew*. |
|---|---|

1. _______________________

2. _______________________

3. _______________________

4. _______________________

5. _______________________

# Topic Introduction

**Text:** _______________________________

**Topic:** _______________________________

**Related Terms:**

1. _______________________________

2. _______________________________

3. _______________________________

4. _______________________________

5. _______________________________

6. _______________________________

7. _______________________________

8. _______________________________

9. _______________________________

10. _______________________________

**The term I know most about is:**

_______________________________

**What I know:**

_______________________________

_______________________________

_______________________________

_______________________________

_______________________________

_______________________________

_______________________________

_______________________________

_______________________________

_______________________________

_______________________________

# Prediction Log

**Text:** _______________________________________

**Prediction #1:** _______________________________________

_______________________________________

**Textual Evidence:** _______________________________________

_______________________________________

**Summary:** _______________________________________

_______________________________________

_______________________________________

_______________________________________

**Prediction #2:** _______________________________________

_______________________________________

**Textual Evidence:** _______________________________________

_______________________________________

**Summary:** _______________________________________

_______________________________________

_______________________________________

_______________________________________

**Prediction #3:** _______________________________

_______________________________

**Textual Evidence:** _______________________________

_______________________________

**Summary:** _______________________________

_______________________________

_______________________________

_______________________________

## Summary

_______________________________

_______________________________

_______________________________

_______________________________

_______________________________

_______________________________

# Object Pronouns

<table>
<tr><td>About Object Pronouns</td><td>

- A pronoun is a word that is used in place of one or more nouns or pronouns.
- An object pronoun completes the meaning of the action verb and tells who or what receives the action of the verb. An object pronoun comes after the verb in a sentence.
- These words are object pronouns: *me, you, him, her, us, them. It* can also be used as an object pronoun.

</td></tr>
</table>

## Find Object Pronouns

Read the paragraph. Circle all the object pronouns you find.

Anna's mother gave her two jugs of cream. Anna took them. Anna poured the cream into the large wooden container. She began to stir it with a paddle. She stirred it for a long time. Then Anna's mother called her. "Anna, stop churning when the cream turns to butter. Then bring it to the kitchen. I will make us fresh biscuits tonight."

# Find It in Your Reading

Write three sentences from your reading that include object pronouns. Circle the object pronouns. Write the noun that each object pronoun replaces.

1. _______________________________________________

_______________________________________________

2. _______________________________________________

_______________________________________________

3. _______________________________________________

_______________________________________________

# Put It in Your Writing

Write three sentences to tell about a time you shared something with someone. Use as many object pronouns as you can in each sentence.

1. _______________________________________________

_______________________________________________

2. _______________________________________________

_______________________________________________

3. _______________________________________________

_______________________________________________

{ DONE ✔ }

AGENDA

## STEP 1 Making Connections

I will connect what I already know to the narrative "Island of the Blue Dolphins" by Scott O'Dell and discuss how life for teenagers in "Island of the Blue Dolphins" was different from today.

## STEP 2 Developing Vocabulary

I will discuss the six vocabulary words: *dingy, hesitate, entice, motion, solemnly,* and *appalling*.

## STEP 3 Practicing Fluency

I will read aloud part of "The Big Hunt" with fluency by practicing phrasing and using punctuation to inform meaning, and I will chart my fluency progress.

## STEP 4 Building Word Study Skills

I will learn, practice, and spell five new high-frequency words.
I will practice recognizing and using words with diphthongs *oi* and *oy*.
I will understand the spelling homework assignment.

## STEP 5 Reading for Understanding

I will review the reading strategy of predicting.
I will learn to use the reading skill of predicting for character, setting, plot, narrator, and problem/solution.

## STEP 6 Applying the Conventions of English

I will review my understanding of verbs.
I will identify and use present tense verbs in my speaking, reading, and writing.

## STEP 7 Writing with Purpose

I will review the stages of the writing process.
I will review the first draft of my narrative and identify ideas for revision.

{ Summarizing My Learning }

# Hidden Clues

Read the clues for each number. Write the correct vocabulary word under each clue. The letters in the boxes will complete the answer to the question at the bottom of the page.

1. Brianna will nod if she decides to bring the drinks to the party.

___ ___ ___ [1] ___ ___ ___

2. Will's dad will tell him not to buy the first car he saw.

[2] ___ ___ [3] ___ ___ ___

3. Elena washed her favorite T-shirt so many times it now looks old and faded.

___ ___ [4] [5] ___

4. Keisha does her homework quietly and seriously.

[6] ___ ___ ___ ___ ___ ___

5. Rich thinks it's awful to see trash dumped all over the street.

___ ___ [7] ___ ___ ___ ___

6. Mr. Harness buys books online because they offer him free shipping.

___ ___ ___ [8] ___ ___

## What does Ramo go back to the village to get?

a ___ f ___ s ___ ___ ___ ___ ___ ___ ___ a r
     1    2  3  4  5    6  7  8

| **Vocabulary** | dingy | entice | solemnly |
| --- | --- | --- | --- |
| | hesitate | motion | appalling |

## Practice Reading Phrases

1. how he got his name

2. too excited to sleep

3. came across a Lakota settlement

4. often heard appalling stories

5. called themselves Americans

## Practice Reading Sentences

1. "Wake up!" Big Bear growled to his son, leaving no doubt as to how he got his name.

2. "I've been too excited to sleep!"

3. "I heard some came across a Lakota settlement," said the other man.

4. Though he had never seen a ghost face, Spotted Horse often heard appalling stories about them.

5. He also knew ghost faces called themselves Americans and spoke a language called English.

## Timed Reading

**{ ROLE OF THE READER }**

Read the passage to your partner as accurately as possible.

Remember, your reading goal is 80 Words Correct Per Minute (WCPM).

**{ ROLE OF THE LISTENER }**

As your partner reads, mark these errors with a strikethrough:

- mispronounced words
- skipped words
- changed words
- added words

Excerpt from
# The Big Hunt

|  | Number of Words |
|---|---|
| "Wake up!" Big Bear growled to his son, leaving no doubt as to | 13 |
| how he got his name. "Today is a big day for you." | 25 |
| "I am awake," said Spotted Horse as he ran out of the tipi. "I've | 39 |
| been too excited to sleep!" | 44 |
| "Meet me at the fire," called Big Bear. "We're having buffalo stew | 56 |
| today." | 57 |
| "I'll be right there," said Spotted Horse. Buffalo stew was his | 68 |
| favorite. An elder made it before every hunt. | 76 |
| As Spotted Horse ate, he overheard two men talking to his father. | 88 |
| "Many more ghost faces are moving west through the Great Plains," | 99 |
| said one. | 101 |
| "I heard some came across a Lakota settlement," said the other | 112 |
| man. "They forced the Lakota to move and ruined their hunt." | 123 |
| Big Bear groaned and shook his head. Spotted Horse looked up | 134 |
| from his stew and shook his head, too. Though he had never seen a | 148 |
| ghost face, Spotted Horse often heard appalling stories about them. | 158 |
| He also knew ghost faces called themselves Americans and spoke a | 169 |
| language called English. | 172 |

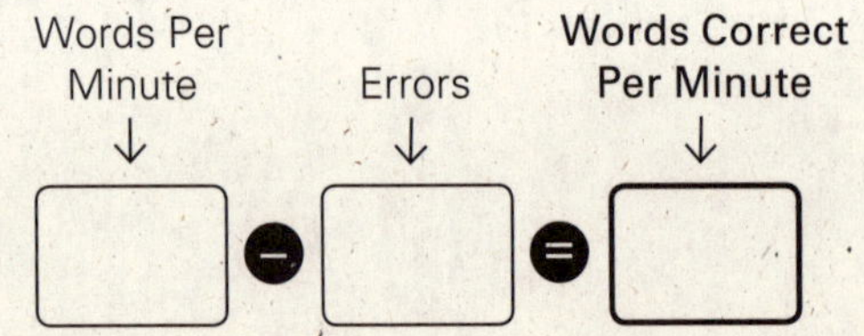

## High-Frequency Words

| | | | | |
|---|---|---|---|---|
| ate | word | having | without | told |
| help | already | care | here | idea |
| little | one | down | getting | funny |

## Words of the Day

__ __ __ __ __   __ __ __ __ __   __ __ __ __

__ __ __ __   __ __ __ __

## Scrambled Letters

Use the scrambled letters below to spell the Words of the Day.

| have | like | must | old | new |
|---|---|---|---|---|

1. o  d  l  = ______

2. a  e  v  h  = ______

3. w  n  e  = ______

4. k  i  l  e  = ______

5. s  t  u  m  = ______

# Word Study Skill

Read the words in the box. Circle five words that have the diphthongs *oi* or *oy*.

| | | | | |
|---|---|---|---|---|
| boy | cure | coil | shirt | boil |
| home | float | toy | burn | toil |

---

# Phonics Practice

Circle the word in each pair with the diphthong *oi*. For each word, underline the letters that make the diphthong sound *oi* or *oy*.

1. oil        enjoy

2. toy        boil

3. ploy        moist

4. oyster        soil

# Apply It

Read the paragraph below. Circle words with the diphthong *oi*. Also circle words with the diphthong *oy*.

Troy waved goodbye to Mr. Brown. Mr. Brown had been a loyal employee of the family farm. But Troy's father could no longer pay Mr. Brown to work on the farm. Troy was sad as he walked past the pig pen. "Oink," squealed the pigs. Troy looked out over the pig pen. He saw something shiny in the soil near Big Boy, his favorite pig. Could it be a coin? Was it a piece of foil? He moved closer. No, it was oil!

# Spell It

| Spelling Tip | Many words contain diphthongs *oi* or *oy*. |
| --- | --- |

1. _______________________________

2. _______________________________

3. _______________________________

4. _______________________________

5. _______________________________

## The Big Hunt

*Part 2 of 4*

Crow's Heart gathered the hunters. He was the hunt leader and wanted to make sure that each man knew exactly what he was supposed to do. Spotted Horse listened carefully and tried to hold back his excitement. Crow's Heart called out the names of the men who would be shooting arrows. It was decided. Spotted Horse would finally have the chance to fire his bow during a hunt.

"Let's head to Sitting Bear Field," said Crow's Heart. "The buffalo wander out in the open and graze this time of day. Big Bear, you take the lead horse and separate the herd. The rest of us will spread out and surround the group. As always, each man should shoot no more than three arrows. We trust that this will provide for us and **preserve** our precious buffalo." ⓫

**preserve** protect

## Notes

1. Why do you think the Native Americans want to preserve their precious buffalo?

_______________________

_______________________

_______________________

_______________________

_______________________

2. What do you think is the problem in this story? How do you predict Spotted Horse will solve it?

_______________________

_______________________

_______________________

_______________________

_______________________

_______________________

_______________________

_______________________

_______________________

The Lakota hunters mounted their horses. Their families cheered as they rode away. When the hunters arrived at the field, Spotted Horse took his place. He looked out over the field. Countless buffalo quietly grazed the landscape in front of him.

Crow's Heart lifted his arm and motioned to Big Bear. As Big Bear charged on his horse, the crowd of American buffalo ran. The ground rumbled as buffalo rushed past the hunters. Many buffalo ran in Spotted Horse's direction. Spotted Horse drew his bow. His heart thumped, and his hands were sweaty and shaking. He fired at one of the buffalo. He watched his arrow stick in the earth. As his first arrow broke under the hoof of a buffalo, Spotted Horse turned his horse and saw another buffalo quickly approaching. ❚❚

## Notes

3. How does Spotted Horse feel when the hunt begins? Underline the evidence in the text to support your answer.

_______________________

_______________________

_______________________

_______________________

_______________________

_______________________

4. What happened after Spotted Horse shot his first arrow? Underline it. What do you predict will happen next?

_______________________

_______________________

_______________________

_______________________

_______________________

_______________________

_______________________

_______________________

_______________________

Without hesitating, he pulled out a second arrow and aimed. He released the arrow. Before he could tell if he'd hit his target, the mighty buffalo crashed to the ground. The earth seemed to shake under the animal's fall. For a moment, Spotted Horse felt lost in the roar and dust that surrounded him.

Big Bear raced over on his horse. "Well done, son!" he shouted. "You were successful on your first hunt!"

Spotted Horse took a deep breath as the sounds of the running herd grew distant. His father leapt from his horse and cut a horn off the buffalo.

"This is your prize for your first kill," Big Bear said.

Spotted Horse smiled and tucked the horn in his **satchel.** He couldn't wait to share the news with his mother. ⏸

**How do Spotted Horse's feelings change from the beginning to the end of the hunt?**

---

**satchel** small bag

## Notes

5. Did Spotted Horse solve his problem? How do you know?

6. What was Spotted Horse's prize for his first buffalo? Circle it.

# Narrative Map: Reading

**Text:** _______________________________________________

## Characters

Main: _______________________________________

_______________________________________

Others: _____________________________________

_______________________________________

_______________________________________

_______________________________________

## Setting

Where: ______________________________________

_______________________________________

_______________________________________

When: _______________________________________

_______________________________________

## Summary

Part 1: ______________________________________

_______________________________________

_______________________________________

Part 2: ______________________________________

_______________________________________

_______________________________________

Part 3: ______________________________________

_______________________________________

_______________________________________

Part 4: ______________________________________

_______________________________________

_______________________________________

# Plot

**BEGINNING**

**MIDDLE**

**END**

Narrator: _______________________________________________

# Problem and Solution

Problem: _______________________

Solution: _______________________

# Present Tense Verbs

| **About Present Tense Verbs** | • A present tense verb expresses what exists or is happening now.<br>• Some present tense verbs express a state of being that exists now. Example: *I am dizzy.*<br>• Some present tense verbs express an action that is happening now. |
| --- | --- |

## Write the Present Tense Verb

Read each sentence. Then write the correct present tense form of the verb in parentheses on the line.

Life (to be) _________________ much easier now than it was 200 years ago. We can (to ride) _________________ bikes, cars, trains, or planes to travel. A person (to buy) _________________ food and other things he or she (to need) _________________ at stores. Many homes (to have) _________________ heat in winter and air conditioning in summer. Every town (to build) _________________ schools and libraries so people can get an education. Our government has passed many laws that (to protect) _________________ people at work, too. However, people still (to work) _________________ hard to take care of their families and be successful.

# Find It in Your Reading

Write three sentences from your reading that include present tense verbs. Underline each present tense verb. Then draw an arrow from each verb to each noun or pronoun that it tells about.

1. _______________________________________________

_______________________________________________

2. _______________________________________________

_______________________________________________

3. _______________________________________________

_______________________________________________

# Put It in Your Writing

Write sentences to describe yourself to a new pen pal. Underline the correct form of the present tense verbs you use in each sentence.

1. _______________________________________________

_______________________________________________

2. _______________________________________________

_______________________________________________

3. _______________________________________________

_______________________________________________

{ DONE ✔ }



## STEP **1** Making Connections

I will connect what I already know to the narrative "Island of the Blue Dolphins" by Scott O'Dell and discuss how life for teenagers in "Island of the Blue Dolphins" was different from today.

## STEP **2** Developing Vocabulary

I will discuss the six vocabulary words: *dingy, hesitate, entice, motion, solemnly,* and *appalling.*

## STEP **3** Practicing Fluency

I will read aloud part of "The Big Hunt" with fluency by practicing phrasing and focusing on conveying emotion and meaning, and I will chart my fluency progress.

## STEP **4** Building Word Study Skills

I will learn, practice, and spell five new high-frequency words.
I will practice recognizing and using words with diphthongs *ou* and *ow*.
I will understand the spelling homework assignment.

## STEP **5** Reading for Understanding

I will review the reading skill of predicting for character, setting, plot, narrator, and problem/solution.
I will review the reading strategy of predicting.

## STEP **6** Applying the Conventions of English

I will review my understanding of present tense verbs.
I will identify and use present progressive tense verbs in my speaking, reading, and writing.

## STEP **7** Writing with Purpose

I will review the stages of the writing process.
I will finish revising my narrative and edit for complete and correct sentences.

{ Summarizing My Learning }

# Crossword Puzzle

Read the clues for each number. Write the correct vocabulary word on the puzzle.

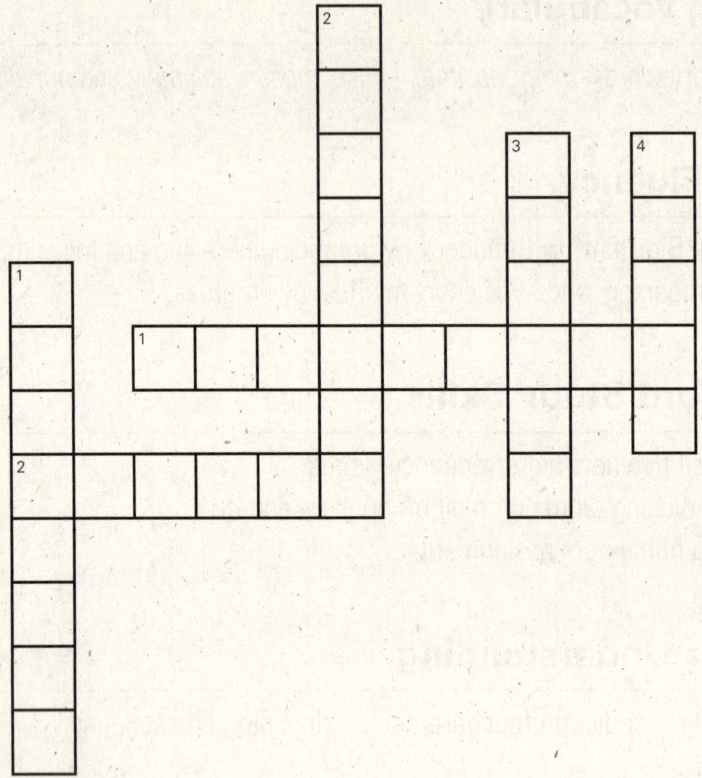

**Across**

1. Leta found the restaurant __________ because it was so dirty.
2. The exciting features will __________ José to buy a new cell phone.

**Down**

1. The hospital visitors talked __________ so they would not wake the patients.
2. Having a puppy is a big job, so you should __________ before buying one too quickly.
3. The clerk will __________ to the next person in line.
4. Carl cleaned his old, __________ carpets.

| Vocabulary | dingy | appalling | solemnly |
| --- | --- | --- | --- |
| | motion | hesitate | entice |

# Practice Reading Phrases

1. finally have the chance
2. no more than three arrows
3. will provide for us
4. as they rode away
5. grazed the landscape

# Practice Reading Sentences

1. Spotted Horse would finally have the chance to fire his bow during a hunt.
2. "As always, each man should shoot no more than three arrows."
3. "We trust that this will provide for us and preserve our precious buffalo."
4. Their families cheered as they rode away.
5. Countless buffalo quietly grazed the landscape in front of him.

# Timed Reading

**{ ROLE OF THE READER }**

Read the passage to your partner as accurately as possible.

Remember, your reading goal is 80 Words Correct Per Minute (WCPM).

**{ ROLE OF THE LISTENER }**

As your partner reads, mark these errors with a strikethrough:

- mispronounced words
- skipped words
- changed words
- added words

Excerpt from
# The Big Hunt

Number of Words

Crow's Heart gathered the hunters. He was the hunt leader and | 11

wanted to make sure each man knew exactly what he was supposed | 23

to do. Spotted Horse listened carefully and tried to hold back his | 35

excitement. Crow's Heart called out the names of the men who would | 47

be shooting arrows. It was decided. Spotted Horse would finally have | 58

the chance to fire his bow during a hunt. | 67

"Let's head to Sitting Bear Field," said Crow's Heart. "The buffalo | 78

wander out in the open and graze this time of day. Big Bear, you take | 92

the lead horse and separate the herd. The rest of us will spread out | 106

and surround the group. As always, each man should shoot no more | 118

than three arrows. We trust that this will provide for us and preserve | 131

our precious buffalo." | 135

The Lakota hunters mounted their horses. Their families cheered | 144

as they rode away. When the hunters arrived at the field, Spotted | 156

Horse took his place. He looked out over the field. Countless buffalo | 168

quietly grazed the landscape in front of him. | 176

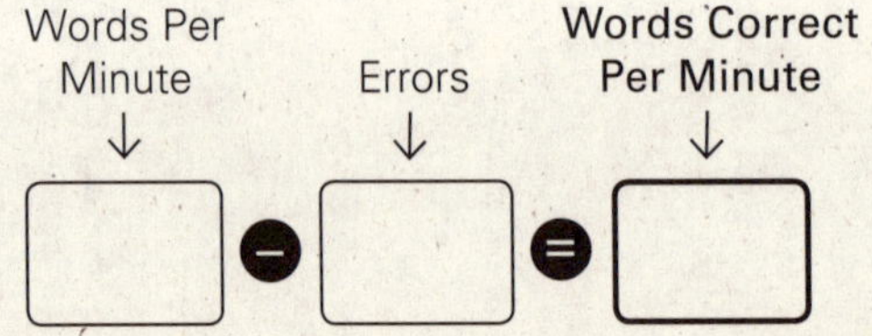

# High-Frequency Words

| | | | | | | |
|---|---|---|---|---|---|---|
| have | little | one | care | without | told | ate |
| word | must | down | here | idea | help | |
| already | having | new | getting | funny | like | old |

---

# Words of the Day

___ ___ _______ ___ ___

___ ___ _______

---

# Word Riddles

Answer the riddles below with the Words of the Day.

| now | take | of | our | eat |
|---|---|---|---|---|

1. Which word has 2 letters? __________

2. Which word would you use to tell
   about something that belongs to us? __________

3. Which word has 3 letters and
   describes what you do with food? __________

4. Which word has a long *a* sound? __________

5. Which word rhymes with *cow?* __________

# Phonics Skill

Read the words in the box. Circle five words that have the diphthongs *ou* or *ow*.

| now | tooth | pick | loud | it |
|-----|-------|------|------|-----|
| cow | box | brown | cloud | with |

---

# Phonics Practice

Circle the word with the diphthong *ou*. For each word, underline the letters that make the diphthong sound *ou* or *ow*.

1. plow      pout

2. noun      cow

3. vow       out

4. meow      mouth

# Apply It

Read the paragraph below. Circle words with the diphthong *ou*. Also circle words with the diphthong *ow*.

Flower counted to ten to calm herself down. It was her first day as a clown. She wanted to wow the crowd with her tricks. Flower vowed to make her parents proud of her. Skipping into the ring, she began to dance around. It was like she was dancing on a cloud. The make-up frown painted on her face did not hide her smile.

# Spell It

| **Spelling Tip** | Many words contain diphthongs *ou* or *ow*. |
|---|---|

1. _______________________________

2. _______________________________

3. _______________________________

4. _______________________________

5. _______________________________

# Quick Write

How do Spotted Horse's feelings change from the beginning to the end of the hunt?

# Prediction Log

**Text:** _______________________________________________

**Prediction #1:** _______________________________________

_______________________________________________

**Textual Evidence:** ____________________________________

_______________________________________________

**Summary:** ____________________________

_______________________________________________

_______________________________________________

_______________________________________________

_______________________________________________

**Prediction #2:** _______________________________________

_______________________________________________

**Textual Evidence:** ____________________________________

_______________________________________________

**Summary:** ____________________________

_______________________________________________

_______________________________________________

_______________________________________________

_______________________________________________

**Prediction #3:** _______________________________

_______________________________

**Textual Evidence:** _______________________________

_______________________________

**Summary:** _______________________________

_______________________________

_______________________________

_______________________________

_______________________________

## Summary

_______________________________

_______________________________

_______________________________

_______________________________

_______________________________

_______________________________

# Present Progressive Tense Verbs

**About Present Progressive Tense Verbs**

- A present tense verb expresses what exists or is happening now.
- The present progressive tense verb expresses a continuing action or state of being. Example: *I am walking to school right now.*
- Form the present progressive tense by adding *-ing* to the main verb in the present tense. Use the correct tense of the *be* verb and use it as the helping verb. Helping verbs are *am, is,* and *are.*
- The helping verbs *am* and *is* are used with most singular subjects. The helping verb *are* is used with the pronoun *you* and all plural subjects. Examples: *I am walking; You are walking; He is walking; She is walking; It is walking; We are walking; You are walking; They are walking.*

## Identify the Present Progressive Tense

Read each sentence. Underline all of the examples of present progressive tense verbs you find. Underline both words that make up the present progressive tense verb.

1. Marilee is calling.

2. She is calling to say that she is feeling better.

3. I am making dinner for us right now.

4. I am watching the oven.

5. My pie is baking, and I do not want it to burn.

6. It is an apple pie, and it is bubbling.

# Find It in Your Reading

Write three sentences from your reading that include the present progressive tense. Underline each example of the present progressive tense. Be sure to underline both words that form the present progressive tense of the verb.

1. _______________________________________________

_______________________________________________

2. _______________________________________________

_______________________________________________

3. _______________________________________________

_______________________________________________

# Put It in Your Writing

Write three sentences to describe things that you are doing right now. Underline the present progressive tense verbs in your sentences.

1. _______________________________________________

_______________________________________________

2. _______________________________________________

_______________________________________________

3. _______________________________________________

_______________________________________________



Practice Book • Unit 1

## STEP **1** Making Connections

{DONE ✔}

I will connect what I already know to a photograph and discuss how life for teenagers of the past was different from today.

## STEP **2** Developing Vocabulary

I will review and complete an assessment of six vocabulary words.

## STEP **3** Practicing Fluency

I will read aloud part of "The Big Hunt" with fluency by practicing phrasing, and I will chart my fluency progress.

## STEP **4** Building Word Study Skills

I will learn, practice, and spell five new high-frequency words.
I will practice recognizing and using words with diphthongs *oi, oy, ou,* and *ow.*
I will complete a spelling test to assess my ability to spell the chapter words.

## STEP **5** Reading for Understanding

I will review the reading strategy of predicting.
I will review the reading skill of predicting for character, setting, plot, narrator, and problem/solution.

## STEP **6** Applying the Conventions of English

I will review my understanding of nouns, pronouns, and present tense verbs.
I will write declarative sentences using the conventions learned in this chapter.

## STEP **7** Writing with Purpose

I will review the stages of the writing process.
I will edit my narrative for word choice, adjectives, punctuation, and spelling.

{Summarizing My Learning}

{AGENDA}

# Show What You Know

Read each question. Check the box beside the best answer.

1. If your mother **hesitates** before taking a new job, she

   ☐ starts right away.

   ☐ thinks about it for a while.

   ☐ turns it down.

   ☐ accepts a different job.

2. Which action would **entice** people to drive their cars less?

   ☐ Build more roads.

   ☐ Raise the speed limit.

   ☐ Make cars bigger.

   ☐ Raise the cost of gasoline.

3. Zack <u>pointed</u> to where Maria should put the box.
   Which word would work best as a substitution for the underlined word?

   ☐ enticed

   ☐ motioned

   ☐ hesitated

   ☐ appalled

4. If you find a movie **appalling,** you might

   ☐ give it a good review.

   ☐ see it again.

   ☐ walk out in the middle.

   ☐ move to another seat.

5. Select the word that has the closest meaning to **dingy.**

   ☐ dirty

   ☐ serious

   ☐ tired

   ☐ bored

6. Someone who is at a _______ would most likely act **solemnly.**

   ☐ carnival

   ☐ supermarket

   ☐ restaurant

   ☐ hospital

## Practice Reading Phrases

1. help move the buffalo
2. used every part of each buffalo
3. but I can be better
4. pulled back on his horse
5. a covered wagon and three people

## Practice Reading Sentences

1. People from the settlement arrived later to help move the buffalo.
2. Spotted Horse's tribe used every part of each buffalo they killed.
3. "I am shooting well, but I can be better."
4. Spotted Horse pulled back on his horse and nearly fell.
5. Behind him was a covered wagon and three people Spotted Horse knew must be the boy's family.

## Timed Reading

**{ ROLE OF THE READER }**

Read the passage to your partner as accurately as possible.

Remember, your reading goal is 80 Words Correct Per Minute (WCPM).

**{ ROLE OF THE LISTENER }**

As your partner reads, mark these errors with a strikethrough:

- mispronounced words
- skipped words
- changed words
- added words

Excerpt from
# The Big Hunt

| | Number of Words |
|---|---|
| People from the settlement arrived later to help move the buffalo. | 11 |
| Everyone worked together to skin the great beasts, cut them into | 22 |
| pieces, and load them onto horses. They were careful not to leave | 34 |
| anything behind. Spotted Horse's tribe used every part of each | 44 |
| buffalo they killed. | 47 |
| When the tribe returned to the settlement, Spotted Horse could | 57 |
| think of nothing but hunting. "Father, I am riding back to the field. Is | 71 |
| that OK?" he asked. | 75 |
| "Why?" asked Big Bear. | 79 |
| "I must practice," said Spotted Horse. "I am shooting well, but I | 91 |
| can be better." | 94 |
| "You may go," laughed Big Bear. "Make sure to return before the | 106 |
| sun falls. We are preparing a feast." | 113 |
| Spotted Horse rode his horse to the field. As he came through | 125 |
| some bushes, Spotted Horse saw a ghost face staring up at him. | 137 |
| Spotted Horse pulled back on his horse and nearly fell. The boy | 149 |
| appeared to be the same age as Spotted Horse, but he had short | 162 |
| blonde hair and wore strange clothes. Behind him was a covered | 173 |
| wagon and three people Spotted Horse knew must be the boy's | 184 |
| family. | 185 |

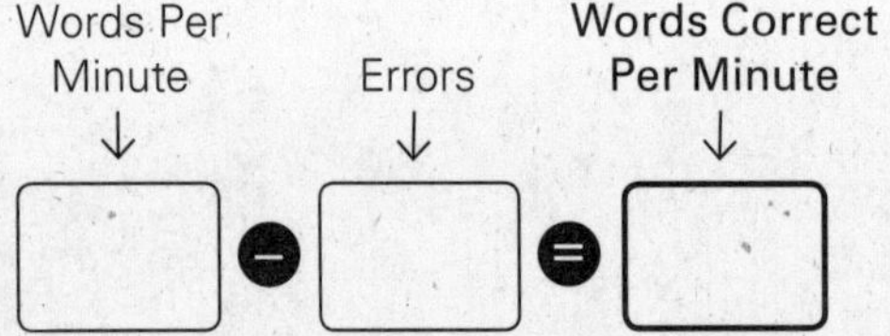

# High-Frequency Words

| | | | | | | |
|---|---|---|---|---|---|---|
| now | take | one | already | eat | getting | idea |
| have | like | of | down | new | told | |
| ate | word | must | our | without | here | |
| little | help | having | old | care | funny | |

# Words of the Day

________   ________   ________   ________

________   ________   ________   ________

# Alphabetical Order

List the Words of the Day in alphabetical order.

| out | please | pretty | enough | ride |
|---|---|---|---|---|

1. ________________________

2. ________________________

3. ________________________

4. ________________________

5. ________________________

# Word Study Skill

Read the words in the box. Circle five words that have the diphthongs *oi, oy, ou,* or *ow.*

| foil | aloud | ploy | today | surface |
|------|-------|------|-------|---------|
| because | clown | aim | drown | basket |

# Phonics Practice

Read the words in the boxes. Write each word in the correct column on the chart.

| clown | toys | cloud | coins | boiled | point | about | brow |

| diphthong *oi* | diphthong *oy* | diphthong *ou* | diphthong *ow* |
|----------------|----------------|----------------|----------------|
|  |  |  |  |

# Apply It

Read the sentences below. For each one, circle the words with the correct diphthong.

1. *oy*   Roy would not let his sister annoy him today.

2. *oi*   He had toiled over the same wooden joint for a week and now he was done.

3. *ou*   Roy wanted to make his dad proud by helping around the farm.

4. *ow*   Now that he was finished fixing the plow, he could finally rest.

# Spell It

| **Spelling Tip** | Many words contain diphthongs *oi, oy, ou,* or *ow.* |
| --- | --- |

1. _______________________________________

2. _______________________________________

3. _______________________________________

4. _______________________________________

5. _______________________________________

## The Big Hunt

*Part 4 of 4*

Spotted Horse soon found the two wagon horses. They were drinking water from a nearby stream. He tied them to his own horse with rope he had made from buffalo **sinews**. Then he returned to the ghost faces. He stopped in front of the man who had earlier drawn his rifle out of fear. The man reached out and took the rope.

"Thank you," he said. He motioned to the boy. The boy climbed inside the wagon. Spotted Horse could not believe how many belongings they carried. He thought of how his people could move their entire camp in a matter of hours. He thought of the **burden** these four people must feel carrying so many things.

**sinews** tissue that connects muscle to bone
**burden** difficulty

### Notes

1. Why do you think Spotted Horse knew to look for the horses by a stream?

________________________________

________________________________

________________________________

________________________________

________________________________

________________________________

2. What do you predict will happen next? What is your evidence?

________________________________

________________________________

________________________________

________________________________

________________________________

________________________________

________________________________

________________________________

The boy emerged from the wagon and held out a sack to Spotted Horse. Inside was a beautiful knife. Spotted Horse studied the knife for some time. Then he remembered Little Crow's stories about the trading post. He realized the boy expected something in return.

Spotted Horse solemnly reached into his satchel. He knew the only valuable thing he owned was the buffalo horn he'd received as a trophy that afternoon. He held the horn out to the boy.

The boy took the horn in his hands. He looked it over and handed it back to Spotted Horse. Spotted Horse, thinking his trade had been refused, tried to return the boy's knife. ⏸

> **Notes**
>
> 3. Was your prediction from question 2 accurate? How was it different from what actually happened?
>
> _______________________
> _______________________
> _______________________
> _______________________
> _______________________
>
> 4. What did Spotted Horse give the boy? Why?
>
> _______________________
> _______________________
> _______________________
> _______________________
> _______________________
> _______________________
> _______________________
> _______________________
> _______________________
> _______________________

The boy waved his hand and pushed the knife back toward Spotted Horse. Then he pointed to the horses. Spotted Horse realized that the knife was being traded for his good deed. He smiled and raised his hand in thanks.

Spotted Horse looked over his shoulder as he rode home. He saw that the family had turned their wagon back on its wheels. As the sun dipped to the horizon, Spotted Horse sped up. He looked forward to getting home. He would tell of the hunt and of the ghost faces he'd met in the field. He'd show off the buffalo horn and the knife he'd received in the trade. He'd wake in the morning and jump in the river. When he saw the children playing, he'd remember even less of what it was to be like them. ⏸

**What is life like for Spotted Horse? How is it different from life today?**

## Notes

5. How does Spotted Horse know that the knife was being traded for his good deed?

6. What predictions does Spotted Horse make about what will happen next? Underline them. Do you think his predictions will be accurate? Why or why not?

# Conventions Review

## Review Plural Nouns

Fill in each line with the correct plural noun.

As the Statue of Liberty comes into view, all the _________________ (family) on the

boat rush to the _________________ (deck). Antonio wraps his _________________ (arm)

around his mother's waist. He has seen many _________________ (city) so far in his short

life, but somehow he knows New York will be different.

## Review Subject Pronouns

Circle the correct subject pronoun to replace the underlined noun in each
sentence.

1. Can <u>Marcus</u> (he, they) mow our lawn?

2. <u>Our lawn</u> (We, It) is starting to look like a jungle.

3. <u>My wife and I</u> (They, We) are on vacation and cannot cut it.

## Review Object Pronouns

Read the paragraph. Circle all the object pronouns you find.

"Can you hand me the photo album?" Grandma asks.

I give her the dusty book. "This picture shows the day your grandfather and I were

married." The picture is old and faded. I examine it closely.

"I think you look a lot like him!" she says with a big smile.

# Review Present Tense Verbs

Read each sentence. Then write the correct present tense form of the verb in parentheses on the line.

My little sister, Carmen, (love) _________________ baseball. She even (say)

_________________ she (want) _________________ to travel back in time to meet Jackie

Robinson. I (think) _________________ she might be a great player herself someday.

# Review Present Progressive Tense

Read each sentence. Underline all the examples of present progressive tense you find. Underline both words that make up the present progressive tense.

1. Right now my class is studying the Civil War.

2. We are learning all about Abraham Lincoln.

3. I study every night, so I am expecting to do well on the chapter test.

# Put It in Your Writing

Write three sentences about the place in which your family lives. Check to make sure your sentences contain plural nouns, subject and object pronouns, and present tense verbs, including the present progressive tense. Example: *He is taking me to my games this year. He* is a subject pronoun; *me* is an object pronoun; *is taking* is a verb in the present progressive tense; *games* is a plural noun.

_______________________________________________________________

_______________________________________________________________

_______________________________________________________________

**STEP 1 Developing Test-Taking Strategies** {DONE ✔}

I will read a test-taking manual.
I will learn strategies for taking multiple-choice tests.



**STEP 2 Assessing My Learning**

I will take a multiple-choice test on skills I learned in this chapter.

**STEP 3 Writing With Purpose**

I will publish the final draft of my narrative.

**STEP 4 Analyzing My Results**

I will identify which questions I answered correctly and which questions I answered
   incorrectly.

**STEP 5 Reinforcing My Learning**

I will reinforce my understanding of using sentence and word clues to find the meaning
   of unknown words.
I will reinforce my understanding of how to include simple supporting facts and details
   in my writing.

**STEP 6 Speaking With Purpose**

I will watch a video of a speech and evaluate the speaker's delivery of the speech.

{Summarizing My Learning}

_______________________________________________

_______________________________________________

_______________________________________________

# Test-Taking Manual
## Before the Test

### Be Prepared

- Know what you will be tested on and study.
- Get a full night's rest.
- Have all your materials (pencil, eraser, calculator, dictionary) at your desk.

### Be Comfortable but Alert

- Make sure you have enough room to work.
- Do not slouch in your chair.

### Stay Relaxed and Confident

- Remember that you are well prepared and can do well.
- Take deep breaths if you feel anxious.
- Do not talk about the test with the other students.

## During the Test

Follow these five steps for each question on the test.

**Step 1:** Determine what the question is asking you to do.

**Step 2:** Try to answer the question in your own words.

**Step 3:** Eliminate any answers you know are incorrect.

**Step 4:** Choose the best answer.

**Step 5:** If time allows, review your answers to each question.

### Example Question

1. **The statue is a <u>monument</u> to the man that founded our town.**

   A. party

   B. built

   C. remembrance

   D. gigantic

# Skills Assessment 2

Read each sentence, and then find the choice that means the same as the underlined word.

1. The dog wagged his tail as he <u>willingly</u> let me take him for a walk.
   - A. sadly
   - B. happily
   - C. helpfully
   - D. slowly

2. Because of the rain, we <u>remained</u> in the house.
   - A. stayed
   - B. left
   - C. played
   - D. worked

3. For <u>enjoyment</u>, my family likes to play board games.
   - A. work
   - B. exercise
   - C. health
   - D. fun

4. I remembered my aunt, but I did not <u>recognize</u> my cousin because she had grown so much.
   - A. understand
   - B. see
   - C. know
   - D. ask

5. I tripped on the rug so many times that now I <u>avoid</u> walking on it.
   - A. keep away from
   - B. usually like
   - C. move toward
   - D. think about

6. I was <u>thrilled</u> about having a birthday because I wanted a new bicycle.
   - A. unhappy
   - B. wishing
   - C. smart
   - D. excited

*Go on to the next page →*

# Skills Assessment 2, continued

**Read this draft of a story, then answer the questions.**

(1) Tillie's camping trip was really fun. (2) They went to a place called Jackson's Lake, and it was beautiful. (3) There were a lot of fun things to do there. (4) During the day, they went on hikes and went swimming. (5) In the evenings they sat around the campfire telling scary stories.

(6) One night, Uncle Gus told a story about a giant bear. (7) First, he described what it looked like. (8) He said that there was a giant bear that lived in the woods that was looking for food. (9) All of a sudden, they heard a noise behind their tent. (10) Tillie jumped up and screamed. (11) Her cousins ran into the tent. (12) Tillie wanted to know what scared her. (13) She walked toward the tent and looked behind it.

*Go on to the next page →*

# Skills Assessment 2, continued

**7. Which detail should be put after sentence 1?**

> (1) Tillie's camping trip was really fun.

A. Camping by a lake is good because of water sports.

B. She went with her cousins and her Uncle Gus.

C. Children love to go camping in the summer.

D. Tillie really enjoys swimming in the summer.

**8. Which of these would be the BEST way to begin sentence 8?**

> (8) He said that there was a giant bear that lived in the woods that was looking for food.

A. Last,

B. Then,

C. Before,

D. Today,

**9. Which detail could be put after sentence 10?**

> (10) Tillie jumped up and screamed.

A. Tillie used to jump a lot when she was little.

B. Screaming is fun when a person is not scared.

C. People all over the campsite could hear her.

D. Some people really know how to scream loudly.

**10. Which detail should be put after sentence 11?**

> (11) Her cousins ran into the tent.

A. Tillie used to run track with her cousins.

B. There were a lot of tents at the campground.

C. Their tent was full of backpacks and coats.

D. They were back in the tent in just seconds.

*Go on to the next page →*

# Skills Assessment 2, continued

**11.** Which of these would be the BEST way to begin sentence 13?

> (13) She walked toward the tent and looked behind it.

A. So,

B. Because,

C. Before,

D. Once,

**12.** Which is the BEST sentence to put at the end of the last paragraph?

A. Luckily, she found that two squirrels were making the noise.

B. It was late at night, and Tillie was getting really tired.

C. There are many stories about bears that bother campers.

D. Uncle Gus bought the tent at a sporting goods store at the mall.

**End of test** ■

# Using Word and Sentence Clues

| **Reminder:**<br>**Finding the**<br>**Meaning of an**<br>**Unknown Word** | • When you come to an unknown word, first look to see if there are any word parts you recognize.<br><br>• Word parts such as prefixes, root words, and suffixes can provide clues to the meaning.<br><br>• Look at the whole sentence for clues. Try to picture what is happening in the sentence. Also try to substitute a different word for the word you are trying to figure out. |
|---|---|

## Clarifying Log

"Oh, no!" Mom cried as we finished our sandwiches in the kitchen. "I think I left Coco's cage open!"

We ran to the living room. She was right. The door to Coco's cage was open, and my pet bird was gone! Mom gave me a regretful look.

"I'm really sorry," she said. "He must be in the house somewhere, right?"

For half an hour we called for Coco, but he didn't make a peep. Usually we couldn't keep him quiet. Eventually, however, we found him sitting quietly on the refrigerator.

"Coco, what were doing up there?" I asked as I carried him back to his cage.

"Sandwiches! Sandwiches!" he cried.

| Words to Clarify ⟶ | regretful | eventually |
|---|---|---|
| 1. Make a quick prediction. | | |
| 2. Look for a word ending, prefix, suffix, or root word. | | |
| 3. Identify the part of speech. | | |

| | | |
|---|---|---|
| **4.** Look for clues in the words and sentences nearby. | | |
| **5.** Make a more informed prediction. | | |
| **6.** Confirm the meaning of the word. | | |

# Identify the Meaning

Read each sentence, then find the choice that means the same as the underlined word.

**1. Ana made a delectable pie with just apples, cinnamon, and a little sugar.**

   **A.** difficult

   **B.** meat

   **C.** tasty

**2. There was not a cloud in the clear, azure sky.**

   **A.** rainy

   **B.** blue

   **C.** above

## Choices & Challenges

On your own piece of paper…

**A.** Use your favorite vocabulary word in a sentence. Include clues to the word's meaning in your sentence.

**B.** Find a word you do not know in a passage in your Anthology. Use what you have learned to write a prediction about its meaning.

**C.** Write to explain how you figured out one of the words in the test items above.

# Supporting Facts and Details

Read the passage from *Skills Assessment 2* on page 158. Then answer the following questions about the narrative.

## Idea Workshop: Narrative

1. In one sentence, summarize the problem.

2. What concrete sensory details show the setting of this narrative?

3. What happened in the beginning? What happened during the middle? What happened in the end?

# Idea Workshop: Narrative

4. After reading this narrative, what would you like to learn more about?

## Which Revision?

Circle the answer that could be added to the narrative to make it better.

**1. Which detail could be added after sentence 8?**

A. The bear was cuddly.

B. She went with her cousins and Uncle Gus.

C. The bear was large and hungry.

**2. Which detail could be added before sentence 10?**

A. It was very quiet.

B. It sounded like bells chiming.

C. It sounded like a monster crashing through the trees.

### Choices & Challenges
On your own piece of paper…

A. Look back at a piece of writing you have done recently. Make notes about where you might add more details.

B. Think of a time when you have done something new. Write sentences to explain how you felt. Include as many details as possible.

C. Find another place in the passage where the author might have added a detail. Write a sentence that he or she might have added.

## STEP 1 Making Connections

{DONE ✔}

I will connect what I already know to a painting and discuss the essential question, *How was life for teenagers of the past different from today?*

## STEP 2 Developing Vocabulary

I will discuss vocabulary words in a cumulative review.

## STEP 3 Practicing Fluency

I will read aloud part of "The Big Hunt" with fluency by practicing phrasing and conveying meaning and emotion, and I will chart my fluency progress.

## STEP 4 Building Word Study Skills

I will learn five new high-frequency words.
I will practice recognizing and using words with the *r*-controlled vowel patterns *–or, –ir, –ur,* and *–er.*
I will understand the spelling homework assignment.

## STEP 5 Reading for Understanding

I will review the genre of narrative.
I will learn to use the reading strategy of questioning.

## STEP 6 Applying the Conventions of English

I will review my understanding of complete and declarative sentences.
I will identify and use interrogative sentences in my speaking, reading, and writing.

## STEP 7 Writing with Purpose

I will review stages of the writing process.
I will deconstruct the narrative prompt and scoring guide, and I will begin prewriting.

{ Summarizing My Learning }

# Practice Reading Phrases

1. studied the knife

2. reached into his satchel

3. held the horn out

4. tried to return the boy's knife

5. raised his hand

# Practice Reading Sentences

1. Spotted Horse studied the knife for some time.

2. Spotted Horse solemnly reached into his satchel.

3. He held the horn out to the boy.

4. Spotted Horse, thinking his trade had been refused, tried to return the boy's knife.

5. He smiled and raised his hand in thanks.

# Timed Reading

**ROLE OF THE READER**

Read the passage to your partner as accurately as possible.

Remember, your reading goal is 80 Words Correct Per Minute (WCPM).

**ROLE OF THE LISTENER**

As your partner reads, mark these errors with a strikethrough:

- mispronounced words
- skipped words
- changed words
- added words

Excerpt from
## The Big Hunt

|  | Number of Words |
|---|---|
| The boy emerged from the wagon and held out a sack to Spotted | 13 |
| Horse. Inside was a beautiful knife. Spotted Horse studied the knife | 24 |
| for some time. Then he remembered Little Crow's stories about the | 35 |
| trading post. He realized the boy expected something in return. | 45 |
| Spotted Horse solemnly reached into his satchel. He knew the | 54 |
| only valuable thing he owned was the buffalo horn he'd received as a | 66 |
| trophy that afternoon. He held the horn out to the boy. | 79 |
| The boy took the horn in his hands. He looked it over and handed | 93 |
| it back to Spotted Horse. Spotted Horse, thinking his trade had been | 105 |
| refused, tried to return the boy's knife. | 112 |
| The boy waved his hand and pushed the knife back toward | 128 |
| Spotted Horse. Then he pointed to the horses. Spotted Horse realized | 134 |
| that the knife was being traded for his good deed. He smiled and | 147 |
| raised his hand in thanks. | 152 |

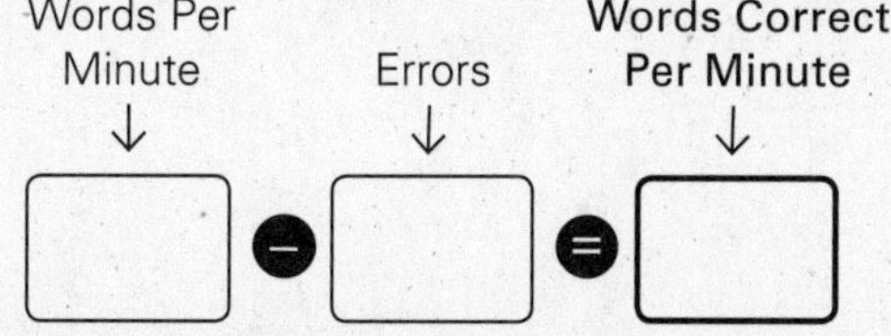

# Words of the Day

Spell each high-frequency word that you hear.

_______________     _______________     _______________

_______________     _______________

# Alphabetical Order

List the Words of the Day in alphabetical order.

| this | short | that | soon | there |
|------|-------|------|------|-------|

1. ______________________________

2. ______________________________

3. ______________________________

4. ______________________________

5. ______________________________

# Word Study Skill

Read the words in the box. Circle four words that have an *r*-controlled vowel sound *(–or, –ir, –ur, –er)*.

**germ**    **hatch**    **huge**    **magic**    **bird**

**burn**    **term**    **puppy**    **city**    **cage**

# Phonics Practice

Circle the word with the correct sound and letter pattern. Underline the letters that make the *r*-controlled vowel sound in each word.

1. *–or*    smirk    major
2. *–ur*    squirm    turn
3. *–er*    ever    birch
4. *–ir*    shirt    stern

# Apply It

Read the paragraph below. Circle words with *r*-controlled vowels *–or*, *–ir*, *–ur*, or *–er*.

Jasper urged his horse home. He had heard a rumor that Old Man Baxter was missing. If Old Man Baxter didn't light the lighthouse, the sailors would crash on the shore. The sea churned. Jasper felt the whirling rain through his shirt. When he got to the lighthouse, he burst up the ladder. On the top, he lit the lantern.

# Spell It

| **Spelling Tip** | If you hear the letter *r* in a word, that word may have one of the *r*-controlled vowels *–ir*, *–or*, *–er*, or *–ur*. |
| --- | --- |

1. _______________________

2. _______________________

3. _______________________

4. _______________________

5. _______________________

# Topic Introduction

**Text:** _______________________________________________

**Topic:** _______________________________________________

**Related Terms:**

1. _______________________________

2. _______________________________

3. _______________________________

4. _______________________________

5. _______________________________

6. _______________________________

7. _______________________________

8. _______________________________

9. _______________________________

10. _______________________________

**The term I know most about is:**

_______________________________

**What I know:**

_______________________________

_______________________________

_______________________________

_______________________________

_______________________________

_______________________________

_______________________________

_______________________________

_______________________________

_______________________________

_______________________________

_______________________________

# Summary Tree

**Text:** _______________________________________________

1.

2.

3.

1.

2.

3.

Where
When
Who
What Happened

1.

2.

3.

1.

2.

3.

**Summary**

# Question Log

**Text:** _______________________________

| Question #1 | Question #2 | Question #3 |
|---|---|---|
|  |  |  |

**On-the-Surface**
*who, where, when, and what happened*

**Under-the-Surface**
*how, why, would, could, and should*

| Question #1 | Question #2 | Question #3 |
|---|---|---|
|  |  |  |

## Summary

_______________________________

_______________________________

# Interrogative Sentences

**About Interrogative Sentences**

- An interrogative sentence asks a question.
- An interrogative sentence ends with a question mark.
- Many interrogative sentences begin with questioning words such as *who, what, when, where, why,* or *how.*

## Write an Interrogative Sentence

Read each declarative sentence. Then write an interrogative sentence to go with it using *who, what, when, where, why,* or *how.*

| SENTENCE | INTERROGATIVE SENTENCE |
|---|---|
| 1. Jim lives in the city. | |
| 2. I love to go to the library. | |
| 3. Panda bears eat bamboo. | |
| 4. We went to the movies last night. | |
| 5. Centerville is a large town. | |

## Find It in Your Reading

Find three interrogative sentences from your reading to write below. Circle the question word in each sentence. Circle the mark at the end of each sentence.

1. _______________________________________________

_______________________________________________

2. _______________________________________________

_______________________________________________

3. _______________________________________________

_______________________________________________

## Put It in Your Writing

Write three interrogative sentences about life 200 years ago. Remember to include a question mark at the end of each one.

1. _______________________________________________

_______________________________________________

2. _______________________________________________

_______________________________________________

3. _______________________________________________

_______________________________________________

{DONE ✔}

## STEP 1 Making Connections

I will connect what I already know to the narrative "The Master Puppeteer" by Katherine Paterson and Haru Wells and discuss how life for the teenager in "The Master Puppeteer" was different from today.

## STEP 2 Developing Vocabulary

I will learn three new vocabulary words: *nudge*, *miserable*, and *devise*.

## STEP 3 Practicing Fluency

I will read aloud part of "Daughter of Liberty" with fluency by practicing phrasing and stressing words with special type treatment, and I will chart my fluency progress.

## STEP 4 Building Word Study Skills

I will learn five new high-frequency words.
I will review recognizing and using words with *r*-controlled vowel patterns *–ar* and *–or*.
I will understand the spelling homework assignment.

## STEP 5 Reading for Understanding

I will review the reading strategy of questioning.
I will learn to use the reading skill of questioning for character, setting, plot, speaker, problem/solution, and theme.

## STEP 6 Applying the Conventions of English

I will review my understanding of interrogative sentences.
I will identify and use subject-verb agreement in my speaking, reading, and writing.

## STEP 7 Writing with Purpose

I will review the stages of the writing process, the writing prompt, and the scoring guide.
I will complete the prewriting stage of the writing process.

{ Summarizing My Learning }



Practice Book • Unit 1

# Hidden Clues

Read the clues for each number. Write the correct vocabulary word under each clue. The letters in the boxes will complete the answer to the question at the bottom of the page.

1. Gas costs a lot of money, so Kate and Tina make plans to carpool to school together.

   __ __ __ __ _[1]_

2. A bad cold makes me feel sore and tired.

   __ _[2]_ __ __ __ __ __ __

3. André will make a trap door to the backyard so his cat can go outside whenever she wants.

   __ __ __ _[3]_ __

4. When the mall is crowded, I try not to bump into other people by mistake.

   __ _[4]_ __ __ __

5. When my dad snores during a movie, we laugh and push his arm to wake him.

   _[5]_ __ __ _[6]_ __ __

6. Marco, our team captain, is very unhappy that he can't play in the soccer game.

   __ __ __ __ _[7]_ __ __ __ __

## Why is Jiro unhappy?

H _ _ _ h _ _ _ y.
   1   2   3    4   5   6   7

| Vocabulary | nudge | miserable | devise |

## Practice Reading Phrases

1. worry more about that butter
2. how to take care of a house
3. count for something
4. when Papa was sick
5. the way it is

## Practice Reading Sentences

1. "Right now, though, you should worry more about that butter."
2. "You'll never marry if you don't know how to take care of a house."
3. "*I'm* smart. Doesn't that count for something?"
4. "When Papa was sick, you ran the whole farm!"
5. "That's just the way it is."

## Timed Reading

{ ROLE OF THE READER }

Read the passage to your partner as accurately as possible.

Remember, your reading goal is 80 Words Correct Per Minute (WCPM).

{ ROLE OF THE LISTENER }

As your partner reads, mark these errors with a strikethrough:

- mispronounced words
- skipped words
- changed words
- added words

Excerpt from
## Daughter of Liberty

| | Number of Words |
|---|---|
| "That may be true," replied Mama. "Right now, though, you | 10 |
| should worry more about that butter." | 16 |
| "*Oh*, Mama!" Sophia said. "The things Papa and the men talk | 27 |
| about are more important!" | 31 |
| "You need to prepare for the day when you are married," said | 43 |
| Mama. "Look at your sister Deborah. She's seventeen and has two | 54 |
| babies already. You'll be her age in just three years. You'll never | 66 |
| marry if you don't know how to take care of a house. How do you | 81 |
| expect to find a smart man to take care of you?" | 92 |
| "*I'm* smart. Doesn't that count for something?" asked Sophia. | 101 |
| "Think of all the things we do. We milk the cows and make cheese. | 115 |
| We smoke meat and put away vegetables for the winter. We make | 128 |
| soap and candles. You keep track of the household money. When | 140 |
| Papa was sick, you ran the whole farm!" | 146 |
| "You have a point, Sophia," Mama said. "However, when women | 156 |
| get married, their husbands are in charge. That's just the way it is." | 169 |

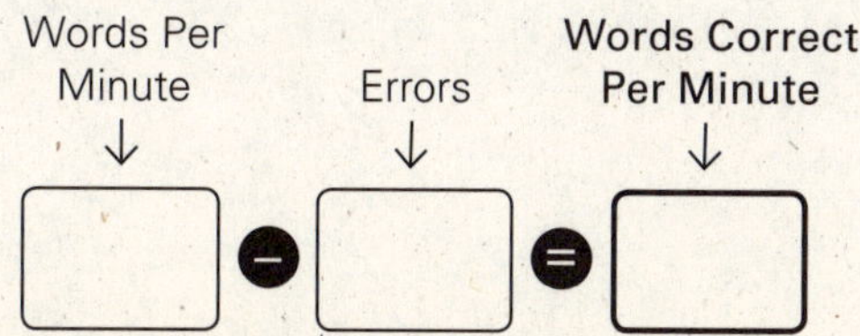

# High-Frequency Words

| this | short | that | soon | there |

# Words of the Day

___ ___ ___ ___      ___ ___ ___ ___ ___      ___ ___ ___ ___ ___

___ ___ ___ ___ ___      ___ ___ ___ ___

# Categorize

Write each Word of the Day under the correct category.

| how | with | under | they | well |

**Word with two syllables**

1. __________

**Words with *th***

2. __________

3. __________

**Words with *w***

4. __________

5. __________

6. __________

**Word that means the opposite of *over***

7. __________

# Word Study Skill

Read the words in the box. Circle five words that have an *r*-controlled vowel sound *(–ar, –or)*.

| | | | | |
|---|---|---|---|---|
| corn | pork | each | harp | laugh |
| art | leave | jar | east | aunt |

# Phonics Practice

Circle the word with the correct sound. Underline the letters that make the *r*-controlled vowel sound in each word.

1. *–or*   orchid   harder
2. *–ar*   ajar   sword
3. *–ar*   export   started
4. *–or*   darts   afford

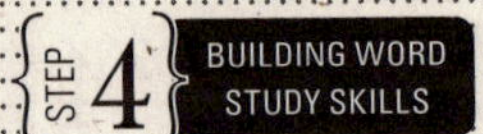

# Apply It

Read the paragraph below. Circle words with the *r*-controlled vowel sound /ar/. Also circle words with the /or/ sound.

Ciara picked up her harp. She began to play. She had worked hard to learn all the music. At first, the notes had sounded too sharp. She played major and minor chords. She practiced over and over until she formed them right. Soon she would play her harp with the organ.

# Spell It

| Spelling Tip | If you hear the letter *r* in a word, that word may have one of the *r*-controlled vowel sounds /or/ or /ar/. |
| --- | --- |

1. _______________________________

2. _______________________________

3. _______________________________

4. _______________________________

5. _______________________________

## Daughter of Liberty

*Part 2 of 6*

The next day, Sophia went to church with her family. The townspeople always gathered to talk after the service. They often talked about the weather, farm animals, and better ways to make candles. Today the men spoke out against the British.

Sophia stood behind her father so she could listen to the men. She had asked him before about the problems with the British. He always avoided her questions. She didn't like **eavesdropping**, but she wanted to know what was going on.

"Good afternoon, Sophia," a voice said, causing her to jump. "It's nice to see you."

It was Seth Lowell, who lived nearby. Sophia knew him from when they went to school together. Sophia had left school soon after she'd learned to read and do math. Even so, she and Seth had remained friends. ⏸

**eavesdropping** listening secretly

## Notes

1. What did the men talk about after church today?

2. What can you tell about Sophia from the second paragraph?

"Hello, Seth," Sophia said, blushing. She knew he had caught her listening to the men. "It's nice to have a day of rest, isn't it?"

"I know what you mean. We've been fixing the fences on our farm all week," said Seth. "I've also joined the Sons of Liberty."

"What's that?" Sophia asked.

"It's a group that fights for the rights of the **colonists**," Seth explained. "We Americans should collect our own taxes and take care of ourselves. That's what we've always done. We shouldn't be forced to live by British rules."

"But what can you do to stand up to the British?" Sophia replied. ⏸

**Notes**

3. What group fights for the colonists' rights?

4. Why does Seth join the Sons of Liberty?

**colonists** people who lived in the 13 British colonies that became the United States

"Well, the British wanted to tax colonists' legal papers and newspapers. They even wanted to tax our playing cards! It was called the Stamp Act, and the Sons of Liberty protested it. Because so many colonists refused to pay the tax, the act was reversed."

"I remember that," Sophia replied. "It still seems like the British treat us unfairly, though."

"That's because they force laws and other taxes on us," Seth said angrily. "They keep soldiers here to watch over us. We will **rebel** against them if we must."

"I wish I could do what you're doing," Sophia said. "You must feel as if you have a real purpose. *The Sons of Liberty*," she sighed. "I like the sound of that." ⏸

{ **How do Sophia and Seth feel about the British? How can you tell?** }

---

**rebel** defy or fight

---

### Notes

{ 5. What did colonists do to protest the Stamp Act? }

{ 6. Based on what you have read so far, what do you think is the theme of this story? }

# Narrative Map: Reading

Text: _______________________________

<table>
<tr><td colspan="2">Characters</td><td>Setting</td></tr>
</table>

**Characters**

Main: _______________________

_______________________

_______________________

Others: _______________________

_______________________

_______________________

**Setting**

Where: _______________________

_______________________

When: _______________________

_______________________

## Summary

Part 1: _______________________________

_______________________________

Part 2: _______________________________

_______________________________

Part 3: _______________________________

_______________________________

Part 4: _______________________________

_______________________________

Part 5: _______________________________

_______________________________

Part 6: _______________________________

_______________________________

# Plot

BEGINNING

_________________________________________________

_________________________________________________

_________________________________________________

_________________________________________________

MIDDLE

_________________________________________________

_________________________________________________

_________________________________________________

_________________________________________________

END

_________________________________________________

_________________________________________________

_________________________________________________

_________________________________________________

Narrator: _________________________________________

# Problem and Solution

Problem: _______________________     Solution: _______________________

_______________________              _______________________

_______________________              _______________________

# Theme

_________________________________________________

_________________________________________________

_________________________________________________

# Subject-Verb Agreement

<table>
<tr><td>About Subject-Verb Agreement</td><td>

- A subject and verb must agree in number.
- Use a singular subject with the singular form of a verb. Example: *Where am I?*
- Use a plural subject with the plural form of a verb. Example: *Where are we?*
- In an interrogative sentence, the verb sometimes appears before the subject. For example: *Is the dog black?*
- To determine the subject of an interrogative sentence and whether the verb agrees with it, try restating the interrogative sentence as a declarative sentence. For example: *Is the dog black? The dog is black.*

</td></tr>
</table>

## Fix the Verb

Underline the subject of each interrogative sentence. Cross out the verb. At the end of the sentence, write the correct form of the verb that agrees with the subject.

1. Is you ready to leave? _______________

2. Are the play about to begin? _______________

3. Which students is sitting in front? _______________

4. Does you want to jump rope now? _______________

5. Do Tita wish to join the group? _______________

6. When is Grandma and Grandpa eating dinner? _______________

# Find It in Your Reading

Write three interrogative sentences from your reading. Circle the subject.
Underline the verbs.

1. _______________________________________________

_______________________________________________

2. _______________________________________________

_______________________________________________

3. _______________________________________________

_______________________________________________

# Put It in Your Writing

Ask three questions about the town or city in which you live. Then answer each
question. Use correct subject-verb agreement in each sentence.

1. _______________________________________________

_______________________________________________

2. _______________________________________________

_______________________________________________

3. _______________________________________________

_______________________________________________

{ DONE ✔ }

## STEP 1 Making Connections

I will connect what I already know to the narrative "The Master Puppeteer" by Katherine Paterson and Haru Wells and discuss how life for the teenager in "The Master Puppeteer" was different from today.

## STEP 2 Developing Vocabulary

I will learn three new vocabulary words: *lament, fortitude,* and *slighted.*

## STEP 3 Practicing Fluency

I will read aloud part of "Daughter of Liberty" with fluency by practicing phrasing and conveying meaning and emotion, and I will chart my fluency progress.

## STEP 4 Building Word Study Skills

I will learn five new high-frequency words.
I will review recognizing and using words with *r*-controlled vowel patterns *–or, –ur, –ir, –er,* and *–ar.*
I will understand the spelling homework assignment.

## STEP 5 Reading for Understanding

I will review the skill of questioning for character, setting, plot, speaker, problem/solution, and theme.
I will review the reading strategy of questioning.

## STEP 6 Applying the Conventions of English

I will review my understanding of verbs.
I will identify and use helping verbs in my speaking, reading, and writing.

## STEP 7 Writing with Purpose

I will review stages of the writing process.
I will use a narrative frame to complete a first draft of my narrative.

{ Summarizing My Learning }

# Crossword Puzzle

Read the clues for each number. Write the correct vocabulary word on the puzzle.

## Across

1. I ________ that my favorite aunt cannot visit this year.
2. Juan showed ________ when he told the bully to leave his little brother alone.
3. Tran felt ________ that his party invitation was lost in the mail.

## Down

1. Dr. Herrera will ________ leaving her patients when she retires after 30 years.
2. An ambulance driver needs ________ to do a good job.
3. I felt ________ when I heard that other schools closed earlier than ours for summer vacation.

| **Vocabulary** | lament | fortitude | slighted |
| --- | --- | --- | --- |

## Practice Reading Phrases

1. townspeople always gathered

2. spoke out against the British

3. what was going on

4. learned to read and do math

5. he had caught her

## Practice Reading Sentences

1. The townspeople always gathered to talk after the service.

2. Today the men spoke out against the British.

3. She didn't like eavesdropping, but she wanted to know what was going on.

4. Sophia had left school soon after she'd learned to read and do math.

5. She knew he had caught her listening to the men.

## Timed Reading

{ **ROLE OF THE READER** }

Read the passage to your partner as accurately as possible.

Remember, your reading goal is 80 Words Correct Per Minute (WCPM).

{ **ROLE OF THE LISTENER** }

As your partner reads, mark these errors with a strikethrough:

- mispronounced words
- skipped words
- changed words
- added words

Excerpt from
# Daughter of Liberty

| | Number of Words |
|---|---|
| The next day, Sophia went to church with her family. The | 11 |
| townspeople always gathered to talk after the service. They often | 21 |
| talked about the weather, farm animals, and better ways to make | 32 |
| candles. Today the men spoke out against the British. | 41 |
| Sophia stood behind her father so she could listen to the men. She | 54 |
| had asked him before about the problems with the British. He always | 66 |
| avoided her questions. She didn't like eavesdropping, but she wanted | 76 |
| to know what was going on. | 82 |
| "Good afternoon, Sophia," a voice said, causing her to jump. "It's | 93 |
| nice to see you." | 97 |
| It was Seth Lowell, who lived nearby. Sophia knew him from | 108 |
| when they went to school together. Sophia had left school soon | 119 |
| after she'd learned to read and do math. Even so, she and Seth had | 133 |
| remained friends. | 135 |
| "Hello, Seth," Sophia said, blushing. She knew he had caught her | 146 |
| listening to the men. "It's nice to have a day of rest, isn't it?" | 160 |
| "I know what you mean. We've been fixing the fences on our farm | 173 |
| all week," said Seth. "I've also joined the Sons of Liberty." | 184 |

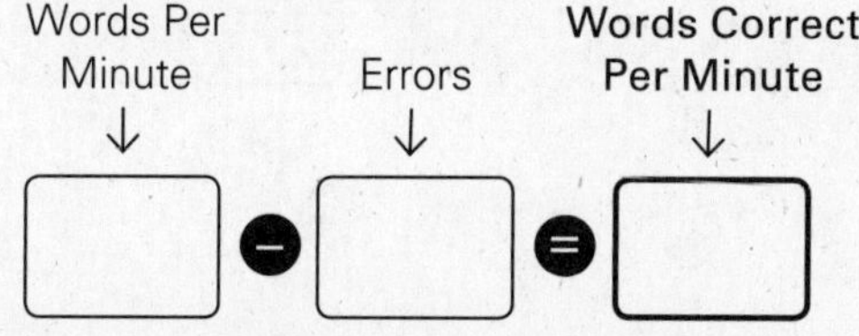

Words Per Minute ↓   −   Errors ↓   =   Words Correct Per Minute ↓

# High-Frequency Words

| how | with | under | soon | there |
|-----|------|-------|------|-------|
| this | short | that | they | well |

# Words of the Day

___ ___ ___   ___ ___ ___   ___ ___ ___

___ ___ ___   ___ ___ ___

# Missing Letters

Write the missing letter or letters for each Word of the Day. Then write the complete word.

1. p ▢▢ k  ·····▶  ___  ·····▶  _______________

2. y e ▢  ·····▶  ___  ·····▶  _______________

3. ▢▢ e d  ·····▶  ___  ·····▶  _______________

4. t ▢▢  ·····▶  ___  ·····▶  _______________

5. ▢ a y  ·····▶  ___  ·····▶  _______________

# Word Study Skill

Read the words in the box. Circle five words that have an *r*-controlled vowel sound.

| | | | | |
|---|---|---|---|---|
| horse | fast | tank | fish | blurt |
| herd | cow | yawn | girl | card |

# Phonics Practice

Read the words in the box. Write each word in the correct column on the chart.

kernel   confirm   conductor   cider

backyard   art   burning   passport

| *or* sound as in *tailor* | *ir* sound as in *firm* | *or* sound as in *boring* | *ur* sound as in *fur* | *er* sound as in *water* | *ar* sound as in *farm* |
|---|---|---|---|---|---|
| | | | | | |

# Apply It

Read the sentences below. For each sentence, circle the words with the correct *r*-controlled vowel sound.

1. *–ar*      Carmen gazed up at the stars in the night sky.

2. *–or* as in *neighbor*      The television blared from the tailor's shop behind her.

3. *–er*      They looked like swirling patterns of glitter.

4. *–ir*      She tried not to dirty her skirt as she lay on the grass.

5. *–or* as in *thorn*      Tonight, an astronaut had orbited around the Earth for the first time.

6. *–ur*      Was that burst of light the spaceship? Or was it just a blur in the sky?

# Spell It

| **Spelling Tip** | The letter combination *–or* can make different *r*-controlled vowel sounds, such as the *–or* in *sailor* or the *–or* in *short*. |
| --- | --- |

1. _______________________________________

2. _______________________________________

3. _______________________________________

4. _______________________________________

5. _______________________________________

# Quick Write

How do Sophia and Seth feel about the British? How can you tell?

# Summary Tree

**Text:** ___________________________________________

1.

2.

3.

1.

2.

3.

Where

When

1.

2.

3.

1.

2.

3.

Who

What
Happened

**Summary**

# Question Log

**Text:** _______________________________________________

|  |  |  |
|---|---|---|
| Question #1 | Question #2 | Question #3 |

**On-the-Surface**
*who, where, when, and what happened*

**Under-the-Surface**
*how, why, would, could, and should*

|  |  |  |
|---|---|---|
| Question #1 | Question #2 | Question #3 |

# Summary

_______________________________________________

_______________________________________________

_______________________________________________

# Helping Verbs

| **About Helping Verbs** | • In some sentences, the verb contains a main verb and one or more helping verbs. Example: *I may ride my bike. May* is the helping verb and *ride* is the main verb.<br>• A helping verb helps the main verb express an action or a state of being.<br>• Some common helping verbs are *may, might, could, must,* and *would*. |
| --- | --- |

## Find the Helping Verb

Read each sentence. Underline the two words that form the verb in each sentence. Circle the helping verbs.

1. I must finish my homework before bed.

2. The boys in her class might visit the museum.

3. We could not believe the size of the crowd!

4. The next train may arrive in an hour.

5. James and Lisa would love to see you at their party.

6. I would go with you.

# Find It in a Paragraph

Read the selection below. Find sentences with helping verbs.
Underline both words that form the verb. Then circle the helping verbs.

"The snow might fall all night," Papa calls to us as Ella and I jump

into bed. "It could be up past your waist by the time you wake up!"

I look at my sister in the bed next to mine and smile.

"Would we build a snowman or a fort tomorrow?" she asks me.

"We must finish our chores first," I tell her. "But after that, Papa says

we may play all afternoon!"

# Put It in Your Writing

Write sentences about a conversation between two people. Be sure to use a
helping verb in each sentence.

1. _______________________________________________

_______________________________________________

2. _______________________________________________

_______________________________________________

3. _______________________________________________

_______________________________________________

{ DONE ✔ }

## STEP 1 Making Connections

I will connect what I already know to the narrative "James Forten: Saved by a Game of Marbles" by Phillip Hoose and discuss how life for the teenager in "James Forten: Saved by a Game of Marbles" was different from today.

## STEP 2 Developing Vocabulary

I will discuss the six vocabulary words: *nudge*, *miserable*, *devise*, *lament*, *fortitude*, and *slighted*.

## STEP 3 Practicing Fluency

I will read aloud part of "Daughter of Liberty" with fluency by practicing phrasing and changing voice to reflect characters, and I will chart my fluency progress.

## STEP 4 Building Word Study Skills

I will learn five new high-frequency words.
I will review recognizing and using words with complex spelling patterns *ou*, *ould*, and *ough*.
I will understand the spelling homework assignment.

## STEP 5 Reading for Understanding

I will review the reading strategy of questioning.
I will review the reading skill of questioning for character, setting, plot, speaker, problem/solution, and theme.

## STEP 6 Applying the Conventions of English

I will review my understanding of verbs.
I will identify and use helping verbs in my speaking, reading, and writing.

## STEP 7 Writing with Purpose

I will review stages of the writing process.
I will review the first draft of my narrative and identify ideas for revision.

{ Summarizing My Learning }

_______________________________________________

_______________________________________________

# Hidden Clues

Read the clues for each number. Write the correct vocabulary word under each clue. The letters in the boxes will complete the answer to the question at the bottom of the page.

1. Lena felt so unhappy when her dog ran away, she cried every night.

__\[1\]_ ___ ___ ___ ___ ___ ___ ___

2. Tomas elbowed his brother to move him out of the blind man's way.

___ ___ ___ _\[2\]_ ___

3. Avi was brave and calm enough to stop the two boys from fighting.

___ ___ _\[3\]_ ___ ___ ___ ___ ___

4. The mean cheerleader looked down on me even after I made the team.

___ ___ ___ _\[4\]_ ___ ___ ___

5. Patricia says that she has not made any friends since her best friend moved away.

_\[5\]_ ___ _\[6\]_ _\[7\]_ ___

6. Marco, our team captain, is writing out a few new plays to help us win the next soccer game.

___ ___ _\[8\]_ ___

## Who were still rich and went to the theater in Jiro's city?

C
___ ___ ___ ___ ___ ___ ___ ___
1   2   3   4   5   6   7   8

| Vocabulary | nudge | miserable | devise |
|---|---|---|---|
| | lament | fortitude | slighted |

## Practice Reading Phrases

1. time to move

2. to get out of the way

3. you should be grateful

4. have some respect

5. every chance we get

## Practice Reading Sentences

1. "He should have given us time to move."

2. "It's your job to get out of the way."

3. "You should be grateful that we send soldiers to protect your western border."

4. "Tell your king to have some respect for us!"

5. "We must stand up to those Redcoats every chance we get."

## Timed Reading

**{ ROLE OF THE READER }**

Read the passage to your partner as accurately as possible.

Remember, your reading goal is 80 Words Correct Per Minute (WCPM).

**{ ROLE OF THE LISTENER }**

As your partner reads, mark these errors with a strikethrough:

- mispronounced words
- skipped words
- changed words
- added words

Excerpt from
## Daughter of Liberty

Number of Words

"Oh!" Mama complained. "He should have given us time to move." — 11

"That is Lieutenant Shaw," the soldier said. "He's busy with the — 22

king's business. What right do you have to object to it? It's your job — 36

to get out of the way." — 42

"How can you say that?" Mama demanded with great fortitude. — 52

"We are British citizens, just like you." — 59

"You colonists think you are treated so badly. People in England — 70

pay much higher taxes than you do," the soldier argued. "You should — 82

be grateful that we send soldiers to protect your western border." — 93

"Protect us?" said Mama. "You march around with your guns and — 104

treat us as if we are prisoners in our own country." — 115

"Then you may wish to tell your men to have some respect for their — 129

king and their country," he said. — 135

"Tell your king to have some respect for us!" Mama shot back. — 147

Mama turned her back to the soldier. She led Sophia away. A — 159

moment later, they heard a voice behind them. — 167

"Well done, Madam Heath. We must stand up to those Redcoats — 178

every chance we get." — 182

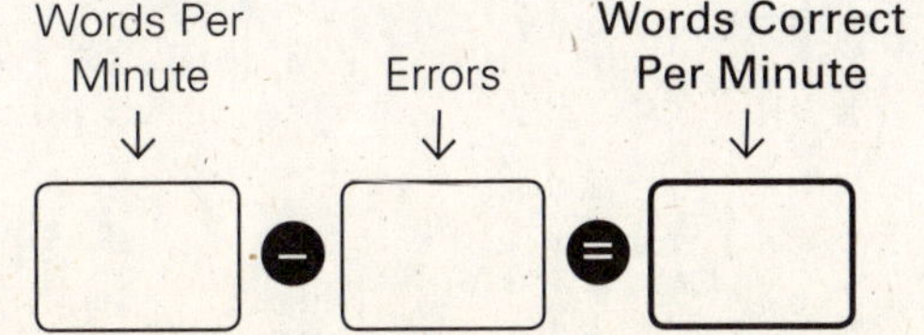

{STEP **4**} BUILDING WORD STUDY SKILLS

## High-Frequency Words

| too | this | with | park | that | soon | they | well |
|---|---|---|---|---|---|---|---|
| how | need | short | under | yes | say | there | |

## Words of the Day

__ __ __ __ __ __ __ __ __ __ __

__ __ __ __ __ __ __

## Scrambled Letters

Use the scrambled letters below to spell the Words of the Day.

| want | after | story | fly | went |
|---|---|---|---|---|

1. l   f   y   =  ______

2. t   a   w   n   =  ______

3. e   w   t   n   =  ______

4. f   a   t   e   r   =  ______

5. r   o   t   y   s   =  ______

# Word Study Skill

Read the words in the box. Circle five words that contain the pattern *ou*.

| | | | | |
|---|---|---|---|---|
| cloud | rule | loft | thaw | loud |
| mouth | cost | scout | poke | drought |

# Phonics Practice

Match each word to a word that has the same ending sound and spelling pattern. For each word, underline the letters *ou*. There will be one word left over.

tough

fought

through

could

dough

should

rough

sought

thorough

# Apply It

Read the paragraph below. Circle words that contain the spelling patterns *ou,* *ould*, and *ough*.

May 6, 1862

Dear Dr. Thorough,

My cousin Sue has a terrible cough. I told her that she ought to see a doctor. She was not sure. I brought her chicken soup to make her better. I thought it would help, but she's been coughing through the night. Could you please check on her?

Sincerely,

Henry Walden

# Spell It

| **Spelling Tip** | Words with spelling patterns *ou, ould,* and *ough* may look similar but sound different. |
| --- | --- |

1. _______________________________

2. _______________________________

3. _______________________________

4. _______________________________

5. _______________________________

## Daughter of Liberty

○—○—○—④—○—○
Part 4 of 6

"Madam Blake, this tea is very unusual," Sophia's mother said politely, making a sour face.

Sophia picked up her cup and took a swallow. The tea wasn't unusual. It was awful. She tried not to make a face.

"This is **sage** tea," Madam Blake said. "I know the tea may seem strange. But I belong to the Daughters of Liberty."

"The Daughters of Liberty?" Sophia asked. "Like the Sons of Liberty?"

"That's right," Madam Blake nodded. "We have made a promise not to buy any more tea from England."

"Why not?" Mama asked. "Tea comforts us, and we've been drinking it our whole lives!"

Sophia laughed. Her mother loved her cups of tea. ⏸

---

**sage** a type of herb used for medicines and cooking

## Notes

{ 1. What have the Daughters of Liberty promised to do? }

_______________________

_______________________

_______________________

_______________________

_______________________

_______________________

_______________________

_______________________

_______________________

{ 2. Why are the Daughters of Liberty protesting? }

_______________________

_______________________

_______________________

_______________________

_______________________

_______________________

"If we buy British tea, we are saying we deserve to be taxed," Madam Blake replied sharply. "So we ladies are **boycotting** British tea."

"It seems like such a small thing," Sophia said. "Does it really matter?"

"It sends a message that we can't be slighted or pushed around. Right now, the British don't listen to us. If we stop buying British **goods**, their businesses will suffer. Since they need our business, they will be forced to listen to us."

"I'll never drink tea again," Sophia declared. "I shall consider it poison!" ▮

**Notes**

3. What does Sophia declare?

4. Should the Daughters of Liberty protest?

**boycotting** not buying
**goods** products

Mama smiled politely. She still looked unsure. "I do love my tea," she lamented. "But then again, I like my self-respect more."

"It doesn't stop at tea," added Madam Blake. "We've devised many plans. We won't buy British cloth, either. We have promised to wear only **homespun** clothes. We have spinning parties where we make our own dresses. Join us! We need more strong women."

"Think about what the soldier said to us today, Mama," said Sophia. "Things like that will keep happening unless we try to make a difference. Let's join the Daughters of Liberty."

"We will think about your group, Madam Blake," said Sophia's mother. "Thank you for the *interesting* tea. We must return home." ⏸

> **What is the main problem in this story? How do you think it will be solved?**

---

**homespun** homemade



## Notes

5. What does Sophia tell her mother?

_______________________

_______________________

_______________________

_______________________

_______________________

6. Why does Sophia want to join the Daughters of Liberty?

_______________________

_______________________

_______________________

_______________________

_______________________

_______________________

_______________________

_______________________

_______________________

_______________________

# Helping Verbs

| About Helping Verbs | • A helping verb helps the main verb to express an action or a state of being. Example: *I will ride my bike.*<br>• The helping verb in a sentence does not always appear right before the main verb. Sometimes, one or more words separate the main verb and the helping verb. Example: *When are you going?*<br>• Some common helping verbs are *am, is, are, will, can,* and *could.* |
| --- | --- |

## Find the Helping Verb, Part II

Read each sentence. Underline the two words that form the verb in each sentence. Circle the helping verbs.

1. The ship's captain could perform amazing tricks for his guests.

2. Will you hand me the broom, please?

3. Shelly's friends can meet us any time this afternoon.

4. He will not tell any jokes in class.

5. I can run faster than anyone on my soccer team.

6. The alarm could ring at any minute.

# Find It in a Paragraph

Read the selection below. Find sentences with helping verbs.
Underline both words that form the verb. Then circle the helping verbs.

Thomas carries the milk pail inside just as the sun rises. He could not imagine how his uncle could milk cows every day at this hour. Back in the city, where his family lives, he would be asleep right now. But at his cousin's farm, everyone gets up before dawn.

*What will they make me do next?* Thomas thinks to himself. Just then, he sees his uncle coming toward him with a horse's saddle.

"You can ride a horse, right?" Thomas's uncle asks with a smile.

"Absolutely!" Thomas exclaims with relief.

# Put It in Your Writing

Write sentences to tell about special talents or skills you have. Make sure to include a helping verb in each sentence.

1. _______________________________________________

_______________________________________________

2. _______________________________________________

_______________________________________________

3. _______________________________________________

_______________________________________________

{ DONE ✔ }

## STEP **1** Making Connections

I will connect what I already know to the narrative "James Forten: Saved by a Game of Marbles" by Phillip Hoose and discuss how life for the teenager in "James Forten: Saved by a Game of Marbles" was different from today.

## STEP **2** Developing Vocabulary

I will discuss the six vocabulary words: *nudge, miserable, devise, lament, fortitude,* and *slighted.*

## STEP **3** Practicing Fluency

I will read aloud part of "Daughter of Liberty" with fluency by practicing phrasing and using punctuation to inform meaning, and I will chart my fluency progress.

## STEP **4** Building Word Study Skills

I will learn five new high-frequency words.
I will review recognizing and using words with complex spelling patterns *al, eigh, ol,* and *wa.*
I will understand the spelling homework assignment.

## STEP **5** Reading for Understanding

I will review questioning for character, setting, plot, speaker, problem/solution, and theme.
I will review the reading strategy of questioning.

## STEP **6** Applying the Conventions of English

I will review my understanding of declarative and interrogative sentences.
I will identify and use the order of main and helping verbs in my speaking, reading, and writing.

## STEP **7** Writing with Purpose

I will review the stages of the writing process.
I will review the narrative prompt and my first draft and edit for subject-verb agreement.

{ Summarizing My Learning }

# Crossword Puzzle

Read the clues for each number. Write the correct vocabulary word on the puzzle.

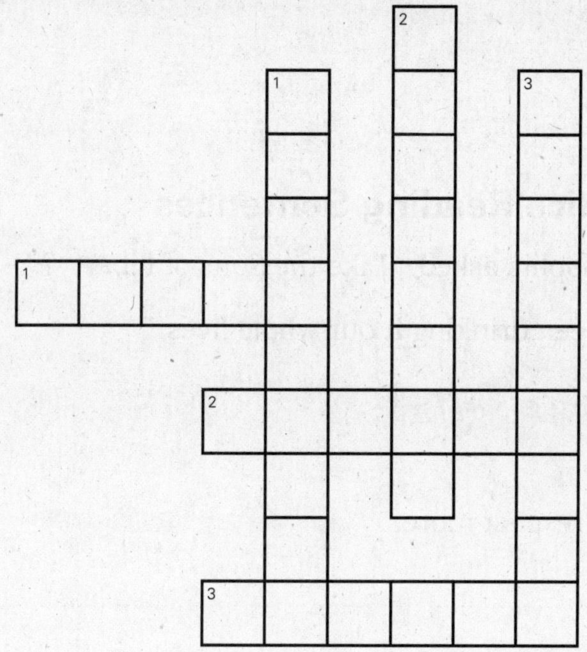

## Across

1. Pedro will _________ David if he does not behave in the library.
2. Emma said how much she will _________ leaving her teacher when she moves.
3. Malik says he will _________ a way to safely fit all of our science projects into the van.

## Down

1. When Chantelle fights with her family, she feels _________.
2. Don felt _________ when he was cut from the baseball team.
3. The dentist said that I showed _________ because I sat quietly while he filled my cavity.

| **Vocabulary** | nudge | miserable | devise |
| --- | --- | --- | --- |
| | lament | fortitude | slighted |

## Practice Reading Phrases

1. Sophia asked

2. drinking it our whole lives

3. really matter

4. I shall consider

5. But then again

## Practice Reading Sentences

1. "The Daughters of Liberty?" Sophia asked. "Like the Sons of Liberty?"

2. "Tea comforts us, and we've been drinking it our whole lives!"

3. "Does it really matter?"

4. "I shall consider it poison!"

5. "But then again, I like my self-respect more."

## Timed Reading

**{ ROLE OF THE READER }**

Read the passage to your partner as accurately as possible.

Remember, your reading goal is 80 Words Correct Per Minute (WCPM).

**{ ROLE OF THE LISTENER }**

As your partner reads, mark these errors with a strikethrough:

- mispronounced words
- skipped words
- changed words
- added words

Excerpt from
# Daughter of Liberty

| | Number of Words |
|---|---|
| "This is sage tea," Madam Blake said. "I know the tea may seem | 13 |
| strange, but I belong to the Daughters of Liberty." | 22 |
| "The Daughters of Liberty?" Sophia asked. "Like the Sons | 31 |
| of Liberty?" | 33 |
| "That's right," Madam Blake nodded. "We have made a promise | 43 |
| not to buy any more tea from England." | 51 |
| "Why not?" asked Mama. "Tea comforts us, and we've been | 61 |
| drinking it our whole lives!" | 66 |
| Sophia laughed. Her mother loved her cups of tea. | 75 |
| "If we buy British tea, we are saying we deserve to be taxed," | 88 |
| Madam Blake replied sharply. "So we ladies are boycotting British tea." | 99 |
| "It seems like such a small thing," Sophia said. "Does it really | 111 |
| matter?" | 112 |
| "It sends a message that we can't be slighted or pushed around. | 124 |
| Right now, the British don't listen to us. If we stop buying British | 137 |
| goods, their businesses will suffer. Since they need our business, they | 148 |
| will be forced to listen to us." | 155 |
| "I'll never drink tea again," Sophia declared. "I shall consider | 165 |
| it poison!" | 167 |
| Mama smiled politely. She still looked unsure. "I do love my tea," | 179 |
| she lamented. "But then again, I like my self-respect more." | 189 |

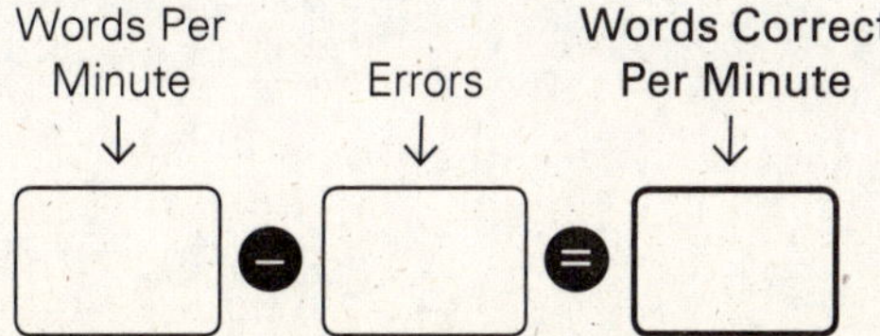

# High-Frequency Words

| | | | | | | |
|---|---|---|---|---|---|---|
| want | this | with | park | soon | went | there |
| too | after | short | under | fly | say | well |
| how | need | story | that | yes | they | |

# Words of the Day

______  ______  ______

______  ______

# Word Riddles

Answer the riddles below with the Words of the Day.

| from | give | her | when | some |
|---|---|---|---|---|

1. Which word has three letters? ____________________

2. Which two words rhyme? ____________________

3. Which word has a silent *h?* ____________________

4. Which word has a short *i* sound? ____________________

# Word Study Skill

Read the words in the box. Circle five words that contain the *al, eigh, ol,* or *wa* patterns.

| | | | | |
|---|---|---|---|---|
| pal | eight | aunt | laugh | stalk |
| water | poke | pole | straw | left |

# Phonics Practice

Circle the word with the correct sound and spelling pattern. Underline the letters in that word that make that sound.

1. **eigh** as in *freight*     they     weight     height
2. **ol** as in *mold*     tool     hollow     sold
3. **al** as in *tall*     bale     already     ballet
4. **wa** as in *want*     water     wade     wait

# Apply It

**Read the paragraph below. Circle words with the complex spelling patterns** *al,* *eigh, ol,* **or** *wa.*

"Don't fall," Lee thought as she rode into the ring. Everyone had told her that Waffle was too old to ride in the show. She was only good for pulling a sleigh of freight. But Lee had trained Waffle since she was a colt. They were going to give it their all for this last show. Waffle neighed to let Lee know she was ready to win.

# Spell It

| **Spelling Tip** | Listen carefully to a word or read it aloud before you try to spell it. |
| --- | --- |

1. _________________________________

2. _________________________________

3. _________________________________

4. _________________________________

5. _________________________________

# Quick Write

What is the main problem in this story? How do you think it will be solved?

# Question Log

**Text:** _________________________________

| Question #1 | Question #2 | Question #3 |
| --- | --- | --- |
|  |  |  |

**On-the-Surface**
*who, where, when, and what happened*

**Under-the-Surface**
*how, why, would, could, and should*

| Question #1 | Question #2 | Question #3 |
| --- | --- | --- |
|  |  |  |

# Summary

_________________________________________

_________________________________________

_________________________________________

# Declarative and Interrogative Sentences

| **About Declarative and Interrogative Sentences** | • A declarative sentence makes a statement and ends with a period. Example: *My shoes are red.*<br>• An interrogative sentence asks a question and ends with a question mark. Example: *Where are my shoes?*<br>• Many interrogative sentences include helping verbs. Often, the helping verb in an interrogative sentence comes before the subject of the sentence. Example: <u>Will</u> you borrow an eraser? |
| --- | --- |

## Rewrite the Sentence

Read each declarative sentence. Rewrite each one as an interrogative sentence. You may use helping verbs such as *will, can,* or *could* to help you. You may also use question words such as *when, where, why,* or *how.*

1. The class will end at 2:00 p.m.

______________________________________________________

2. Marco can move here from Mexico.

______________________________________________________

3. Sam can go to the store.

______________________________________________________

4. There could be money left over.

______________________________________________________

# Find It in Your Reading

Write three interrogative sentences from your reading. Circle the helping verbs or question words in each sentence.

1. _______________________________________________

_______________________________________________

2. _______________________________________________

_______________________________________________

3. _______________________________________________

_______________________________________________

# Put It in Your Writing

Write interrogative sentences telling what you would like to learn about life before the American Revolution. Make sure to include helping verbs or question words in your sentences.

1. _______________________________________________

_______________________________________________

2. _______________________________________________

_______________________________________________

3. _______________________________________________

_______________________________________________

{ DONE ✔ }

## STEP 1 Making Connections

I will connect what I already know to a painting and discuss the essential question: *How was life for teenagers of the past different from today?*

AGENDA

## STEP 2 Developing Vocabulary

I will review and complete an assessment of six vocabulary words.

## STEP 3 Practicing Fluency

I will read aloud part of "Daughter of Liberty" with fluency by practicing phrasing and stressing words with special type treatment, and I will chart my fluency progress.

## STEP 4 Building Word Study Skills

I will learn, practice, and spell five new high-frequency words.
I will review recognizing and using words with complex spelling patterns *ou, ould, ough, al, eigh, ol,* and *wa.*
I will understand the spelling homework assignment.

## STEP 5 Reading for Understanding

I will review the reading strategy of questioning.
I will learn to use the reading skill of questioning for character, setting, plot, speaker, problem/solution, and theme.

## STEP 6 Applying the Conventions of English

I will review my understanding of declarative and interrogative sentences and helping verbs.
I will write declarative and interrogative sentences using helping verbs.

## STEP 7 Writing with Purpose

I will review the stages of the writing process.
I will edit my narrative for word choice, present and past tense verbs, and spelling.

{ Summarizing My Learning }

_______________________________________

_______________________________________

# Show What You Know

Read each question. Check the box beside the best answer.

1. If you show **fortitude** when driving alone for the first time, you—

   ☐ complain about it.
   ☐ do it calmly.
   ☐ drive fast.
   ☐ feel sad.

2. What would most likely happen if you were to **nudge** an angry dog?

   ☐ The dog would calm down.
   ☐ The dog would get hungry.
   ☐ The dog would fall asleep.
   ☐ The dog would bark.

3. Kara <u>figured out</u> a way to stay for an extra week.

   Which word would work best as a substitution for the underlined words?

   ☐ devised
   ☐ lamented
   ☐ slighted
   ☐ nudged

4. If an activity made you feel **miserable,** what would you do?

   ☐ Do it again.
   ☐ Tell other people to try it.
   ☐ Say good things about it.
   ☐ Stop doing it.

5. Select the word that has the most similar meaning to **slighted.**

   ☐ unhappy
   ☐ insulted
   ☐ excited
   ☐ tired

6. Someone who is _______ about something would most likely **lament** it.

   ☐ mad
   ☐ in danger
   ☐ sad
   ☐ calm

## Practice Reading Phrases

1. this is a good idea

2. a new set of clothing

3. the homespun clothes we already have

4. beautiful English fabric

5. would not be the same

## Practice Reading Sentences

1. "Why don't you think this is a good idea?"

2. "It can take *a year* to make a new set of clothing."

3. "I suppose we can start with the homespun clothes we already have."

4. Sophia and her mother had bought beautiful English fabric several months before.

5. Wearing a plain white dress would not be the same.

## Timed Reading

{ **ROLE OF THE READER** }

Read the passage to your partner as accurately as possible.

Remember, your reading goal is 80 Words Correct Per Minute (WCPM).

{ **ROLE OF THE LISTENER** }

As your partner reads, mark these errors with a strikethrough:

- mispronounced words
- skipped words
- changed words
- added words

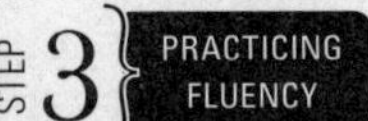

Excerpt from
# Daughter of Liberty

| | Number of Words |
|---|---|
| "Why don't you think this is a good idea?" Sophia asked when | 12 |
| they arrived home. "Don't you want the British to stop treating | 23 |
| us badly?" | 25 |
| "Sophia, you understand how much work it takes to make the | 36 |
| clothes we have already, don't you?" her mother replied. "Can you | 47 |
| imagine how hard it will be to make new clothes? We will have to | 61 |
| spend even more time making wool into thread. Then we'll have to | 73 |
| weave the thread into cloth. It can take *a year* to make a new set of | 89 |
| clothing." | 90 |
| "Well," Sophia said. "I suppose we can start with the homespun | 101 |
| clothes we already have." | 105 |
| "What about your new green dress?" her mother asked. "Will you | 116 |
| still wear that to the dance next week?" | 124 |
| "Oh, my green dress," Sophia said. She didn't know how to reply. | 136 |
| Sophia and her mother had bought beautiful English fabric several | 146 |
| months before. They had made the dress specifically for the big | 157 |
| dance. With her mother's help, Sophia had even stitched little blue | 168 |
| flowers into the sleeves. Wearing a plain white dress would not be | 180 |
| the same. | 182 |

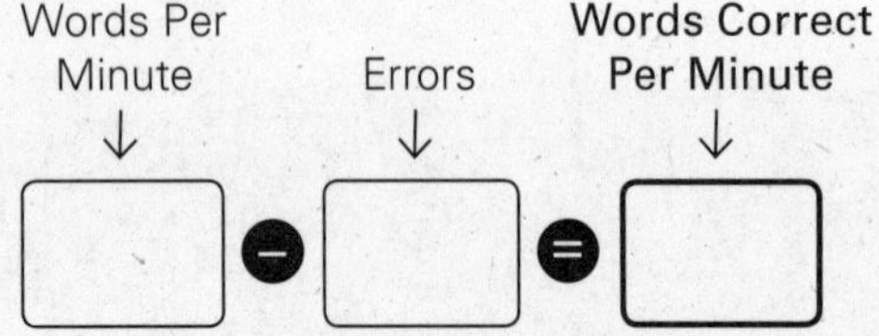

# High-Frequency Words

| from | how | after | short | park | soon | yes | went | there |
|------|-----|-------|-------|------|------|-----|------|-------|
| want | this | need | her | under | when | they | say | |
| too | give | with | story | that | fly | some | well | |

# Words of the Day

# Alphabetical Order

List the Words of the Day in alphabetical order.

think    giving    won't    just    open

1. ______________________________________________

2. ______________________________________________

3. ______________________________________________

4. ______________________________________________

5. ______________________________________________

# Word Study Skill

Read the words in the box. Circle five words that have the *ould, ough, al, eigh, ol,* or *wa* pattern.

| | | | | |
|---|---|---|---|---|
| would | pose | proud | wash | though |
| old | cone | could | pony | |

# Phonics Practice

Read the words in the box. Write each word in the correct column on the chart.

| weigh | swamp | fought | borough |
|---|---|---|---|
| gold | should | ball | alter |

| *ould* as in *could* | *ough* as in *thorough* | *ough* as in *bought* | *al* as in *alright* | *eigh* as in *neigh* | *ol* as in *mold* | *wa* as in *water* |
|---|---|---|---|---|---|---|
| | | | | | | |

# Apply It

Read the sentences below. For each one, circle the words with the correct spelling pattern.

1. *ould* — "Could you run down to the store?" asked Mom. "Would you, please?"

2. *ough* as in *thorough* — "I don't have flour to make the dough."

3. *al* — Mom always bakes a pie for the "Best Pie" stall at the fair.

4. *eigh* — Last year, our eighty-year-old neighbor won for her apple pie.

5. *ol* — This year, Mom is trying out an old recipe for polka dot pie.

6. *wa* — I like watching her pies bake in the oven as the smell wafts down the street.

# Spell It

| Spelling Tip | A letter combination may make different sounds in different words. |
|---|---|

1. _______________________________

2. _______________________________

3. _______________________________

4. _______________________________

5. _______________________________

## Daughter of Liberty

*Part 6 of 6*

The days before the dance passed quickly. Sophia hardly had time to think. She had always been busy with chores, but now there were even more. Still, she felt good about what she was doing. Sophia and her mother put away the green dress. They spent all their free time creating a new one that didn't use products from England.

At first Sophia's father didn't like what they were doing. He didn't think women should be involved in the struggle. However, his feelings toward the British changed his mind. In the end, taking a stand made the whole family feel proud. They faced the soldiers in town with their heads held high.

## Notes

1. What was Sophia so busy doing?

_______________________

_______________________

_______________________

_______________________

_______________________

_______________________

_______________________

_______________________

_______________________

_______________________

2. What does it mean to face something with your head held high?

_______________________

_______________________

_______________________

_______________________

_______________________

On the night of the dance, Sophia felt nervous. She watched people dancing around the big barn. It sparkled with the light of a hundred candles. She saw girls in dresses of blue, red, green, and brown. The boys wore their finest suits.

Fiddlers played lively tunes. Rows of dancers spun around the room. Sophia couldn't help thinking that she looked silly in her simple, homemade dress.

Then Seth walked over to Sophia. "Would you like some spearmint tea?" he asked. He offered a teacup. "You look lovely tonight."

Sophia blushed. "I know I am only wearing a homespun dress, but—"

"You are a Daughter of Liberty, aren't you?" Seth asked. ⏸

## Notes

3. What were people doing when Sophia got to the dance?

4. Sophia thought she looked silly in her homemade dress. What does this tell you about what Sophia is like?

Sophia gave him a wide smile. "How did you know?"

"Everyone knows about your efforts. You are a great help to the cause," Seth said, smiling back at her. "It's easy for people to say that they won't use British goods. The Daughters of Liberty make it possible for people to follow through on their promises. Creating new clothes and teas helps people to avoid British goods."

"So it doesn't bother you to see girls looking so plain?" Sophia asked.

"Sophia, you wear the clothes of a **patriot**," Seth replied. "And in them, you look prettier than you could in the finest silk England could offer." ⏸

**How might the lives of these teens be different if they lived in modern times?**

---

**patriot** a person who supports and defends his or her country

## Notes

5. What does Seth say about how Sophia looks in her dress?

6. How do you think Seth's words make Sophia feel about being a Daughter of Liberty?

# Conventions Review

## Review Declarative and Interrogative Sentences

Read each sentence. Then write an interrogative sentence to go with it using question words *who, what, when, where, why,* or *how.*

| DECLARATIVE SENTENCE | INTERROGATIVE SENTENCE |
|---|---|
| 1. George Washington was the first President of the United States. | |
| 2. Dui's grandparents live in Vietnam. | |

## Review Interrogative Sentences with Subject-Verb Agreement

Underline the subject of each interrogative sentence. Cross out the verb. At the end of the sentence, write the correct form of that verb to agree with the subject.

1. Does you have anything to drink? _______________

2. How many tiles does you need for the new floor? _______________

3. Is they allowed to have visitors? _______________

## Review Declarative Sentences with Helping Verbs

Read each sentence. Underline the two words that make up the verb in each sentence. Circle the helping verbs.

1. She would not watch the movie with us.

2. Mrs. Arguello's husband may travel to the Great Wall of China.

3. I might buy a new coat for the winter.

## Review Verbs and Helping Verbs

Read each sentence. Underline the two words that make up the verb in each sentence. Circle the helping verbs.

1. Can you send my letter this week?

2. The new town hall could open by next week.

3. All my friends will agree on our next trip.

## Review Declarative and Interrogative Sentences

Read the declarative sentences below. Rewrite each as an interrogative sentence.

1. Kelly was assigned to Mr. Maru's class.

_______________________________________________

2. There are 48 states in the continental U.S.

_______________________________________________

## Put It in Your Writing

Write three sentences telling what your hometown might have been like when you were born. Include both declarative and interrogative sentences.

1. _______________________________________________

_______________________________________________

2. _______________________________________________

_______________________________________________

3. _______________________________________________

_______________________________________________

## STEP 1 Developing Test-Taking Strategies {DONE ✔}

I will read a test-taking manual.
I will learn strategies for taking multiple-choice tests.

## STEP 2 Assessing My Learning

I will take a multiple-choice test on skills I learned in this chapter.

## STEP 3 Writing With Purpose

I will publish the final draft of my narrative.

## STEP 4 Analyzing My Results

I will identify which questions I answered correctly and which questions I answered
   incorrectly.
I will analyze incorrect answers and correct them.

## STEP 5 Reinforcing My Learning

I will reinforce my understanding of characters, setting, and plot.
I will reinforce my understanding of theme.

## STEP 6 Speaking With Purpose

I will watch a video of a speech and analyze the organization of the speech.
I will also organize my speech by creating an outline.

{Summarizing My Learning}

_______________________________________________

_______________________________________________

_______________________________________________

# Test-Taking Manual
## Before the Test

### Be Prepared

- Know what you will be tested on and study.
- Get a full night's rest.
- Have all your materials (pencil, eraser, calculator, dictionary) at your desk.

### Be Comfortable but Alert

- Make sure you have enough room to work.
- Do not slouch in your chair.

### Stay Relaxed and Confident

- Remember that you are well prepared and can do well.
- Take deep breaths if you feel anxious.
- Do not talk about the test with the other students.

---

## During the Test

Follow these five steps for each question on the test.

**Step 1:** Determine what the question is asking you to do.

**Step 2:** Try to answer the question in your own words.

**Step 3:** Eliminate any answers you know are incorrect.

**Step 4:** Choose the best answer.

**Step 5:** If time allows, review your answers to each question.

### Example Question

**1. Who had promised to teach Luisa to ride a bike?**

   **A.** Luisa's mother

   **B.** Luisa's friends

   **C.** Luisa's father

   **D.** Luisa's sister

# Skills Assessment 3

**Directions:** Read this article, and then answer the questions.

## Flying Down the Street

1    Luisa was ten years old, and all of her friends knew how to ride a bike. She wanted to learn how to ride a bike more than anything. It looked like so much fun! At least a thousand times a day, Luisa imagined herself flying down the street on a bike with her hair streaming behind her.

2    Luisa's father had promised to teach her to ride, but she did not have a bike. No one in her family had a bike, and her parents could not afford to buy one. Luisa asked everyone she knew, "Do you have a bike I could borrow?" "No, sorry," was the usual answer.

3    One day, Luisa decided to try one more time. She asked her neighbors, Marta and John.

4    "Hmm, you know, I think Joey's old bike is still out in the shed. Why don't you go look?" Marta answered.

5    Joey had been a friend of Luisa's father when they were children. Luisa tried to imagine how old this bike might be. Even if his bike was still in the shed, chances were it would not work. Luisa went to the shed to check it out anyway. She climbed through a lot of junk and finally saw a dusty old bike. John helped her get it out of the shed. A huge smile came across Luisa's face when she saw that it seemed to work. Luisa scrubbed hard and the bike cleaned up well. Better yet, it worked!

6    Then the hard work began. True to his word, Luisa's father helped her learn to ride. In her dreams, it only took one try down the street, and she could ride by herself. She quickly learned that it would not be that easy. Again and again, Luisa's father ran next to her to steady the bike. Halfway down the block he would let go, and she would try to ride on her own. She always fell. Luisa's knees were cut and bleeding, but she did not let that stop her. Something told her not to give up.

7    Finally, after many tries, Luisa sailed down the rest of the street on her own. She had done it! She could ride a bike. She stopped at the end of the street, turned around, and rode home. Luisa could hear her father cheering.

8    From that day on, Luisa rode everywhere. She rode to her friends' houses. She rode to the park. She rode with her friends on weekends. She loved to feel the wind whipping through her hair!

*Go on to the next page* →

# Skills Assessment 3, continued

**1.** Read this sentence from paragraph 1.

> At least a thousand times a day, Luisa imagined herself flying down the street on a bike with her hair streaming behind her.

**This sentence shows that Luisa probably**

- A. does not like her hair.
- B. likes to daydream.
- C. owns a bicycle.
- D. wants to fly someday.

**2.** **When Luisa's father was a child, who was his friend?**

- A. Marta
- B. Joey
- C. John
- D. Luisa

**3.** **Where does Luisa finally find a bike to ride?**

- A. in her neighbor's shed
- B. at her uncle's house
- C. in her father's shed
- D. at a bicycle store

**4.** **What does Luisa learn in paragraph 5?**

- A. All sheds are full of dusty old junk.
- B. It is easy to learn to ride on a brand new bike.
- C. Her father used to have a lot of friends.
- D. Old things can still be useful and good.

**5.** **If Luisa had not asked Marta and John for a bike, she probably would**

- A. not know anything about them.
- B. ask her mother to teach her to ride.
- C. not have learned to ride a bike.
- D. learn to roller-skate instead.

**6.** **Luisa falls many times, and she**

- A. scrapes her knees.
- B. does not ride anymore.
- C. bends her bicycle.
- D. cries in front of her father.

*Go on to the next page →*

# Skills Assessment 3, continued

7. **Which line from the story tells you that Luisa will finally learn to ride?**

   A. "Luisa's father had promised to teach her to ride, but she did not have a bike."

   B. "They were as old as her grandparents, so she did not think they would have a bike."

   C. "Again and again, Luisa's father ran next to her to steady the bike."

   D. "Luisa's knees were cut and bleeding, but she did not let that stop her."

8. **What does the author teach us in paragraph 6?**

   A. Life is not always like it is in a dream.

   B. All children should learn to ride a bicycle.

   C. One should let go when teaching someone to ride.

   D. Running next to a bike rider is dangerous.

9. **Which is the MOST important event in the story?**

   A. Luisa asked to borrow a bike.

   B. Luisa cleans the old bicycle.

   C. Luisa rides the bike on her own.

   D. Luisa's father cheers her on.

10. **In this story, Luisa is a person who**

   A. is afraid to ride a bike.

   B. does not give up easily.

   C. always talks too much.

   D. wants to make new friends.

*Go on to the next page* →

# Skills Assessment 3, continued

11. **Which word BEST describes Luisa's father in this story?**

    A. helpful

    B. worried

    C. unhappy

    D. brave

12. **Which is a theme in the story?**

    A. It is easy to ride a bike.

    B. Fathers are the best teachers.

    C. Practice brings success.

    D. Girls should repair bikes.

**End of test** ■

# Character, Setting, and Plot

**Reminder: Identifying Character, Setting, and Plot**

- A character is a person or animal in a story.
- The setting is the place and time of a story.
- The plot is the main events of a story that include a beginning, middle, and end.

## Our Special Summer Vacation

1  The summer of 2006 was special. We decided to spend our family's summer vacation at my grandparents' home on the beach.

2  We drove two hours out of the city and arrived in the late afternoon. My grandparents' house is amazing. It is right on the beach. All we could see from their deck were the dunes and the ocean. The reflection of the sun sparkled on the ocean. I wanted to go swimming right away, but my father said to get ready for dinner.

3  My grandfather grilled hamburgers and hot dogs, and my grandmother made her potato salad for dinner. My sister and I shucked corn and made a big green salad. We sat at the long, wood table on the deck and watched the moon rise over the ocean. For dessert, my grandmother served a scrumptious fruit salad inside a hollowed-out watermelon. It looked almost too good to eat.

4  Every day of that vacation was wonderful. We splashed in the ocean like playful dolphins and built enormous sand castles. My grandfather taught us how to body surf and liked to show off his own body-surfing skills. What a thrill it was to ride a wave all the way into shore! I really wanted to stay longer than two weeks, but I knew I had to go back to school after Labor Day.

5  All too soon we returned to the city. I was happy to see my friends and to sleep in my own room. It felt good to be home, but I smiled to myself every time I thought about our stay on the beach. I look forward to another summer vacation at my grandparents' house.

## Choices & Challenges

On your own piece of paper...

**A.** Write about a vacation your family has taken. Where did you go? What did you do?

**B.** Write about the beach setting. What do you see, hear, smell, taste, and feel?

**C.** Write about a vacation that the author may have taken to her grandparents' house in the winter. What would be the same? What would be different?

# Summary Tree

**Text:** _______________________________________________

**Summary**

| Reminder: Theme | • Theme is what the story reveals about life. |

# Narrative Map

Look back at "Our Special Summer Vacation." Identify the characters, setting, the main events of the plot, and the theme. Use the Narrative Map to record your information.

## Characters

Main: _______________________

_______________________

Others: _______________________

_______________________

_______________________

## Setting

Where: _______________________

_______________________

_______________________

When: _______________________

_______________________

_______________________

## Plot

Beginning: _______________________

_______________________

Middle: _______________________

_______________________

End: _______________________

_______________________

## Theme

_______________________

# Identify Character, Setting, Plot, and Theme

Turn back to page 243 and reread the story "Our Special Summer Vacation." Then answer these questions. Use your notes from the Narrative Map on page 245 to help you.

1. **Who is the main character of this story?**
   A. the author's grandfather
   B. the author's grandmother
   C. the author

2. **Where was the grandparents' house?**
   A. at the beach
   B. in the mountains
   C. in the city

3. **At the end of the story, the narrator**
   A. has dinner.
   B. goes home to the city.
   C. learns to body surf.

4. **What is the theme of this story?**
   A. There is no place like home.
   B. Summer vacations are the most fun.
   C. Family gatherings create special memories.

---

### Choices & Challenges
On your own piece of paper…

**A.** Write a different story with the same theme.

**B.** Write about the author's next family vacation to her grandparents' house.

**C.** Write about a gathering your family has had. What happened? Why was it special?

---

## STEP **1** Assessing My Learning

{DONE ✔}

I will take a multiple-choice test on skills I learned in this unit.



## STEP **2** Speaking With Purpose

I will practice giving my speech with my partner.
I will get and give feedback to my partner about the speeches.

## STEP **3** Discussing the Essential Question

I will review all the texts from the unit.
I will discuss the texts and the unit's essential question with my partner.
I will write a reflection about the essential question.

{Summarizing My Learning}

_______________________________________________

_______________________________________________

_______________________________________________

# Discussing the Essential Question

Think about each theme question and how it helps you answer the essential question. Discuss each theme question with your partner. Write down your thoughts.

How are teenagers today different from teenagers in the past? Give examples from the texts.

How were teens in the 19th century different from teens today? Give examples from the texts.

How were teens growing up in the 1700s different from teens today? Give examples from the texts.

# Reflect on the Essential Question

Think about this unit's essential question. Using your prior knowledge from all texts and activities you have read and done, write everything you know about this question.

> How was life for teenagers of the past different from today? Why?

## STEP **1** Making Connections

{DONE ✔}

I will connect what I already know to a painting.
I will discuss the essential question *How are people affected by natural disasters?*

## STEP **2** Developing Vocabulary

I will discuss vocabulary words in a cumulative review.

## STEP **3** Practicing Fluency

I will read aloud part of "Daughter of Liberty" with fluency by practicing phrasing
and changing voice to reflect characters and I will chart my fluency progress.

## STEP **4** Building Word Study Skills

I will learn five new high-frequency words.
I will practice recognizing and using words with the silent letter *h* and the silent letter pattern *gn*.
I will understand the spelling homework assignment.

## STEP **5** Reading for Understanding

I will learn the genre of expository text.
I will learn to use the reading strategy of on-the-surface and under-the-surface reading with
nonfiction text.

## STEP **6** Applying the Conventions of English

I will review my understanding of verbs.
I will identify and use action verbs in the past tense in my speaking, reading, and writing.

## STEP **7** Writing with Purpose

I will review the stages of the writing process.
I will deconstruct the problem/solution prompt and scoring guide.
I will begin prewriting using the *Topic Toss.*

{Summarizing My Learning}

______________________________________________

______________________________________________

## Practice Reading Phrases

1. some spearmint tea

2. wearing a homespun dress

3. make it possible for people

4. it doesn't bother you

5. the finest silk England could offer

## Practice Reading Sentences

1. "Would you like some spearmint tea?"

2. "I know I am only wearing a homespun dress, but—"

3. "The Daughters of Liberty make it possible for people to follow through on their promises."

4. "So it doesn't bother you to see girls looking so plain?"

5. "And in them, you look prettier than you could in the finest silk England could offer."

## Timed Reading

**{ ROLE OF THE READER }**

Read the passage to your partner as accurately as possible.

Remember, your reading goal is 85 Words Correct Per Minute (WCPM).

**{ ROLE OF THE LISTENER }**

As your partner reads, mark these errors with a strikethrough:

- mispronounced words
- skipped words
- changed words
- added words

Excerpt from
# Daughter of Liberty

| | Number of Words |
|---|---|
| Fiddlers played lively tunes. Rows of dancers spun around the | 10 |
| room. Sophia couldn't help thinking that she looked silly in her | 21 |
| simple, homemade dress. | 24 |
| Then Seth walked over to Sophia. "Would you like some | 34 |
| spearmint tea?" he asked. He offered a teacup. "You look lovely | 45 |
| tonight." | 46 |
| Sophia blushed. "I know I am only wearing a homespun | 56 |
| dress, but—" | 58 |
| "You are a Daughter of Liberty, aren't you?" Seth asked. | 68 |
| Sophia gave him a wide smile. "How did you know?" "Everyone | 79 |
| knows all about your efforts. You are a great help to the cause," | 92 |
| Seth said, smiling back at her. "It's easy for people to say that they | 106 |
| won't use British goods. The Daughters of Liberty make it possible for | 118 |
| people to follow through on their promises. Creating new clothes and | 129 |
| teas helps people avoid British products." | 135 |
| "So it doesn't bother you to see girls looking so plain?" | 146 |
| Sophia asked. | 148 |
| "Sophia, you wear the clothes of a patriot," Seth replied. "And | 159 |
| in them, you look prettier than you could in the finest silk England | 172 |
| could offer." | 174 |

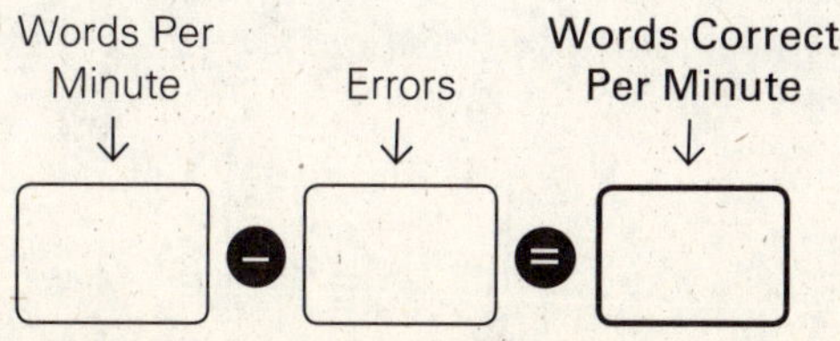

# Unit 2 High-Frequency Word List

*(**Bold Words** = Most frequently misspelled)*

| | | | |
|---|---|---|---|
| **before** | made | wanted | **been** |
| maybe | those | hold | together |
| walk | call | **then** | never |
| live | cold | bring | show |
| **what** | **could** | used | try |
| over | use | far | bear |
| thank | or | **were** | **that's** |
| them | pull | hurt | only |
| **who** | **every** | light | **would** |
| may | wash | carry | warm |
| put | ship | past | sick |
| round | read | **always** | bread |
| **again** | why | full | own |
| around | seen | keep | **ready** |
| gave | table | mind | turned |
| outside | page | clean | **their** |
| goes | **know** | grow | slow |
| **says** | found | kind | brother |
| **any** | sleep | **because** | lady |
| teach | work | place | start |
| these | better | time | easy |
| **by** | **once** | myself | |
| both | done | shall | |

# Words of the Day

___ ___ ___ ___ ___   ___ ___ ___   ___ ___ ___ ___ ___ ___

___ ___ ___ ___ ___ ___

# Alphabetical Order

List the Words of the Day in alphabetical order.

**before**  **maybe**  **walk**  **live**  **what**

1. ___ ___ ___ ___ ___ ___

2. ___ ___ ___ ___ ___

3. ___ ___ ___ ___ ___ ___

4. ___ ___ ___ ___ ___

5. ___ ___ ___ ___ ___

# Word Study Skill

Read the words in the box. Circle five words that have a silent letter *h* or silent letter *gn* pattern.

| | | | | |
|---|---|---|---|---|
| **gnat** | **you've** | **being** | **ghost** | **boxes** |
| **gnome** | **reign** | **shelf** | **book** | **echo** |

# Phonics Practice

Underline the silent letter *h* or silent letter pattern *gn* in each word. Put a line through the word without a silent letter.

1. hairy      sign      ghost

2. gnat      chaos      groan

3. honest      hundred      cologne

4. yellow      rhyme      gnaw

# Apply It

As you read, circle at least five words that have a silent letter or silent letter pattern. You may circle more than five words with silent letters.

Sara was exhausted when she got home. For hours her class had practiced the plays and songs for Heritage Day. They were honoring their ancestors. They were studying and designing posters of the foreign countries where they came from.

"What are we having for dinner, Papa?" Sara asked as she gnawed on a breadstick. She knew he would whip up a yummy meal. When her papa was a boy in Italy, his mother taught him how to cook. They had to gather wheat to make pasta! It was a sign of the times. "Can we please have spaghetti?" Sara begged. Her stomach was rumbling.

# Spell It

| **Spelling Tip** | Remember that some words contain the silent letter *h* or silent letter pattern *gn*. |
| --- | --- |

1. ___________________________

2. ___________________________

3. ___________________________

4. ___________________________

5. ___________________________

# Reading Tree: Expository

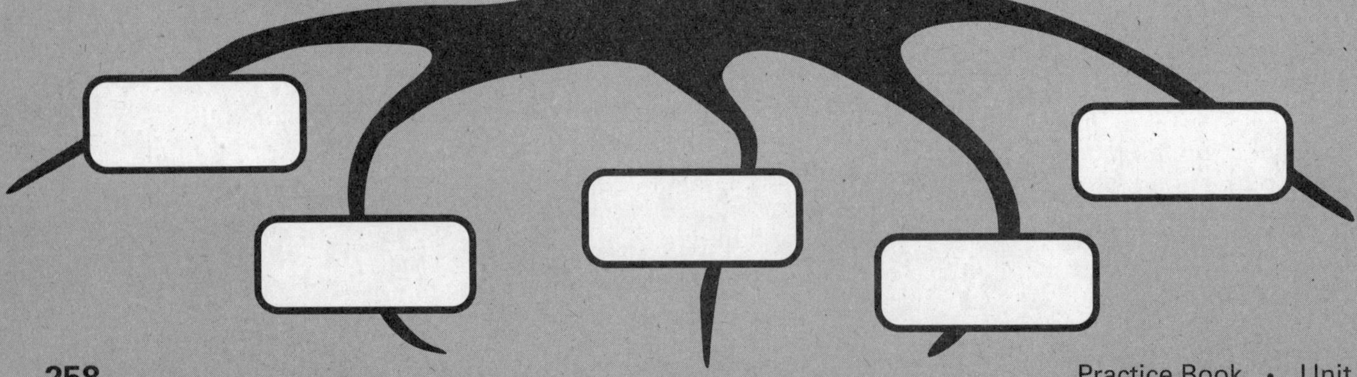

# Topic Introduction

**Text:** ______________________________________

**Topic:** ______________________________________

Related Terms:

1. ______________________________

2. ______________________________

3. ______________________________

4. ______________________________

5. ______________________________

6. ______________________________

7. ______________________________

8. ______________________________

9. ______________________________

10. ______________________________

The term I know most about is:

______________________________

What I know:

______________________________

______________________________

______________________________

______________________________

______________________________

______________________________

______________________________

______________________________

______________________________

______________________________

______________________________

______________________________

______________________________

# Summary Tree

**Text:** ___________________________________________

1.

2.

3.

1.

2.

3.

1.

2.

3.

1.

2.

3.

Where

When

Who

What Happened

**Summary**

_______________________________________________
_______________________________________________
_______________________________________________
_______________________________________________

# Action Verbs in the Past Tense

<table>
<tr><td>About Action Verbs in the Past Tense</td><td>

- For many verbs, form the past tense by adding –ed to the present tense form of the verb. Examples: *surf, surfed; walk, walked*
- To form the past tense of most regular verbs that end in –e, add only –d. Examples: *save, saved; hope, hoped*
- To form the past tense of some verbs that end in a consonant, double the final consonant before adding –ed. Examples: *pat, patted; step, stepped; knit, knitted*

</td></tr>
</table>

## Find the Action Verbs in the Past Tense

Read each sentence. Underline the action verbs in the past tense in each sentence.

1. We mixed the dough before we baked the bread.

2. Mr. Lewis always remembers the time I helped him.

3. I love the scrapbook that Sophia created.

4. Have you ever visited the Museum of Science?

5. Darien scraped, cleaned, and then painted the wall.

6. The frog hopped across the path and plopped into the pond.

7. Mario dropped the ball right next to first base.

8. Jamie shoveled and carted all of the dirt before he planted his garden.

# Find It in Your Reading

Write three sentences from your reading that include verbs in the past tense. Underline the verbs in the past tense. Circle the ending that was added to form the past tense.

1. _______________________________________________

_______________________________________________

2. _______________________________________________

_______________________________________________

3. _______________________________________________

_______________________________________________

# Put It in Your Writing

Write three sentences about a natural disaster that happened in the past. Include at least one action verb in the past tense in each sentence.

_______________________________________________

_______________________________________________

_______________________________________________

_______________________________________________

**{ DONE ✔ }**

## STEP **1** Making Connections

I will connect what I already know to the informative text "What If the Polar Ice Caps Melted?" by Katherine Friedman.

I will discuss how people are affected by natural disasters in "What If the Polar Ice Caps Melted?"

## STEP **2** Developing Vocabulary

I will learn three new vocabulary words: *cycle, reflect,* and *formidable*.

## STEP **3** Practicing Fluency

I will read aloud part of "Rebuilding New Orleans" with fluency by practicing phrasing and using punctuation to inform meaning and I will chart my fluency progress.

## STEP **4** Building Word Study Skills

I will learn five new high-frequency words.

I will practice recognizing and using words with the silent letter patterns *kn* and *mb*.

I will understand my spelling homework assignment.

## STEP **5** Reading for Understanding

I will review the reading strategies on-the-surface and under-the-surface reading.

## STEP **6** Applying the Conventions of English

I will review my understanding of verbs.

I will identify and use *be* verbs in the past tense in my speaking, reading, and writing.

## STEP **7** Writing with Purpose

I will review stages of the writing process, problem/solution prompt, and scoring guide.

I will complete the prewriting stage using the *Problem/Solution Organizer* and *Evidence Organizer* to identify a problem and possible solutions and to outline details for my letter.

### { Summarizing My Learning }

_____________________________________________

_____________________________________________

# Hidden Clues

Read the clues for each number. Write the correct vocabulary word under each clue. The letters in the boxes will complete the answer to the question at the bottom of the page.

1. The light that bounced off the windshield blinded me.

___ ___ ___ ___ ___ [1] ___

2. The new quarterback is huge!

___ ___ ___ ___ ___ [2] ___ ___ ___

3. Each day, the flowers open, grow toward the sun, and close.

___ ___ [3] ___ ___

4. Ken sees his image in the mirror.

___ ___ ___ ___ ___ ___ [4]

5. No one bothers the captain of the wrestling team because he is very strong.

___ ___ ___ [5] ___ ___ ___ ___ ___ ___

6. The moon is full tonight, like it was last month.

[6] ___ ___ ___ ___

## Where are most of the polar ice caps?

A n ___ r ___ ___ ___ a
    1  2   3  4  5  6

| Vocabulary | cycle | reflect | formidable |
|---|---|---|---|

## Practice Reading Phrases

1. wonderful mix of cultures
2. one of the most important
3. to the U.S. economy
4. parts of New Orleans
5. cost billions of dollars

## Practice Reading Sentences

1. It has beautiful buildings and a wonderful mix of cultures.
2. New Orleans is also one of the most important port cities in the United States.
3. The products made in New Orleans are important to the U.S. economy.
4. However, parts of New Orleans are not safe for people to live or build businesses.
5. It would cost billions of dollars to rebuild New Orleans and the levees to protect it.

## Timed Reading

**{ ROLE OF THE READER }**

Read the passage to your partner as accurately as possible.

Remember, your reading goal is 85 Words Correct Per Minute (WCPM).

**{ ROLE OF THE LISTENER }**

As your partner reads, mark these errors with a strikethrough:

- mispronounced words
- skipped words
- changed words
- added words

Excerpt from
## Rebuilding New Orleans

Number<br>of Words

New Orleans is a very special city. It is the birthplace of jazz — 13

music. It is also home to many delicious foods, such as gumbo. It has — 27

beautiful buildings and a wonderful mix of cultures. New Orleans is — 38

also one of the most important port cities in the United States. A port — 52

city is a place that sends and receives products and goods. Much of — 65

the nation's grain is shipped out of New Orleans, and much of the — 78

nation's oil is shipped in. Products such as steel, rubber, and coffee — 90

are also traded through the Port of New Orleans. The products made — 102

in New Orleans are important to the U.S. economy. — 111

However, parts of New Orleans are not safe for people to live or — 124

build businesses. Most of the city is below sea level, and it is sinking. — 138

Because the sea is slowly rising, the problem is getting worse. Nearly — 150

all of the properties damaged by Katrina were built in areas of the — 163

city that are below sea level. It is very costly to protect and repair — 177

these areas. It would cost billions of dollars to rebuild New Orleans — 189

and the levees to protect it. Scientists insist that they can design the — 202

new, safer levees. However, some people wonder if rebuilding New — 212

Orleans will be worth the cost. — 218

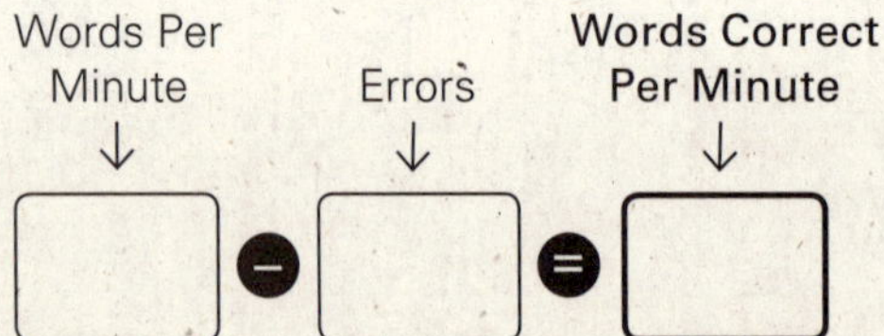

## High-Frequency Words

before    maybe    walk    live    what

## Words of the Day

__ __ __ __ __    __ __ __ __ __    __ __ __ __

__ __ __ __    __ __ __ __

## Categorize

Write each Word of the Day under the correct category.

over    thank    them    who    may

**Word with two syllables**

1. __________

**Words with 3 letters**

2. __________

3. __________

**Words with *th***

4. __________

5. __________

# Word Study Skill

Read the words in the box. Circle five words that have the silent letter patterns *kn* or *mb*.

| | | | | |
|---|---|---|---|---|
| **knead** | **read** | **tomb** | **lamb** | **sent** |
| **now** | **limb** | **play** | **knob** | **stand** |

# Phonics Practice

Underline the silent letter patterns *kn* or *mb* in each word. Put a line through the word without a silent letter.

1. knew      crumb      amber

2. December      lamb      knee

3. climb      knock      nine

4. kite      knight      plumber

# Apply It

As you read, circle at least five words that have a silent letter pattern. You may circle more than five words with silent letters.

Emily watched her father shear the lambs. When he was done, she picked up all the wool until her arms felt numb. Her job was to comb through the wool to get the knots out. Emily wrapped a bit of wool around the knuckle on her thumb. She knew the soft wool would make a nice knitted scarf for her brother.

# Spell It

| **Spelling Tip** | Remember that some words contain the silent letter patterns *kn* or *mb*. |
|---|---|

1. _______________________________________

2. _______________________________________

3. _______________________________________

4. _______________________________________

5. _______________________________________

## Rebuilding New Orleans *by Allison Welch*

*Part 2 of 2*

Karen was upset by what happened to the citizens of New Orleans. She decided to write a letter to a newspaper about whether the city should be rebuilt.

Dear Editor,

We've all seen the chaos and damage Hurricane Katrina caused in New Orleans. Before rebuilding, it's important for us to understand what happened to the city and why. New Orleans is surrounded by water. The city rests below sea level. Before the storm, levees were used to stop water from spilling into the city. The levees were massive, but they could not withstand the force of Hurricane Katrina.



1. Why does Karen say that it is important to understand what happened to the city and why?

2. To whom did Karen write her letter?

When Hurricane Katrina hit the Gulf Coast on August 29, 2005, intense winds swept through New Orleans. The water surrounding the city rose. The levees broke, and most of the city was soon under water. Buildings crumbled. Roads buckled. Over a thousand people died, and nearly a million people lost their homes.

Many citizens of New Orleans were forced to leave. Most wish to return home. We must help them rebuild their homes and city. Some people argue that the process will be too costly. They say New Orleans will never be safe from storms. However, experts have proven these arguments wrong. ❿

## Notes

3. How do you think the author feels about the citizens of New Orleans?

_______________________

_______________________

_______________________

_______________________

_______________________

_______________________

_______________________

_______________________

_______________________

_______________________

_______________________

4. When did Hurricane Katrina hit the Gulf Coast?

_______________________

_______________________

_______________________

_______________________

_______________________

There are several ways to rebuild a safer New Orleans. Many areas, such as the historic French Quarter, made it through the storm. This is because such areas were built on higher land. More of the city can be rebuilt on higher land. Scientists have shown that areas people feel are at risk can also be built on rafts or stilts to keep them safe from flooding. Low-lying areas that flooded do not need to be used for homes and businesses. **Wetlands** can be restored in these areas. Stronger, taller levees have also been designed and can be built to protect the city from storms.

New Orleans can be safe, and rebuilding is well worth the cost. New Orleans is important for the United States' economy. The city's history, people, food, and music are also important to the nation's sense of culture. The people of New Orleans have an exciting chance to construct a safer version of their city with the same great heart. We *must* offer them all the support they need. ⏸

**How are people affected by natural disasters?**

---

**wetlands**  low-lying areas of land that have wet, spongy soil

### Notes

5. Why did areas such as the French Quarter make it through the storm?

6. How does the author feel about New Orleans?

# Problem/Solution Analyzer

Topic: _______________________________

Problem: _______________________________

| Solution | Evidence | Concern |
|---|---|---|
|  |  |  |

# *Be* Verbs in the Past Tense

| **About *Be* Verbs in the Past Tense** | • The past tense of the verb *be* is formed differently than other verbs.<br>• Use *was* and *were* for the past tense of *be*: *I <u>was</u>, he <u>was</u>, she <u>was</u>, it <u>was</u>, you <u>were</u>, we <u>were</u>, they <u>were</u>.* |
| --- | --- |

## Find the *Be* Verbs in the Past Tense

Read each sentence. Underline the *be* verbs in the past tense.

1. She was angry that we were late.

2. I was four years old when Grandpa moved to California.

3. What were they thinking?

4. All the members of the chorus were ready to begin.

5. Carmen and Francis were happy when the cake arrived.

6. Did you find out where Kelsey was all day?

7. It was no surprise to me that the picnic was fun.

8. We were all home safely before dark.

## Find It in Your Reading

Write three sentences from your reading that include *be* verbs in the past tense. Underline the *be* verbs.

1. _______________________________________________

_______________________________________________

2. _______________________________________________

_______________________________________________

3. _______________________________________________

_______________________________________________

## Put It in Your Writing

Write three sentences about how you felt the last time you experienced a storm. Include at least one past tense form of the verb *be* in each sentence.

_______________________________________________

_______________________________________________

_______________________________________________

_______________________________________________

{DONE ✓}

## STEP 1 Making Connections

I will connect what I already know to the informative text "What If the Polar Ice Caps
Melted?" by Katherine Friedman.
I will discuss how people are affected by natural disasters in "What If the Polar Ice Caps Melted?"

## STEP 2 Developing Vocabulary

I will learn three new vocabulary words: *vanish, rapt,* and *expanse.*

## STEP 3 Practicing Fluency

I will read aloud part of "Rebuilding New Orleans" with fluency by practicing phrasing and
stressing words with special type, and I will chart my fluency progress.

## STEP 4 Building Word Study Skills

I will learn five new high-frequency words.
I will review recognizing and using words with the silent letter *h* and the silent letter patterns
*gn, kn,* and *mb.*
I will understand my spelling homework assignment.

## STEP 5 Reading for Understanding

I will review the reading strategies on-the-surface and under-the-surface reading.
I will learn to use the reading strategy, summarizing.

## STEP 6 Applying the Conventions of English

I will review my understanding of verbs in the present tense.
I will identify and use verbs in the present progressive tense in my speaking, reading, and writing.

## STEP 7 Writing with Purpose

I will review stages of the writing process.
I will review prewriting with the *Evidence Organizer.*
I will write first drafts using the problem/solution frame.

{Summarizing My Learning}

________________________________________

________________________________________

**276**

# Crossword Puzzle

Read the clues for each number. Write the correct vocabulary word on the puzzle.

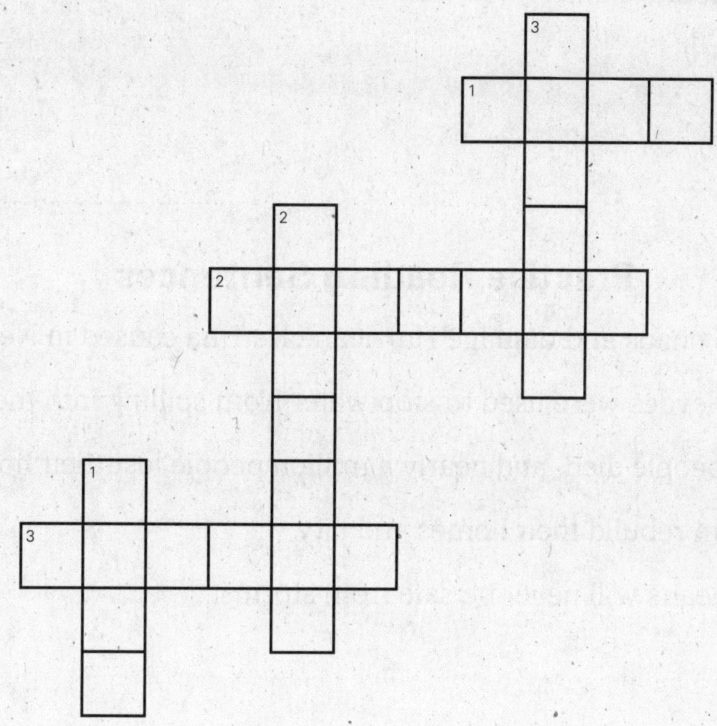

**Across**

1. I am ________ by the baseball game and cannot stop watching it.
2. The businessman built a parking lot on the ________.
3. My dessert would ________ if I asked my brother to watch it for me!

**Down**

1. Babies are ________ by their mothers' voices.
2. The farmer added the ________ of land to his farm.
3. When it's time to do dishes, my sister will ________.

| Vocabulary | vanish | rapt | expanse |
| --- | --- | --- | --- |

# Practice Reading Phrases

1. the chaos and damage

2. to stop water from spilling into

3. nearly a million people

4. their homes and city

5. never be safe

# Practice Reading Sentences

1. We've all seen the chaos and damage Hurricane Katrina caused in New Orleans.

2. Before the storm, levees were used to stop water from spilling into the city.

3. Over a thousand people died, and nearly a million people lost their homes.

4. We must help them rebuild their homes and city.

5. They say New Orleans will never be safe from storms.

# Timed Reading

**{ ROLE OF THE READER }**

Read the passage to your partner as accurately as possible.

Remember, your reading goal is 85 Words Correct Per Minute (WCPM).

**{ ROLE OF THE LISTENER }**

As your partner reads, mark these errors with a strikethrough:

- mispronounced words
- skipped words
- changed words
- added words

Excerpt from
# Rebuilding New Orleans

|  | Number of Words |
|---|---|

Karen was upset by what happened to the citizens of New — 11

Orleans. She decided to write a letter to a newspaper about whether — 23

the city should be rebuilt. — 28

Dear Editor, — 30

We've all seen the chaos and damage Hurricane Katrina caused — 40

in New Orleans. Before rebuilding, it's important for us to understand — 51

what happened to the city and why. New Orleans is surrounded — 62

by water. The city rests below sea level. Before the storm, levees — 74

were used to stop water from spilling into the city. The levees were — 87

massive, but they could not withstand the force of Hurricane Katrina. — 98

When Hurricane Katrina hit the Gulf Coast on August 29, 2005, — 109

intense winds swept through New Orleans. The water surrounding — 118

the city rose. The levees broke, and most of the city was soon under — 132

water. Buildings crumbled. Roads buckled. Over a thousand people — 141

died, and nearly a million people lost their homes. — 150

Many citizens of New Orleans were forced to leave. Most wish — 161

to return home. We must help them rebuild their homes and city. — 173

Some people argue that the process will be too costly. They say — 185

New Orleans will never be safe from storms. However, experts have — 196

proven these arguments wrong. — 200

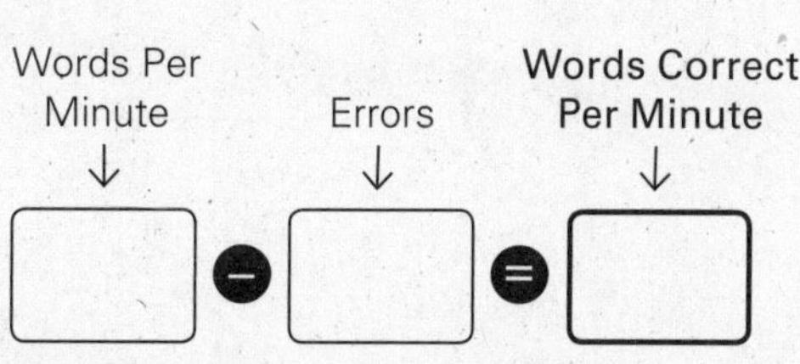

## High-Frequency Words

| before | maybe | walk | live | what |
|--------|-------|------|------|------|
| over | thank | them | who | may |

## Words of the Day

___ ___ ___ ___        ___ ___ ___ ___ ___

___ ___ ___ ___        ___ ___ ___ ___

## Missing Letters

Write the missing letter or letters for each Word of the Day. Then write the complete word.

1. p ▨ t ·····▶ _______ ·····▶ _______________

2. ▨▨▨ u n d ·····▶ _______ ·····▶ _______________

3. g a ▨▨ ·····▶ _______ ·····▶ _______________

4. r ▨▨ n d ·····▶ _______ ·····▶ _______________

5. ▨▨▨ i n ·····▶ _______ ·····▶ _______________

# Word Study Skill

Read the words in the box. Circle five words that have the silent letter *h* or the silent letter patterns *gn, kn,* or *mb*.

| | | | | |
|---|---|---|---|---|
| **chorus** | **ivy** | **know** | **react** | **child** |
| **gnaw** | **tie** | **crumb** | **cookie** | **comb** |

# Phonics Practice

Read the words in the box. Write each word in the correct column on the chart.

| | | | |
|---|---|---|---|
| **design** | **hour** | **knowledge** | **climb** |
| **lamb** | **gnat** | **honest** | **knife** |

| silent letter pattern *gn* | silent *h* | silent letter pattern *kn* | silent letter pattern *mb* |
|---|---|---|---|
| | | | |

# Apply It

Read the sentences below. For each one, circle the words with the correct letter pattern.

1. *kn*    Two knights knocked on Mr. Comb's front door.

2. *gn*    The lamplighter had resigned. It was the end of his reign.

3. *mb*    The knights now wanted Comb to climb up and light the lamps.

4. *gh*    The knights came in out of the ghostly fog.

# Spell It

| **Spelling Tip** | Many words are spelled with silent letters such as the silent letter *h* or silent letter patterns *gn, kn*, and *mb*. |
|---|---|

1. __________________________

2. __________________________

3. __________________________

4. __________________________

5. __________________________

# Topic Introduction

**Text:** _______________________________________________

**Topic:** _______________________________________________

Related Terms:

1. _______________________________

2. _______________________________

3. _______________________________

4. _______________________________

5. _______________________________

6. _______________________________

7. _______________________________

8. _______________________________

9. _______________________________

10. _______________________________

The term I know most about is:

_______________________________

What I know:

_______________________________

_______________________________

_______________________________

_______________________________

_______________________________

_______________________________

_______________________________

_______________________________

_______________________________

_______________________________

_______________________________

_______________________________

_______________________________

# Summary Tree

**Text:** _______________________________

1.

2.

3.

---

1.

2.

3.

---

1.

2.

3.

---

1.

2.

3.

Where

When

Who

What Happened

**Summary**

# Present Progressive Tense Verbs

| **About Verbs in the Present Progressive Tense** | • A verb in the present tense expresses what exists or is happening now.<br>• A verb in the present progressive tense expresses a continuing action or state of being. Helping verbs include *am, are,* and *is*. Example: *I am eating lunch.*<br>• Form the present progressive tense by using the correct form of *be (am, is, are)* in a sentence and then adding *–ing* to the base form of the main verb in the present tense. Example: *They sing. They are singing.* In some cases, you may need to drop the final *-e, -es,* or *s* before adding *-ing,* as in *make, making.* In other cases, you may need to double the final consonant before adding *-ing,* as in *run, running.* |
| --- | --- |

## Form the Present Progressive Tense

Read each sentence below. On each blank line, write the present progressive tense of the verb written underneath.

1. The storm ______________________.
   comes

2. Everyone in town ____________________ to see if it will hit land.
   watches

3. People ____________________ it passes by.
   hope

4. If it does hit town, however, we ____________________ to go to a shelter.
   prepare

5. I ____________________ scared but also a little excited.
   feel

# Find It in Your Reading

Read the letter below. Find sentences with verbs in the present progressive tense. Underline the sentences. Then circle the verbs in the present progressive tense in each.

Dear Uncle Max,

Thanks so much for your letter. I am writing to you from camp. I miss Mom and Dad, but I love it here. The camp is in the woods and every day I swim and hike. I am learning to paddle a canoe. I am making lots of new friends, too. Tonight, there is supposed to be a big storm. Everyone is waiting to see if there will be lightning. I hope it doesn't come near my tent. See you next week.

Love,

Tim

# Put It in Your Writing

Write three sentences about what your family or school is doing to prepare for an emergency. Include one verb in the present progressive tense in each sentence.

_______________________________________________

_______________________________________________

_______________________________________________

_______________________________________________

**286**

## STEP **1** Making Connections

{DONE ✔}

I will connect what I already know to the expository text "Into the Volcano" by Donna O'Meara.
I will discuss how people in "Into the Volcano" are affected by natural disasters.

## STEP **2** Developing Vocabulary

I will discuss the six vocabulary words: *cycle, reflect, formidable, vanish, rapt,* and *expanse.*

## STEP **3** Practicing Fluency

I will read aloud part of "Rebuilding New Orleans" with fluency by practicing phrasing and
using punctuation to inform meaning.
I will chart my fluency progress.

## STEP **4** Building Word Study Skills

I will learn five new high-frequency words.
I will practice recognizing and using words in the *–ay, –ade, –ose* and *–oast* word families.
I will understand my spelling homework assignment.

## STEP **5** Reading for Understanding

I will review the reading strategy of summarizing.
I will learn to use the reading skill of summarizing for the main idea and supporting details in
expository text.

## STEP **6** Applying the Conventions of English

I will review my understanding of verbs in the past tense.
I will identify and use verbs in the past progressive tense in my speaking, reading, and writing.

## STEP **7** Writing with Purpose

I will review the stages of the writing process.
I will review my first draft.
I will revise my first draft for ideas using the *Idea Workshop*.

{Summarizing My Learning}

# Hidden Clues

Read the clues for each number. Write the correct vocabulary word under each clue. The letters in the boxes will complete the answer to the question at the bottom of the page.

1. The light that shines on the lake is too strong for my eyes.

___ ___ ___ [1] ___ ___ ___

2. I could not stop staring at the hot air balloons!

___ [2] ___ ___

3. I walk my dog before breakfast and after supper every day.

___ ___ ___ [3] ___

4. There was enough room for all of our tents on the open field.

___ ___ ___ [4] ___ ___ ___

5. The new sports stadium is gigantic!

___ ___ [5] [6] [7] ___ ___ ___ ___

6. My fears just disappeared once I started the race.

___ ___ [8] ___ ___

## According to many experts, why are the ice caps melting?

g ___ ___ o b ___ ___ w ___ ___ ___ ___ ___ g
1    2  3    4  5  6  7  8

| Vocabulary | cycle | reflect | formidable |
|---|---|---|---|
| | vanish | rapt | expanse |



Practice Book • Unit 2

## Practice Reading Phrases

1. such as the historic French Quarter

2. used for homes and businesses

3. stronger, taller levees

4. well worth the cost

5. history, people, food, and music

## Practice Reading Sentences

1. Many areas, such as the historic French Quarter, made it through the storm.

2. Low-lying areas that flooded do not need to be used for homes and businesses.

3. Stronger, taller levees have also been designed and can be built to protect the city from storms.

4. New Orleans can be safe, and rebuilding is well worth the cost.

5. The city's history, people, food, and music are also important for the nation's sense of culture.

## Timed Reading

**{ ROLE OF THE READER }**

Read the passage to your partner as accurately as possible.

Remember, your reading goal is 85 Words Correct Per Minute (WCPM).

**{ ROLE OF THE LISTENER }**

As your partner reads, mark these errors with a strikethrough:

- mispronounced words
- skipped words
- changed words
- added words

Excerpt from
# Rebuilding New Orleans

<table>
<tr><td></td><td>Number<br>of Words</td></tr>
</table>

There are several ways to rebuild a safer New Orleans. Many | 11

areas, such as the historic French Quarter, made it through the storm. | 23

This is because such areas were built on higher land. More of the city | 37

can be rebuilt on higher land. Scientists have shown that areas people | 49

feel are at risk can also be built on rafts or stilts to keep them safe | 65

from flooding. Low-lying areas that flooded do not need to be used | 77

for homes and businesses. Wetlands can be restored in these areas. | 88

Stronger, taller levees have also been designed and can be built to | 100

protect the city from storms. | 105

New Orleans can be safe, and rebuilding is well worth the cost. | 117

New Orleans is important for the United States' economy. The city's | 128

history, people, food, and music are also important for the nation's | 139

sense of culture. The people of New Orleans have an exciting chance | 151

to construct a safer version of their city with the same great heart. | 164

We *must* offer them all the support they need. | 173

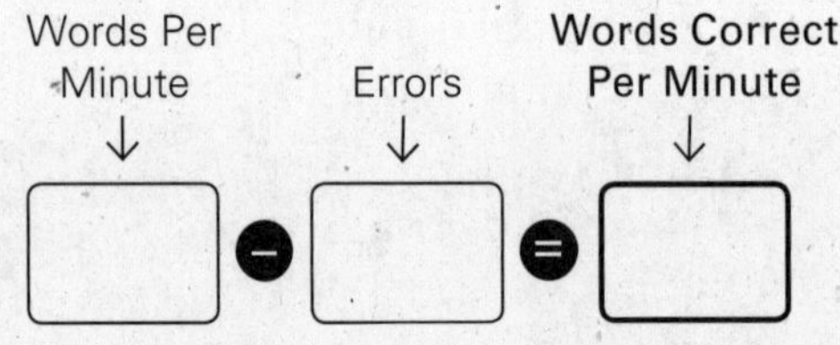

## High-Frequency Words

| | | | | |
|---|---|---|---|---|
| before | maybe | walk | live | what |
| over | thank | them | who | may |
| put | round | again | around | gave |

## Words of the Day

_____ _____ _____ _____

_____ _____

## Scrambled Letters

Use the scrambled letters below to spell the Words of the Day.

| outside | goes | says | any | teach |
|---|---|---|---|---|

1. y  a  s  s   =  _____

2. c  h  e  a  t   =  _____

3. n  a  y   =  _____

4. s  i  d  o  u  t  e   =  _____

5. o  e  s  g   =  _____

# Word Study Skill

Read the words in the box. Circle five words that belong to the *-ade, -ay, -ose,* or *-oast* word families.

> | | | | | |
> |---|---|---|---|---|
> | **nose** | **ray** | **flowers** | **shade** | **fun** |
> | **tray** | **weeds** | **sun** | **coast** | **hour** |

# Phonics Practice

Circle the word that belongs to the correct word family. Underline the ending –ade, –ay, –ose, or –oast in each word.

1. **–ade**    suppose    glade    boast    sway

2. **–ay**    coastal    grade    stray    those

3. **–ose**    disclose    roasted    trade    maybe

4. **–oast**    hose    clay    lemonade    toast

# Apply It

Read the sentences below. In each sentence, there are two words that belong to the same word family. Circle them and write the ending they share on the line.

1. He joined the army to oppose the king and those who supported him.  _______________

2. Today is the day.  _______________

3. Wade sharpened his blade.  _______________

4. I ate some toast once the roast was in the oven.  _______________

# Spell It

| **Spelling Tip** | Listen carefully to a word before you try to spell it. |

1. _______________________________

2. _______________________________

3. _______________________________

4. _______________________________

5. _______________________________

## Wildfires in the West *by Linda B. Ross*

*Part 2 of 4*

Another way to fight wildfires is to set a backfire. That is when firefighters start a fire themselves! The fire they start is small. It is right in the path of the wildfire. The backfire burns trees and brush. This leaves no fuel for the wildfire. Without anything to burn, the wildfire gets smaller. Then the firefighters can control and put out both fires.

Airplanes and helicopters, called water bombers, are also used to fight wildfires. They drop huge amounts of water on a wildfire. However, water itself is often not enough. The airplanes and helicopters also drop chemicals on wildfires. The chemicals help cool the fire down. Flying over a fire can be very dangerous. The aircraft experience a lot of **turbulence** flying so low over the fire. They can also be damaged by the intense heat that reflects off the burning surface.

**turbulence**  irregular motion or shaking

### Notes

1.  When wildfires get out of control, what is one solution firefighters use?

_______________________

_______________________

_______________________

_______________________

2.  Why do firefighters have different ways to fight wildfires?

_______________________

_______________________

_______________________

_______________________

_______________________

_______________________

_______________________

_______________________

_______________________

_______________________

Airplanes and helicopters are also used to drop smokejumpers into wildfire areas. Smokejumpers are special firefighters. Their job is very tough. They are dropped into areas that are difficult to reach from land. Hundreds of smokejumpers work in the West. Most of them work only during fire season. The rest of the year they keep themselves busy with jobs other than firefighting. Then, each summer, they return to fight wildfires.

Some wildfires simply can't be controlled, no matter what firefighters try. In 1988 a fire **ignited** in Yellowstone National Park as a result of lightning. Strong winds were causing the fire to spread. The wildfires were quickly consuming **acres** of land. It seemed as though the park might vanish into the flames. ⏸

**acres**  a unit of land measure equal to 43,560 square feet
**ignited**  caught fire

## Notes

3. When do smokejumpers work?

4. What does the author mean when she says, "It seemed as though the park might vanish into the flames"?

Firefighters from all over the U.S. came to help. They worked all day and night. Despite their efforts, the wildfires raged on. At last, nature itself put out the fires. The wildfires were drenched by rainfall on September 10. The next day snow fell. Although some fires continued burning until November, the worst was over.

More than 25,000 firefighters had come to help. They used hundreds of fire engines and planes. Two people died, and about 67 buildings were destroyed. The wildfires also had a big effect on wildlife. Many trees and plants were destroyed. As a result, many animals starved to death because their food sources had burned. Over time, new plants began to sprout. Burnt areas came back to life, but the damage was great and lasting. The wildfires burned more than 1 million acres. ⏸

**What are some solutions firefighters use to put out wildfires?**

## Notes

5. What were the effects of the 1988 fire in Yellowstone National Park?

6. Why do you think that firefighters came from all over the U.S. to help?

# Information Log

**Text:** _______________________________________________

| { **Subject** } | { **Notes** } |
| --- | --- |
| There are many ways to fight wildfires. | |
| Some wildfires can't be controlled, such as in Yellowstone National Park in 1988. | |

**On-the-Surface**
*who, where, when, and what happened*

**Under-the-Surface**
*how, why, would, could, and should*

## Reflection

_______________________________________________
_______________________________________________
_______________________________________________

# Verbs in the Past Progressive Tense

| **About Past Progressive Tense** | • A verb in the past tense expresses action or a state of being taking place in the past.<br>• A verb in the past progressive tense expresses a continuing action or state of being that has been continuing in the past. Helping verbs are *was* and *were*. Example: *We were reading.*<br>• The past progressive tense is formed by using the correct past tense form of the *be* verb (*was, were*) as a helping verb and adding *–ing* to the base form of the main verb. |
|---|---|

## Form the Past Progressive Tense

Read each sentence. On the blank lines, write the past progressive tense of the verbs written underneath.

1. I _______________________ that my mom could drive us home.
   hope

2. We _______________________ in the gym after school.
   meet

3. The waves _______________________ on the beach.
   crash

4. He told me that he _______________________ at the supermarket first.
   stop

5. She _______________________ computer models to track the storm.
   use

## Find It in Your Reading

Write three sentences from your reading that include verbs in the past progressive tense. Underline each helping and main verb.

1. ___________________________________________

___________________________________________

2. ___________________________________________

___________________________________________

3. ___________________________________________

___________________________________________

## Put It in Your Writing

Write three sentences describing the last rain storm you experienced. Include one verb in the past progressive tense in each sentence.

___________________________________________

___________________________________________

___________________________________________

___________________________________________

___________________________________________

{DONE ✔}

## STEP 1 Making Connections

I will connect what I already know to the expository text "Into the Volcano" by Donna O'Meara.
I will discuss how people in "Into the Volcano" are affected by natural disasters.

## STEP 2 Developing Vocabulary

I will discuss the six vocabulary words: *cycle, reflect, formidable, vanish, rapt,* and *expanse.*

## STEP 3 Practicing Fluency

I will read aloud part of "Wildfires in the West" with fluency by practicing phrasing and
conveying emotion and meaning.
I will chart my fluency progress.

## STEP 4 Building Word Study Skills

I will learn five new high-frequency words.
I will practice recognizing and using words in the *–ive, –ied, –ue,* and *–eam* word families.
I will understand my spelling homework assignment.

## STEP 5 Reading for Understanding

I will review the reading strategy of summarizing.
I will use the reading skill of summarizing for main idea and supporting details in expository text.

## STEP 6 Applying the Conventions of English

I will review my understanding of nouns and verbs in the past tense.
I will identify and use subject-verb agreement with verbs in the past and past progressive tenses
in my speaking, reading, and writing.

## STEP 7 Writing with Purpose

I will review stages of the writing process.
I will review *Idea Workshop* and the problem/solution prompt.
I will edit for correct use of compound verbs using *Editor's Workshop.*

{Summarizing My Learning}

# Crossword Puzzle

Read the clues for each number. Write the correct vocabulary word on the puzzle.

**Across**

1. Please pull down the blinds because I can't see with all the light in the room.
2. That car is the biggest one on the road.
3. My stomach ache will go away after I eat.

**Down**

1. I get tired every afternoon at 4:00.
2. My neighbor needs to find a large open lot to build her new home.
3. I love camping because I can sit and watch a campfire for hours.

| **Vocabulary** | cycle | reflect | formidable |
| --- | --- | --- | --- |
| | vanish | rapt | expanse |

# Practice Reading Phrases

1. a great effect
2. By the time they reach Southern California
3. burst into flames
4. risk their lives
5. other methods to stop the fire

# Practice Reading Sentences

1. Wind has a great effect on how quickly a fire spreads.
2. By the time they reach Southern California the winds are hot and dry.
3. When a wildfire moves through a pine forest, the trees burst into flames!
4. Each year thousands of firefighters risk their lives trying to control wildfires.
5. Firefighters must then try other methods to stop the fire.

# Timed Reading

**{ ROLE OF THE READER }**

Read the passage to your partner as accurately as possible.

Remember, your reading goal is 85 Words Correct Per Minute (WCPM).

**{ ROLE OF THE LISTENER }**

As your partner reads, mark these errors with a strikethrough:

- mispronounced words
- skipped words
- changed words
- added words

Excerpt from
# Wildfires in the West

| | Number of Words |
|---|---|
| Wind has a great effect on how quickly a fire spreads. In Southern | 13 |
| California, Santa Ana winds blow wildly. The winds come from | 23 |
| the Sierra Nevada and Rocky Mountains. By the time they reach | 34 |
| Southern California the winds are hot and dry. They make wildfires | 45 |
| move fast. | 47 |
| Another reason parts of the West have so many wildfires is that | 59 |
| some trees burn more easily than others. In the West, there are many | 72 |
| pine forests. Pine trees contain resin, which burns quickly. When a | 83 |
| wildfire moves through a pine forest, the trees burst into flames! | 94 |
| Wildfires can last for days, weeks, or even months. Homes and | 105 |
| other buildings can be destroyed. The damage can cost millions of | 116 |
| dollars. Sometimes people lose their lives. | 122 |
| Each year thousands of firefighters risk their lives trying to control | 132 |
| wildfires. They know there are many ways to stop a wildfire from | 143 |
| spreading. One way is to make a firebreak. To do this, firefighters | 156 |
| cut down trees and brush that lie in a fire's path. Then they clear the | 169 |
| trees and brush away. When the fire reaches the break, it has nothing | 182 |
| to burn. If all goes well, the fire burns out. However, sometimes | 196 |
| wind blows the fire across the break. Firefighters must then try other | 206 |
| methods to stop the fire. | 214 |

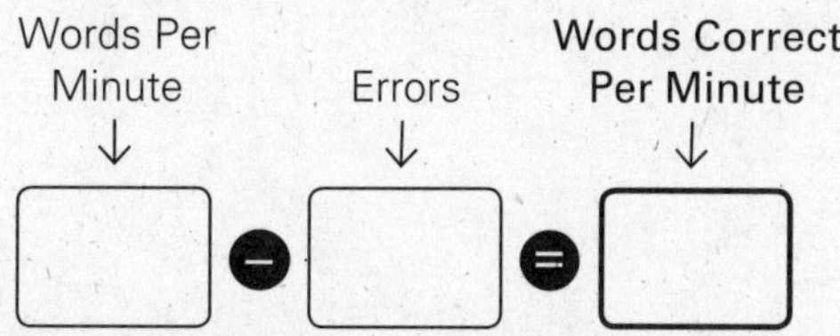

# High-Frequency Words

| before | outside | round | them | live | any | gave |
|--------|---------|-------|------|------|-----|------|
| over | maybe | goes | again | who | what | teach |
| put | thank | walk | says | around | may | |

# Words of the Day

__ __ __ __ __ __    __ __ __ __ __

__ __ __ __    __ __ __ __ __

# Word Riddles

Answer the riddles below with the Words of the Day.

| these | by | both | made | those |
|-------|----|----|------|-------|

1. Which is the shortest word on the list? ______________________

2. Which word rhymes with *cheese*? ______________________

3. Which words end in silent *e*? ______________________

4. Which word ends in *th*? ______________________



Practice Book • Unit 2

# Word Study Skill

Read the words in the box. Circle five words that are in the *–ive, –ied, –ue,* or *–eam* word families.

| | | | | |
|---|---|---|---|---|
| **tied** | **took** | **today** | **say** | **clue** |
| **pay** | **glue** | **give** | **book** | **beam** |

# Phonics Practice

Circle the word that belongs to the correct word family. Underline the ending *–ive, –ied, –ue,* or *–eam* in each word.

1. *–ive* as in *give*        cried        festive        jive
2. *–ive* as in *survive*        thrive        glue        dream
3. *–ied* as in *died*        cue        drive        fried
4. *–ied* as in *pitied*        gleam        tried        carried
5. *–ue*        blue        deprive        steam
6. *–eam*        active        scream        issue

# Apply It

Read the sentences below. In each sentence, there are two words that belong to the same family. Circle them and write the ending they share on the line.

1. Clive climbed down the stairs to the archive. ________

2. He found a clue that there was something of great value there. ________

3. Sue nearly cried out when she spied a key inside. ________

4. I had a dream I was swimming in a stream. ________

5. Mom was not worried as we emptied the giant trunk. ________

6. I will give Sam some wood to build a place for his dogs to live. ________

# Spell It

| **Spelling Tip** | Listen carefully to a word before you try to spell it. A letter combination may make different sounds in different words. |
| --- | --- |

1. ________________________________

2. ________________________________

3. ________________________________

4. ________________________________

5. ________________________________

# Quick Write

What are some solutions firefighters use to put out wildfires?

# Summary Tree

Text: ___________________________________________

1.

2.

3.

1.

2.

3.

1.

2.

3.

1.

2.

3.

Where

When

Who

What
Happened

**Summary**

# Subject–Verb Agreement

**About Subject-Verb Agreement**

- A subject and verb must agree in number. If the subject of a sentence is singular, the verb in the sentence must be singular. If the subject is plural, the verb must be plural.
- To form common past tense verbs, you add *–d* or *–ed* to the present tense. Sometimes, you change the final *–y* in the present tense to an *–i* and add *–ed*. Examples: *smile, smiled; laugh, laughed; worry, worried*.
- To form the past progressive tense of a verb, use the helping verbs *was* or *were* and add *–ing* to the base form of the main verb. Remember, the subject and helping verb must agree in number.

## Make Subjects and Verbs Agree

Read each sentence. Write the correct past tense and past progressive tense form of the verb that agrees with the subject of each sentence.

|  | PAST | PAST PROGRESSIVE |
|---|---|---|
| 1. They look. | | |
| 2. The sailors talk. | | |
| 3. Michelle hurries. | | |
| 4. I work. | | |

# Find It in Your Reading

Write three sentences from your reading that include verbs in the past or past progressive tenses and correct subject-verb agreement. Circle the subject in each sentence. Underline the verb in each sentence.

1. _______________________________________________________________

   _______________________________________________________________

2. _______________________________________________________________

   _______________________________________________________________

3. _______________________________________________________________

   _______________________________________________________________

# Put It in Your Writing

Write three sentences telling about a brush fire. Make sure to include a past or past progressive tense verb with correct subject-verb agreement in each sentence.

1. _______________________________________________________________

   _______________________________________________________________

2. _______________________________________________________________

   _______________________________________________________________

3. _______________________________________________________________

   _______________________________________________________________

{DONE ✔}

## STEP **1** Making Connections

I will connect what I already know to a painting.
I will discuss the essential question, *How are people affected by natural disasters?*

## STEP **2** Developing Vocabulary

I will review and complete an assessment of six vocabulary words.

## STEP **3** Practicing Fluency

I will read aloud part of "Wildfires in the West" with fluency by practicing phrasing and
   using punctuation to inform meaning and I will chart my fluency progress.

## STEP **4** Building Word Study Skills

I will learn five new high-frequency words.
I will review recognizing and using words in the *−ay, −ade, −ose, −oast, −ive, −ied, −ue,* and
   *−eam* word families.
I will take a spelling test.

## STEP **5** Reading for Understanding

I will review the reading strategy of summarizing.
I will review the reading skill of summarizing for main idea and supporting details in expository
   text.

## STEP **6** Applying the Conventions of English

I will review my understanding of subject-verb agreement in the present progressive, past,
   and past progressive tenses.
I will write declarative sentences using the conventions learned in this chapter.

## STEP **7** Writing with Purpose

I will review stages of the writing process.
I will edit for word choice, correct use of pronouns, spelling, and punctuation.

{Summarizing My Learning}

# Show What You Know

Read each question. Check the box beside the best answer.

1. If the symptoms of a cold **vanish,** you—

   ☐ get sicker.
   ☐ need new medicine.
   ☐ feel better.
   ☐ make someone else sick.

2. Which object would be *least* useful when bright light **reflects** into your eyes?

   ☐ sunglasses
   ☐ window shades
   ☐ car visor
   ☐ mirror

3. Kayla was **fascinated** by the pictures in the art museum.

   Which word would work best as a substitution for the underlined word?

   ☐ formidable
   ☐ rapt
   ☐ expanse
   ☐ vanished

4. If something in nature follows a **cycle,** it—

   ☐ repeats again and again.
   ☐ reflects light and heat.
   ☐ happens one time.
   ☐ disappears.

5. Select the word that has the most similar meaning to *formidable*.

   ☐ boring
   ☐ missing
   ☐ fascinating
   ☐ threatening

6. An **expanse** is a ________ area.

   ☐ small, wooded
   ☐ large, dry
   ☐ wide, open
   ☐ narrow, flat

## Practice Reading Phrases

1. start a fire
2. anything to burn
3. airplanes and helicopters
4. drop smokejumpers into wildfire areas
5. jobs other than firefighting

## Practice Reading Sentences

1. That is when firefighters start a fire themselves!
2. Without anything to burn, the wildfire gets smaller.
3. The airplanes and helicopters also drop chemicals on wildfires.
4. Airplanes and helicopters are also used to drop smokejumpers into wildfire areas.
5. The rest of the year they keep themselves busy with jobs other than firefighting.

## Timed Reading

**{ ROLE OF THE READER }**

Read the passage to your partner as accurately as possible.

Remember, your reading goal is 85 Words Correct Per Minute (WCPM).

**{ ROLE OF THE LISTENER }**

As your partner reads, mark these errors with a strikethrough:

- mispronounced words
- skipped words
- changed words
- added words

Excerpt from
# Wildfires in the West

|  | Number of Words |
|---|---|
| Another way to fight wildfires is to set a backfire. That is when | 13 |
| firefighters start a fire themselves! The fire they start is small. It is | 26 |
| right in the path of the wildfire. The backfire burns trees and brush. | 39 |
| This leaves no fuel for the wildfire. Without anything to burn, the | 51 |
| wildfire gets smaller. Then the firefighters can control and put out | 62 |
| both fires. | 64 |
| Airplanes and helicopters, called water bombers, are also used | 73 |
| to fight wildfires. They drop huge amounts of water on a wildfire. | 85 |
| However, water itself is often not enough. The airplanes and | 95 |
| helicopters also drop chemicals on wildfires. The chemicals help cool | 105 |
| the fire down. Flying over a fire can be very dangerous. The aircraft | 118 |
| experience a lot of turbulence flying so low over the fire. They can | 131 |
| also be damaged by the intense heat that reflects off the burning | 143 |
| surface. | 144 |
| Airplanes and helicopters are also used to drop smokejumpers | 153 |
| into wildfire areas. Smokejumpers are special firefighters. Their | 161 |
| job is very tough. They are dropped into areas that are difficult to | 174 |
| reach from land. Hundreds of smokejumpers work in the West. Most | 185 |
| of them work only during fire season. The rest of the year they | 198 |
| keep themselves busy with jobs other than firefighting. Then, each | 208 |
| summer, they return to fight wildfires. | 214 |

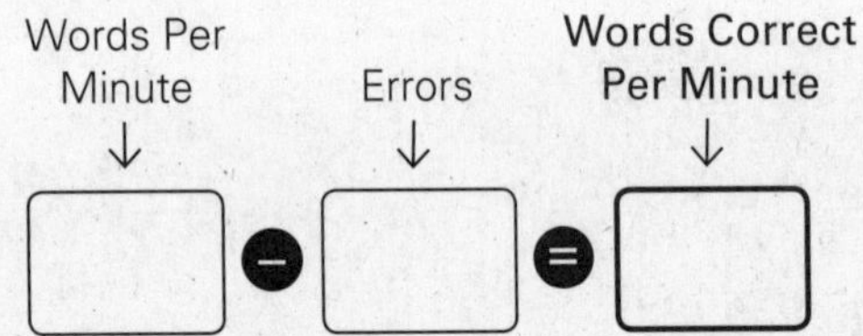

# High-Frequency Words

| before | these | goes | again | who | what | those |
| over | maybe | by | says | around | may | |
| put | thank | walk | both | any | gave | |
| outside | round | them | live | made | teach | |

# Words of the Day

____ ____ ________

_______

# Alphabetical Order

List the Words of the Day in alphabetical order.

| call | cold | could | use | or |

1. __________________
2. __________________
3. __________________
4. __________
5. ____________

# Word Study Skill

Read the words in the box. Circle five words that belong to the *–ade, –ay, –ose,* *–oast, –ive, –ied, –ue,* or *–eam* word families.

| | | | | |
|---|---|---|---|---|
| **blade** | **crew** | **live** | **too** | **view** |
| **say** | **month** | **dream** | **roast** | **family** |

# Phonics Practice

Read the words in the box. Write each one next to the word below that belongs to the same word family.

| | | | | |
|---|---|---|---|---|
| **toast** | **gleam** | **strive** | **forgive** | **chose** |
| **married** | **tray** | **decade** | **sue** | **dried** |

1. cream _______________________________
2. five _______________________________
3. olive _______________________________
4. boast _______________________________
5. worried _______________________________
6. propose _______________________________
7. holiday _______________________________
8. lied _______________________________
9. value _______________________________
10. trade _______________________________

# Apply It

Read the sentences below. For each one, circle the words in the correct word family.

1. *–ade* — "Do you want some lemonade before you go?" asked Mrs. Jade.

2. *–ay* — "When I get back," Jay called as he ran off to the schoolyard.

3. *–ose* — "I suppose the other boys were already there," he thought.

4. *–oast* — Jay would sometimes boast that he could run faster than any of them.

5. *–ive* as in *cursive* — They were going to give him a chance to prove it.

6. *–ive* as in *alive* — Jay could thrive on competition. He wanted to win.

7. *–ied* as in *spied* — At the starting line, he looked down to make sure his shoes were tied.

8. *–ied* as in *copied* — When someone yelled "go," Jay hurried down the path.

9. *–ue* — He ran faster than smoke rises out a chimney flue.

10. *–eam* — Jay heard a scream of excitement from the crowd as he finished first.

# Spell It

| Spelling Tip | Listen carefully to a word before you try to spell it. A letter combination may make different sounds in different words. |
|---|---|

1. ______________________     4. ______________________

2. ______________________     5. ______________________

3. ______________________

## Wildfires in the West *by Linda B. Ross*

*Part 4 of 4*

Although many states have wildfire problems, California has more fires than most. Each year, the state experiences thousands of wildfires. The summers are dry in California. With the heat and strong winds, small fires can quickly grow out of control.

In 2003 wildfires swept through southern California. They were among the state's worst natural disasters in history. Communities from Los Angeles to San Diego burned. Fires destroyed homes and forests. In total, almost 750,000 acres burned. ⏸

### Notes

1. How many acres burned in the 2003 wildfires in California?

2. How do you think the people of Southern California felt about the 1993 wildfires?

Nearly 15,000 firefighters fought these wildfires. As the fires raged, thousands of people were forced to leave their homes. Many lost their houses and belongings, and at least 20 people died.

Years have passed since these natural disasters **ravaged** southern California. However, many people are still rebuilding. Starting over takes a long time. When the weather is bad, building stops. Bad rainstorms, for example, can delay building for weeks to months at a time. Despite delays, most people are hopeful. They consider themselves lucky. They are happy to watch their new homes and businesses slowly come to life. They are happy to be alive. ⓫

## Notes

3. Would you consider yourself lucky if you were still rebuilding from the 2003 wildfires? Why or why not?

___________________________

___________________________

___________________________

___________________________

___________________________

___________________________

___________________________

___________________________

4. What is delaying the rebuilding in Southern California?

___________________________

___________________________

___________________________

___________________________

___________________________

___________________________

**ravaged**   damaged or destroyed

There are some ways to prevent the 2003 **tragedy** in California from repeating itself. One way is to have controlled fires. Controlled fires are set by firefighters to separate tree groupings and areas dense with brush. These fires create firebreaks, which stop wildfires from spreading. Controlled fires are also good because they clear out old plants and allow new plants room to grow. Starting controlled fires in cycles throughout the year could save property and help forests stay healthy.

It's not possible to prevent all wildfires. However, there are things people can do to protect their homes. People can build their houses with materials that resist fire. They can also clear the property around their homes to create firebreaks like the ones firefighters create during controlled burns.

Wildfires are a fact of life in the West. However, there is something we can all do. We can practice good safety habits and protect our homes and land from fires caused by careless behavior. Doing so could save lives, homes, and many of our natural resources. ⏸

**How are people affected by wildfires?**

tragedy awful event

## Notes

5. What are two reasons that controlled fires are a good idea?

6. What is the author's message in this text? How can you tell?

# Information Log

**Text:** ______________________________

<table>
<tr><td>{ Subject }</td><td>{ Notes }</td></tr>
<tr><td>California has more wildfires than most other states.</td><td></td></tr>
<tr><td>2003 southern California wildfires: one of state's worst natural disasters</td><td></td></tr>
<tr><td>What people can do</td><td></td></tr>
</table>

**On-the-Surface**
*who, where, when, and what happened*

**Under-the-Surface**
*how, why, would, could, and should*

## Reflection

______________________________
______________________________
______________________________

# Conventions Review

## Review Verbs in the Present Progressive Tense

On the blank lines, write the present progressive form of the verbs written underneath.

1. Fires _________________________ next to the highway.
   burn

2. Smoke _________________________ from the trees.
   billow

## Review Action Verbs in the Past Tense

Read each sentence. Circle the subject. Underline all past tense action verbs.

1. Lauren watched the sailboats as she jogged through the park.

2. Over one hundred students arrived for the fundraiser.

3. We listened to the hall monitor and hurried to class.

## Review Being Verbs in the Past Tense

Read each sentence. Underline the past tense *be* verbs in each sentence.

1. Lupita was the last person to climb the mountain.

2. Everyone was in the room so we were ready to begin our presentations.

3. Why were they late to class?

## Review Verbs in the Past Progressive Tense

Read each sentence. On the blank line, write the past progressive tense form of the verb written underneath.

1. The audience _______________________.
   wait

2. All the dancers _______________________ backstage.
   practice

## Review Subject-Verb Agreement with Past and Past Progressive Tense Verbs

Read each sentence. Write the correct form of the past tense and past progressive tense to agree with each subject.

| | PAST | PAST PROGRESSIVE |
|---|---|---|
| 1. Adnan carves. | _____________ | _____________ |
| 2. They tally. | _____________ | _____________ |

## Put It in Your Writing

Write three declarative sentences to tell about natural disasters that threaten your area. Use correct subject-verb agreement. Also include examples of present progressive, past tense, past progressive tense, and verbs.

_______________________________________________

_______________________________________________

_______________________________________________

{ DONE ✔ }

## STEP **1** Developing Test-Taking Strategies

I will read a test-taking manual.
I will learn strategies for taking multiple-choice tests.

## STEP **2** Assessing My Learning

I will take a multiple-choice test on skills I learned in this chapter.

## STEP **3** Writing with Purpose

I will publish the final draft of my problem/solution letter.

## STEP **4** Analyzing My Results

I will identify which questions I answered correctly and which questions I answered
incorrectly.

## STEP **5** Reinforcing My Learning

I will reinforce my understanding of verbs in past progressive tense.
I will reinforce my understanding of silent letters *h*, *g*, *k*, and *b*.

## STEP **6** Speaking with Purpose

I will watch a video of a speech and summarize its meaning.

{ Summarizing My Learning }

# Test-Taking Manual
## Before the Test

### Be Prepared

- Know what you will be tested on and study.
- Get a full night's rest.
- Have all your materials (pencil, eraser, calculator, dictionary) at your desk.

### Be Comfortable but Alert

- Make sure you have enough room to work.
- Do not slouch in your chair.

### Stay Relaxed and Confident

- Remember that you are well prepared and can do well.
- Take deep breaths if you feel anxious.
- Do not talk about the test with the other students.

## During the Test

Follow these five steps for each question on the test.

**Step 1:** Determine what the question is asking you to do.

**Step 2:** Try to answer the question in your own words.

**Step 3:** Eliminate any answers you know are incorrect.

**Step 4:** Choose the best answer.

**Step 5:** If time allows, review your answers to each question.

## Example Question

1. **Which is the BEST way to combine these two sentences?**

   We gave Karen a party. She was happy.

   **A.** We gave Karen a party she was happy.

   **B.** We gave Karen a party, or she was happy.

   **C.** We gave Karen a party, and she was happy.

   **D.** We gave Karen a party, but she was happy.

# Skills Assessment 4

**1. Which is an interrogative sentence?**

   A.  We ate dinner at Grandma's on Sunday.

   B.  Who came for dinner last night?

   C.  The dinner was wonderful!

   D.  If your aunt comes, invite her over, too.

**2. Read this part of a sentence.**

All the students _______

**Which words correctly complete the sentence?**

   A.  home after school, didn't they?

   B.  in the museum with their teacher.

   C.  came to the gym for the game.

   D.  playing basketball on Thursday.

**3. Read this part of a sentence.**

My mother and I _______

**Which words correctly complete the sentence?**

   A.  to bake cookies.

   B.  enjoy eating cookies.

   C.  into the market.

   D.  in the kitchen.

**4. Which choice correctly fills the blank?**

_______ enjoys climbing on the rocks.

   A.  I

   B.  My friends

   C.  He

   D.  My friends and I

**5. Which choice correctly fills the blank?**

Ruby fell and got hurt while she _______ to the park after school.

   A.  was racing

   B.  were racing

   C.  is race

   D.  race

**6. Which verb correctly fills the blank?**

My friends _______ reading good books.

   A.  does like

   B.  liking

   C.  likes

   D.  like

**Go on to the next page →**

# Skills Assessment 4, continued

**7. Which underlined word is NOT spelled correctly?**

> Spider monkeys clime up a favorite tree to sleep at night.

A. Spider

B. clime

C. favorite

D. night

**8. Which underlined word is NOT spelled correctly?**

> He used their nife to cut the rope off the fence post.

A. used

B. their

C. nife

D. rope

**9. Which underlined word is NOT spelled correctly?**

> On game daze, Zachary always hopes for sunshine.

A. daze

B. always

C. hopes

D. for

**10. Which underlined word is NOT spelled correctly?**

> Can you believe that some animals have more than one stomack?

A. believe

B. animals

C. than

D. stomack

**11. Which underlined word is NOT spelled correctly?**

> The city bus leaves the corner at half past the our.

A. leaves

B. corner

C. half

D. our

**12. Which underlined word is NOT spelled correctly?**

> "The gost story is scary," the children said.

A. gost

B. scary

C. children

D. said

**End of test** ■

# Verbs in the Past Progressive Tense

**Reminder:
About Past
Progressive Tense**

- A verb in the past tense expresses action or a state of being taking place in the past.
- The past progressive tense expresses a continuing action taking place in the past, or something that took place over time. For example: *We were reading.*
- Form the past progressive tense by using the correct past-tense form of to be (was, were) as a helping verb and adding –ing to the plural present tense of the main verb.

## Form the Past Progressive Tense

Read each sentence. Write the verb in the past progressive tense to correctly complete each sentence.

1. The team _________________ the stadium.
   enter

2. The fans _________________.
   cheer

3. The players _________________ to the crowd.
   wave

4. The referee _________________ a whistle.
   blow

5. The game _________________.
   start

## Find It in Your Reading

Read the story below. Find sentences with verbs in the past progressive tense. Underline the sentences. Then circle the verbs in the past progressive tense in each.

Everyone was hoping to get tickets to the big concert next month. I was waiting in line with all of my friends and classmates. I was not expecting to get tickets because I was at the back of the line. Then I was picked by the radio station to win free tickets. Now I am hanging out backstage with the musicians. I was standing in the right place at the right time!

# Choose the Verb

Which choice correctly fills the blank?

1. **My friends _______ for clothes when they saw our teacher at the mall.**
   A. shopping
   B. was shopping
   C. were shopping

2. **I found a new job while I _______ at another one.**
   A. work
   B. is working
   C. was working

3. **You missed the first half of the game because you _______ your homework.**
   A. was finishing
   B. were finishing
   C. am finishing

4. **It _______, so Chen bought an umbrella.**
   A. is raining
   B. was raining
   C. were raining

# Write Sentences with Past Progressive Tense Verbs

## Choices & Challenges
On your own piece of paper…

**A.** Rewrite each sentence on this page with a different subject and the correct past progressive tense verb.

**B.** Write a letter to a friend that tells what you did one time while you were waiting for a bus or train. Use the past progressive tense to write the letter. When you are finished, circle the verbs in the past progressive tense.

**C.** Create four new test questions about past progressive tense verbs.

# Silent Letters *h, g, k,* and *b*

| **Reminder: About Silent Letters *h, g, k,* and *b*** | • Some words, such as *whale* and *echo*, include a silent *h*.<br>• Some words, such as *resign* and *gnome*, include a silent *g*.<br>• Some words, such as *knead* and *knob*, include a silent *k*. The letter *k* appears before the letter *n* in these words.<br>• Some words, such as *tomb* and *limb*, include a silent *b*. The letter *b* appears after the letter *m* in these words. |
| --- | --- |

## Phonics Practice

Circle the word with the silent letter *h* or *k*. For each word, underline the silent *h, g, k,* or *b*.

1. comb      honor

2. rhythm      design

3. gnat      knife

4. white      gnaw

5. know      thumb

## Apply It

Read the sentences below. Circle the words with the silent letters *h, g, k,* or *b*.

I don't know where I put the Chess Club dues. I doubt that I lost them, but they are missing. There is no rhyme or reason for the loss. If I don't find the money soon, the club will be in debt. I will have to resign as treasurer and there will be a campaign to find a new one.

# Find the Misspelled Word

Which underlined word is NOT spelled correctly?

1. **The club's motto is, "Wen in doubt, ask for help."**

   **A.** wen

   **B.** doubt

   **C.** help

2. **During the storm, the tree lost a huge lim and hundreds of leaves.**

   **A.** huge

   **B.** lim

   **C.** leaves

3. **All of the dogs I know love to naw on bones and chew toys.**

   **A.** know

   **B.** naw

   **C.** chew

4. **The door was so rusty that it was impossible to turn the nob.**

   **A.** rusty

   **B.** was

   **C.** nob

## Choices & Challenges
On your own piece of paper…

**A.** Rewrite the four sentences on this page so that all of the words in the sentence are spelled correctly.

**B.** Identify and write four sentences that include words with silent letters *h, g, k,* or *b* from your Anthology, pages 74–93. Circle the words that include the silent letter and underline the silent letter.

**C.** Write a sentence that includes a word with the silent letter *h.* Repeat for words with the silent letters *g, k,* and *b.*

{ DONE ✔ }

## STEP **1** Making Connections

I will connect what I already know to a photograph and discuss the essential question
*How are people affected by natural disasters?*

## STEP **2** Developing Vocabulary

I will discuss vocabulary words in a cumulative review.

## STEP **3** Practicing Fluency

I will read aloud part of "Wildfires in the West" with fluency by practicing phrasing and
conveying emotion and meaning.
I will chart my fluency progress.

## STEP **4** Building Word Study Skills

I will learn five new high-frequency words.
I will practice recognizing and using words in the *–all, –ance,* and *–aught* word families.
I will understand the spelling homework assignment.

## STEP **5** Reading for Understanding

I will review the expository genre.
I will learn to use the reading strategy of clarifying with expository text.

## STEP **6** Applying the Conventions of English

I will review my understanding of articles.
I will identify and use articles to form complete subjects in my speaking, reading, and writing.

## STEP **7** Writing with Purpose

I will review the stages of the writing process.
I will deconstruct the *Writing Prompt: Problem/Solution* and *Scoring Guide: Problem Solution.*
I will brainstorm to select a focus using *Topic Toss: Problem Solution.*

{ Summarizing My Learning }

_______________________________________________

_______________________________________________

_______________________________________________

## Practice Reading Phrases

1. burned within a canyon
2. flames and burning timber
3. gone up in flames
4. days without sleep
5. filled with smoke

## Practice Reading Sentences

1. However, it spread quickly because it burned within a canyon.
2. This caused flames and burning timber to float out over the area.
3. By the next morning, 10,000 acres had gone up in flames.
4. Many of them worked for days without sleep.
5. The canyons were dark and filled with smoke.

## Timed Reading

**{ ROLE OF THE READER }**

Read the passage to your partner as accurately as possible.

Remember, your reading goal is 85 Words Correct Per Minute (WCPM).

**{ ROLE OF THE LISTENER }**

As your partner reads, mark these errors with a strikethrough:

- mispronounced words
- skipped words
- changed words
- added words

Excerpt from
# Wildfires in the West

|  | Number of Words |
|---|---|
| Luckily the fire was noticed early. However, it spread quickly | 10 |
| because it burned within a canyon. A canyon is like a chimney. It | 23 |
| has a draft of air that moves flames upward. Santa Ana winds were | 36 |
| blowing over 40 miles per hour that day. This caused flames and | 48 |
| burning timber to float out over the area. Topanga Canyon is also | 60 |
| crowded with chaparrals. These groups of trees are small and thick. | 71 |
| Their leaves are stiff and oily. They catch fire very easily and helped | 84 |
| the fire spread. | 87 |
| In minutes, the fire had spread 200 acres. It raged out of control. | 100 |
| By the next morning, 10,000 acres had gone up in flames. | 111 |
| More than 7,000 firefighters fought the formidable wildfire. They | 120 |
| came from all over California. They came from other states, too. | 131 |
| Many of them worked for days without sleep. | 139 |
| Helicopters were also kept busy. They lifted water from the ocean | 150 |
| and dumped it out over the fire. They flew back and forth. In one | 164 |
| hour, they made 750 water drops! Pilots even flew at night, which | 176 |
| was very dangerous. The canyons were dark and filled with smoke. | 187 |
| The helicopter pilots could hardly see. | 193 |

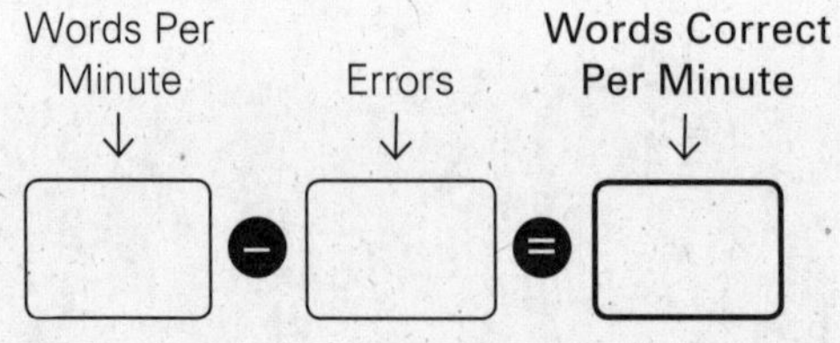

# Words of the Day

# Alphabetical Order

List the Words of the Day in alphabetical order.

| pull | every | wash | ship | read |

1. ___________ ___________ ___________ ___________ ___________
2. ___________ ___________ ___________ ___________
3. ___________ ___________ ___________ ___________
4. ___________ ___________ ___________ ___________
5. ___________ ___________ ___________ ___________

# Word Study Skill

Read the words in the box. Circle five words that belong to the *-aught, -all,* or *-ance* word families.

| | | | | |
|---|---|---|---|---|
| **tall** | **tote** | **wrote** | **dance** | **shield** |
| **caught** | **field** | **call** | **yield** | **taught** |

# Phonics Practice

Circle the words that belong to the correct word family.

| | | | | |
|---|---|---|---|---|
| 1. *–aught* | bought | caught | cold | naught |
| 2. *–all* | fowl | shall | mall | crawl |
| 3. *–ance* | lance | ants | trance | response |
| 4. *–all* | stall | doll | wall | bell |

# Apply It

Read the sentences below. In each sentence, there are two words that belong to the same word family. Circle them and write the ending they share on the line.

1. Martin tried to hit a home run, but the ball hit a wall. ______

2. One glance at the hill told me there was no chance of climbing it. ______

3. All the men in Leon's family are tall. ______

4. Min was distraught about camp until her sister taught her to swim. ______

# Spell It

| Spelling Tip | Remember that words in a word family share the same ending sound and spelling. |
| --- | --- |

1. ______________________________________

2. ______________________________________

3. ______________________________________

4. ______________________________________

5. ______________________________________

# Topic Introduction

**Text:** _______________________________________________

**Topic:** _______________________________________________

| Related Terms: | The term I know most about is: |
|---|---|
| 1. _________________________ | _________________________ |
| | **What I know:** |
| 2. _________________________ | _________________________ |
| | _________________________ |
| 3. _________________________ | _________________________ |
| | _________________________ |
| 4. _________________________ | _________________________ |
| | _________________________ |
| 5. _________________________ | _________________________ |
| | _________________________ |
| 6. _________________________ | _________________________ |
| | _________________________ |
| 7. _________________________ | _________________________ |
| | _________________________ |
| 8. _________________________ | _________________________ |
| | _________________________ |
| 9. _________________________ | _________________________ |
| | _________________________ |
| 10. ________________________ | _________________________ |

# Text Feature Log

**Text:** ____________________________________________

| Text Feature | Purpose | Example |
|---|---|---|
|  |  |  |
|  |  |  |
|  |  |  |
|  |  |  |

# Summary

____________________________________________

____________________________________________

____________________________________________

# Articles

| **About Articles** | <ul><li>Articles are the common adjectives *a, an,* and *the.* Articles modify nouns. Articles may appear anywhere in a sentence, but they always modify nouns. Example: <u>*An* apple *a* day</u> keeps <u>*the*</u> doctor away.</li><li>Use the article *a* before a singular noun that begins with a consonant sound. Example: <u>*a* tree</u></li><li>Use the article *an* before a singular noun that begins with a vowel sound. Example: <u>*an* ant</u></li><li>Use the article *the* with either singular or plural nouns. Example: <u>*the* car,</u> <u>*the* cars</u></li></ul> |
|---|---|

## Find the Article and Subject

Circle the best article to complete each sentence. Then write the complete subject of the sentence at the end of the line.

1. (A, An) book fell from the shelf. _______________

2. (An, The) family camped for three days. _______________

3. (The, A) sisters waited anxiously. _______________

4. Yesterday (a, an) artist visited our class. _______________

5. After (the, an) earthquakes, people moved away. _______________

# Find It in Your Reading

Write three sentences from your reading that have articles in the complete subject. Circle all articles in each sentence. Underline the complete subject.

1. _______________________________________________

_______________________________________________

2. _______________________________________________

_______________________________________________

3. _______________________________________________

_______________________________________________

# Put It in Your Writing

Write at least three sentences about the equipment used to play your favorite sport. Use as many articles as you can in each sentence.

_______________________________________________

_______________________________________________

_______________________________________________

_______________________________________________

_______________________________________________

{DONE ✔}

## STEP **1** Making Connections

I will connect what I already know to the expository text "Disaster! Droughts" by Dennis Brindell Fradin and discuss how people are affected by natural disasters.

## STEP **2** Developing Vocabulary

I will learn three new vocabulary words: *frequent*, *survive*, and *devastation*.

## STEP **3** Practicing Fluency

I will read aloud part of "Wildfires in the West" with fluency by practicing phrasing and using punctuation to inform meaning.
I will chart my fluency progress.

## STEP **4** Building Word Study Skills

I will learn five new high-frequency words.
I will practice recognizing and using words in the *–ield, –ink,* and *–inge* word families.
I will understand the spelling homework assignment.

## STEP **5** Reading for Understanding

I will review the reading strategy of clarifying.
I will learn to use the reading skill of clarifying for text features.

## STEP **6** Applying the Conventions of English

I will review my understanding of nouns.
I will identify and use adjectives in my speaking, reading, and writing.

## STEP **7** Writing with Purpose

I will review the problem/solution prompt and scoring guide.
I will complete the prewriting stage using *Topic Toss, Problem/Solution Organizer,* and *Evidence Organizer.*

{Summarizing My Learning}

# Hidden Clues

Read the clues for each number. Write the correct vocabulary word under each clue. The letters in the boxes will complete the answer to the question at the bottom of the page.

1. Omar goes to the movies every weekend.

___ ___ ___ ___ ___ ___ [1] ___ ___

2. Floods wiped out the whole town.

___ ___ ___ ___ ___ ___ ___ ___ [2] ___ ___

3. The disease made Anna sick for many months, but she is better now.

___ ___ ___ [3] ___ ___ ___

4. It has been raining every afternoon.

___ ___ ___ ___ ___ ___ ___ [4] ___

5. Michael watered that droopy plant, and it's blooming for the first time.

___ ___ [5] ___ ___ ___ ___ ___

6. Everything breaks when we let our bird and hamster out of their cages.

___ ___ ___ [6] ___ ___ ___ ___ ___ [7] ___ [8]

## What causes a drought?

___ o ___ l ___ t ___ l e ___ ___ ___ ___
1   2   3   4   5  6  7  8

**Vocabulary** | frequent     survive     devastation

## Practice Reading Phrases

1. lifted water from the ocean
2. In one hour
3. a great deal of damage
4. a mind of its own
5. more fires than most

## Practice Reading Sentences

1. They lifted water from the ocean and dumped it out over the fire.
2. In one hour, they made 750 water drops!
3. The wildfire burned over 16,000 acres and caused a great deal of damage.
4. The firefighters fought hard, but the fire had a mind of its own.
5. Although many states have wildfire problems, California has more fires than most.

## Timed Reading

**ROLE OF THE READER**

Read the passage to your partner as accurately as possible.

Remember, your reading goal is 85 Words Correct Per Minute (WCPM).

**ROLE OF THE LISTENER**

As your partner reads, mark these errors with a strikethrough:

- mispronounced words
- skipped words
- changed words
- added words

Excerpt from
# Wildfires in the West

|  | Number of Words |
|---|---|

More than 7,000 firefighters fought the formidable fire. They came from all over California. They came from other states, too. Many of them worked for days without sleep. — 10 / 22 / 28

Helicopters were also kept busy. They lifted water from the ocean and dumped it out over the fire. They flew back and forth. In one hour, they made 750 water drops! Pilots even flew at night, which was very dangerous. The canyons were dark and filled with smoke. The helicopter pilots could hardly see. — 39 / 53 / 65 / 76 / 82

The wildfire burned over 16,000 acres and caused a great deal of damage. It roared through canyons and neighborhoods for 10 days. Three people died, and many others were injured. Over 400 homeowners lost their homes to the fire. — 93 / 103 / 114 / 121

The firefighters fought hard, but the fire had a mind of its own. In the end, they couldn't stop it. The fire finally stopped on its own when the winds slowed down. — 134 / 148 / 153

Although many states have wildfire problems, California has more fires than most. Each year, the state experiences thousands of wildfires. The summers are dry in California. With the heat and strong winds, small fires can quickly grow out of control. — 161 / 171 / 183 / 193

Words Per Minute → [ ] − Errors → [ ] = Words Correct Per Minute → [ ]

# High-Frequency Words

> pull   every   wash   ship   read

# Words of the Day

__ __ __ __ __     __ __ __ __ __ __     __ __ __ __ __ __ __ __

__ __ __ __ __ __ __ __ __ __

# Categorize

Write each Word of the Day under the correct category.

> why

> seen

> table

> page

> know

**Words for things**

1. ______________________

2. ______________________

**Word with *h***

3. ______________________

**Words with 4 letters**

4. ______________________

5. ______________________

6. ______________________

# Word Study Skill

Read the words in the box. Circle five words that belong to the *-inge*, *-ink*, or *-ield* word families.

| | | | | |
|---|---|---|---|---|
| **field** | **wink** | **hinge** | **today** | **shield** |
| **rail** | **twelve** | **pink** | **tomorrow** | **shell** |

## Phonics Practice

Circle the words that belong to the correct word family.

1. **–inge**    tinge    singe    range    bang
2. **–ink**    bank    sink    blank    blink
3. **–ield**    wield    heeled    sailed    wild
4. **–ield**    bailed    cornfield    yield    kneeled

# Apply It

Read the sentences below. In each sentence, there are two words that belong to the same word family. Circle them and write the ending they share on the line.

1. Farmer Bai's wheat field did not produce the yield he had wanted. ______________

2. I tried not to cringe when the hinge on the door squeaked. ______________

3. Jordan took a drink of water and placed his glass in the sink. ______________

4. "We will have to rethink our plan," Carl said with a wink. ______________

# Spell It

| **Spelling Tip** | Listen carefully to a word before you try to spell it. |

1. ______________________________

2. ______________________________

3. ______________________________

4. ______________________________

5. ______________________________

## The Black Plague *by Nori Yoshida*

**2** — *Part 2 of 2*

### The Black Death's Effect on Population

The Black Death had a huge effect on the populations of Europe and Asia. In Florence, Italy, for example, the disease killed more than 60,000 people. No one was safe from the plague, and **economies** were damaged throughout the world.

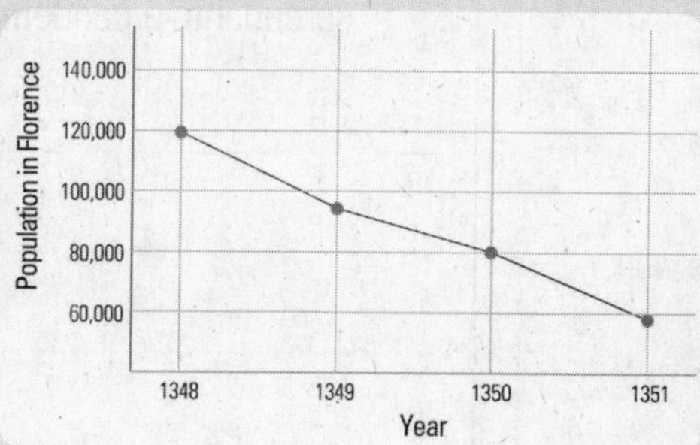


### The Uncontrollable Plague

Most efforts to control and treat the Black Death were useless. This is because nobody knew what caused the plague or how the disease was passed on to humans.

- Perfumes, vinegar, and magic potions were said to treat the disease.

- Many believed bloodletting would cure the plague. During this process, large amounts of blood were drained from infected humans.

- In parts of Italy, citizens thought that cats and dogs were to blame for the plague. They killed the animals. This only meant that there were fewer cats and dogs to kill the plague-infected rats.

There were few ways to control the Black Death. In some cities, healthy people were separated from sick people. In other cities, all incoming ships were blocked. The plague still spread, but not as badly as in areas where the people did nothing.

**economies** systems of managing money and resources

## Notes

1. How many people died from the bubonic plague in Florence?

2. Why do you think the economies of the world were damaged by the bubonic plague?

## Timeline of the Plague

Breakthroughs in medicine are the reasons we can now successfully treat many diseases. The invention of the **vaccine** in 1796 had the greatest effect on fighting the bubonic plague. Unfortunately, this discovery came centuries after the Black Death. Other advances in medicine have helped people stay healthier and stronger. This helps people better fight disease.

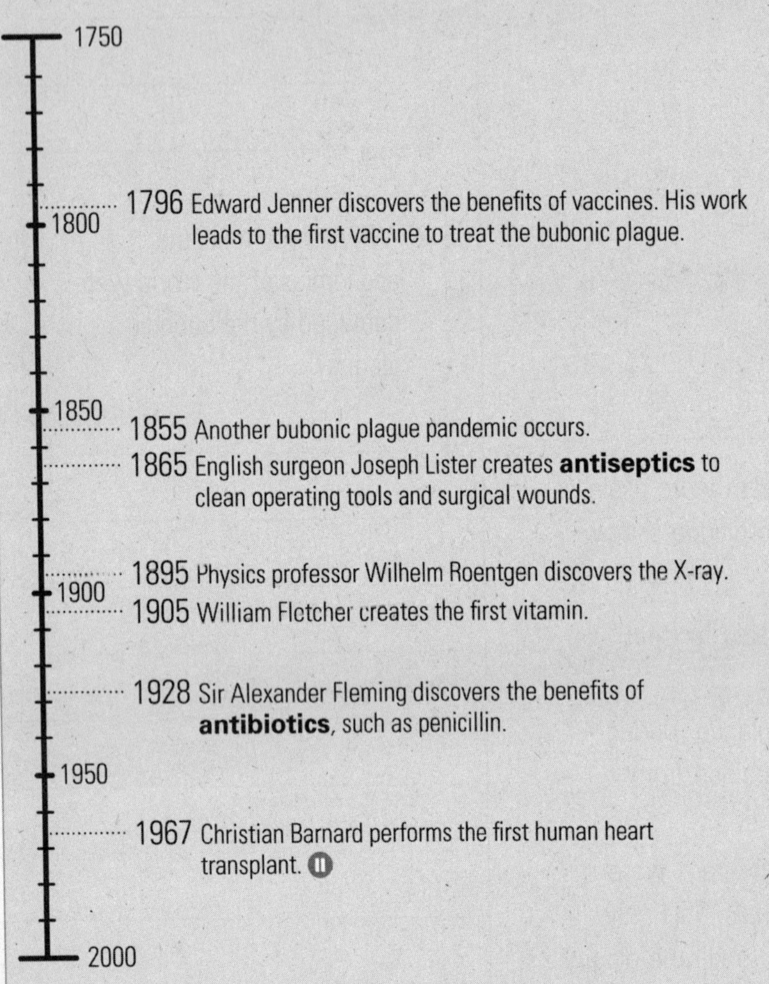


**vaccine** shot given to protect against a disease
**antiseptics** substances that slow the growth of bacteria in open living tissue
**antibiotics** a type of medicine that fights bacteria

### Notes

3. When did another pandemic occur?

4. Why do you think the disease spread into a pandemic in 1855?

Cases of the bubonic plague have dropped greatly in the last century. However, the bacteria that cause the plague still exist. The bacteria can be found in certain animals in parts of the world. Plague cases in humans are also sometimes reported.

Luckily, the disease is now treatable, thanks to breakthroughs in medicine. Medical discoveries will continue to help people cure diseases and prevent pandemic disasters like the Black Death from occurring in the future. ⏸

{ **How are people affected by widespread disease?** }

**Notes**

{ 5. What are the reasons why the plague is treatable? }

{ 6. Could there be another bubonic plague pandemic? }

# Clarifying Log

| Words to Clarify → | | | |
|---|---|---|---|
| 1. Make a quick prediction. | | | |
| 2. Look for a word ending, prefix, suffix, or root word. | | | |
| 3. Identify the part of speech. | | | |
| 4. Look for clues in pictures or other words in the sentence. | | | |
| 5. Make a more informed prediction. | | | |
| 6. Confirm the meaning of the word. | | | |

# Adjectives

| **About Adjectives** | • An adjective is a word that is used to modify a noun or pronoun.<br>• Many adjectives tell how many, which one, or what kind.<br>Examples: _one bee_, _that bee_, _angry bee_.<br>• An adjective usually comes before the noun or pronoun it modifies. |

## Find the Adjectives

Read the passage. Underline the adjectives. Write each adjective in the correct column on the chart.

On Friday, a huge storm hit Centerville. Heavy rain pounded the area. About three hundred people lost electricity. Strong winds and lightning knocked down trees and power lines. Mayor Carol Bernard said, "This storm was the biggest storm in ten years. I'm glad no one was hurt!"

| How many | Which one | What kind |
|---|---|---|
|  |  |  |
|  |  |  |
|  |  |  |
|  |  |  |
|  |  |  |

# Find It in Your Reading

Write three sentences from your reading that include adjectives. Circle the adjectives. Underline the noun that each adjective modifies.

1. _______________________________________________

   _______________________________________________

2. _______________________________________________

   _______________________________________________

3. _______________________________________________

   _______________________________________________

# Put It in Your Writing

Write sentences to tell about a meal you ate recently. Remember to use as many adjectives as you can in each sentence.

_______________________________________________

_______________________________________________

_______________________________________________

_______________________________________________

_______________________________________________

_______________________________________________

AGENDA

{ DONE ✔ }

## STEP **1** Making Connections

I will connect what I already know to the expository text "Disaster! Droughts" by
Dennis Brindell Fradin and discuss how people in "Disaster! Droughts" are affected by
natural disasters.

## STEP **2** Developing Vocabulary

I will learn three new vocabulary words: *pasture, salvage,* and *turmoil.*

## STEP **3** Practicing Fluency

I will read aloud part of "Wildfires in the West" with fluency by practicing phrasing and
conveying emotion and meaning.
I will chart my fluency progress.

## STEP **4** Building Word Study Skills

I will learn five new high-frequency words.
I will review, practice, and spell words in the *–all, –ance, –aught, –ield, –ink,* and *–inge*
word families.
I will understand the spelling homework assignment.

## STEP **5** Reading for Understanding

I will review the reading skill of clarifying for text features.
I will learn to use the strategy of predicting with expository text.

## STEP **6** Applying the Conventions of English

I will review my understanding of nouns.
I will identify and use common and proper nouns in my speaking, reading, and writing.

## STEP **7** Writing with Purpose

I will review my prewriting.
I will use a writing frame to complete a first draft about how to help people after a
natural disaster.

{ Summarizing My Learning }

# Crossword Puzzle

Read the clues for each number. Write the correct vocabulary word on the puzzle.

## Across

1. Lauro tried to _________ the wet library book by drying it with a hair dryer.
2. Jade saw horses in a _________ near her grandmother's farm.
3. Danny's life has been in _________ ever since he lost his wallet.

## Down

1. Miguel is building his house near the _________ so he can see the animals from his porch.
2. Camika tried to _________ the plate, but there were too many small pieces.
3. Judith's life is in _________ because she moved to a new school.

| Vocabulary | pasture | salvage | turmoil |
|---|---|---|---|



Practice Book • Unit 2

# Practice Reading Phrases

1. forced to leave

2. these natural disasters

3. for weeks to months

4. slowly come to life

5. room to grow

# Practice Reading Sentences

1. As the fires raged, thousands of people were forced to leave their homes.

2. Years have passed since these natural disasters ravaged Southern California.

3. Bad rainstorms, for example, can delay building for weeks to months at a time.

4. They are happy to watch their new homes and businesses slowly return to life.

5. Controlled fires are also good because they clear out old plants and allow new plants room to grow.

# Timed Reading

**ROLE OF THE READER**

Read the passage to your partner as accurately as possible.

Remember, your reading goal is 85 Words Correct Per Minute (WCPM).

**ROLE OF THE LISTENER**

As your partner reads, mark these errors with a strikethrough:

- mispronounced words
- skipped words
- changed words
- added words

Excerpt from
# Wildfires in the West

Number of Words

Nearly 15,000 firefighters fought these wildfires. As the fires | 9

raged, thousands of people were forced to leave their homes. Many | 20

lost their houses and belongings. At least 20 people died. | 30

Years have passed since these natural disasters ravaged Southern | 39

California. However, many people are still rebuilding. Starting over | 48

takes a long time. When the weather is bad, building stops. Bad | 60

rainstorms, for example, can delay building for weeks to months | 70

at a time. Despite delays, most people are hopeful. They consider | 81

themselves lucky. They are happy to watch their new homes and | 92

businesses slowly return to life. They are happy to be alive. | 103

There are some ways to prevent the 2003 tragedy in California | 114

from repeating itself. One way is to have controlled fires. Controlled | 125

fires are set by firefighters to separate tree groupings and areas thick | 137

with brush. These fires create firebreaks, which stop wildfires from | 147

spreading. Controlled fires are also good because they clear out old | 158

plants and allow new plants room to grow. Starting controlled fires | 169

in cycles throughout the year could save property and help forests | 180

stay healthy. | 182

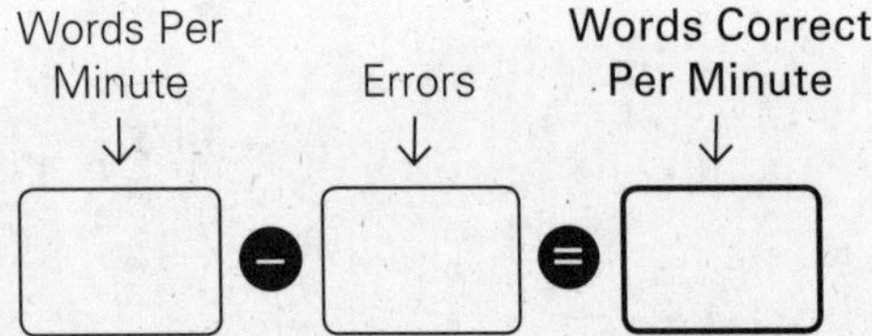

# High-Frequency Words

| pull | every | wash | ship | read |
|------|-------|------|------|------|
| why | seen | table | page | know |

# Words of the Day

______ ______ ______ ______          ______ ______

______ ______ ______          ______ ______

# Missing Letters

Write the missing letter or letters for each Word of the Day. Then write the complete word.

1. **w o** ▮▮  · · · · ▶ ______  · · · · ▶ ____________

2. **f** ▮▮▮ **d**  · · · · ▶ ______  · · · · ▶ ____________

3. ▮▮▮ **t e r**  · · · · ▶ ______  · · · · ▶ ____________

4. **o n** ▮▮  · · · · ▶ ______  · · · · ▶ ____________

5. ▮▮ **e e p**  · · · · ▶ ______  · · · · ▶ ____________

# Word Study Skill

Read the words in the box. Circle five words that belong to the *-all, -ance, -aught, -ield, -ink,* or *-inge* word families.

| | | | | |
|---|---|---|---|---|
| yield | think | caught | flute | win |
| fold | mall | lot | fell | field |

# Phonics Practice

Read the words in the box. Write each one next to the word below that belongs to the same word family.

| | | | |
|---|---|---|---|
| squall | think | prance | shield |
| blink | tinge | taught | fall |

1. binge   _________________

2. sink   _________________

3. caught   _________________

4. hall   _________________

5. advance _________________

6. field   _________________

7. wink   _________________

8. wall   _________________

# Apply It

Read the sentences below. For each one, circle the words in the correct word family.

1. *–ink*      Carla spent all day picking out a pink dress to wear.

2. *–inge*     The dress was long, with a fringe on the bottom.

3. *–ance*     "I want to look nice for the dance," she told her mother.

4. *–ield*     Dad drove her to the field behind her school where the dance would be held.

5. *–aught*    There she saw Mr. Rothberg, the man who taught her math class.

6. *–all*      "You are not dressed for fall!" he said to Carla.

7. *–ink*      "I think I will go get some juice to drink," she told him.

8. *–all*      Soon Carla heard someone call her name. It was her best friend Lee!

# Spell It

| **Spelling Tip** | If you are not sure how to spell a word, try saying it aloud slowly to yourself first. |
| --- | --- |

1. __________________________________

2. __________________________________

3. __________________________________

4. __________________________________

5. __________________________________

# Text Feature Search

**Text:** _______________________________________________

**Example**

How many?

Captions

_______________________________________________

How many?

Title, Subtitle

_______________________________________________

_______________________________________________

How many?

Boldface, Italics

_______________________________________________

_______________________________________________

How many?

Visual Aids (charts, maps, graphs, etc.)

_______________________________________________

_______________________________________________

**Summary**

_______________________________________________

_______________________________________________

# Prediction Log

Text: _______________________________________________

**Prediction #1:** _______________________________________________

_______________________________________________

**Textual Evidence:** _______________________________________________

_______________________________________________

**Summary:** _______________________________________________

_______________________________________________

_______________________________________________

_______________________________________________

**Prediction #2:** _______________________________________________

**Textual Evidence:** _______________________________________________

_______________________________________________

**Summary:** _______________________________________________

_______________________________________________

_______________________________________________

_______________________________________________

**Prediction #3:** _______________________________

_______________________________

**Textual Evidence:** _______________________________

_______________________________

**Summary:** _______________________________

_______________________________

_______________________________

_______________________________

## Summary

_______________________________

_______________________________

_______________________________

_______________________________

_______________________________

_______________________________

_______________________________

_______________________________

# Common and Proper Nouns

| **About Common and Proper Nouns** | • A common noun is a word that names any one of a group of people, places, things, or ideas. A common noun does not begin with a capital letter. Examples: city, state, holiday.<br>• A proper noun is a word that names a particular person, place, thing, or idea. A proper noun begins with a capital letter. Examples: Ella, Pete, Encino, Labor Day |
|---|---|

## What Kind of Noun?

Read each sentence. Circle the common nouns. Underline the proper nouns.

1. The girl gave Louis a card on Valentine's Day.

2. The Pacific Ocean stretches to Asia.

3. The librarian took two books off the shelf for Mr. Rodriguez.

4. Kelly has lots of questions about the test on Monday.

5. How many cups of sugar does Mr. Lewis use in his lemonade?

# Find It in Your Reading

Write three sentences from your reading that include common and proper nouns. Circle the common nouns. Underline the proper nouns.

1. _______________________________________________

_______________________________________________

2. _______________________________________________

_______________________________________________

3. _______________________________________________

_______________________________________________

# Put It in Your Writing

Write at least three sentences that tell about a place you have visited. Remember to capitalize any proper nouns you use.

_______________________________________________

_______________________________________________

_______________________________________________

_______________________________________________

_______________________________________________

**366**

AGENDA

## STEP 1 Making Connections

{ DONE ✔ }

I will connect what I already know to the article "Living Through Katrina" by Eric Shocket and discuss how people in "Living Through Katrina" are affected by natural disasters.

## STEP 2 Developing Vocabulary

I will discuss the six vocabulary words *frequent, survive, devastation, pasture, salvage,* and *turmoil.*

## STEP 3 Practicing Fluency

I will read aloud part of "Tsunamis: The Ocean's Killer Waves" with fluency by practicing phrasing and using punctuation to inform meaning.
I will chart my fluency progress.

## STEP 4 Building Word Study Skills

I will learn five new high-frequency words.
I will practice recognizing and using words in the *–ouch, –ought,* and *–old* word families.
I will understand the spelling homework assignment.

## STEP 5 Reading for Understanding

I will review the reading strategy of predicting.
I will learn to use the reading skill of predicting for the main idea, supporting details, and problem/solution.

## STEP 6 Applying the Conventions of English

I will review my understanding of proper nouns and adjectives.
I will identify and use capitalization with proper adjectives in my speaking, reading, and writing.

## STEP 7 Writing with Purpose

I will review my first draft.
I will complete an *Idea Workshop* to revise for ideas.

{ Summarizing My Learning }

_______________________________________

_______________________________________

# Hidden Clues

Read the clues for each number. Write the correct vocabulary word under each clue. The letters in the boxes will complete the answer to the question at the bottom of the page.

1. Joyce and Kenny are going to fix up this old car and make it run again.

2. Nita has lunch with her grandparents every Sunday.

3. Louisa is moving the horse into the field so it can feed on natural grass.

4. Mr. Edwards is busy after school taking care of his son and his mother-in-law.

5. Reno cleaned the tank, and now the sick fish are doing better.

6. The fire burned down the entire building.

## How many people on Earth today have too little food to eat?

h __ __ __ __ b __ __ l __ __ __
  1  2  3   4    5  6  7  8  9

| Vocabulary | frequent | survive | devastation |
|---|---|---|---|
| | pasture | salvage | turmoil |

# Practice Reading Phrases

1. pulled a plug

2. flopped around helplessly

3. scooped up fish

4. pushed and tossed

5. things that would float

# Practice Reading Sentences

1. It was as if someone had pulled a plug at the floor of the ocean.

2. Boats tipped over in the sand, and fish flopped around helplessly.

3. Some scooped up fish, while others took pictures of the unusual sight.

4. Huge rocks were pushed and tossed like small stones.

5. Some grabbed onto things that would float: a door, a log, a sign.

# Timed Reading

{ **ROLE OF THE READER** }

Read the passage to your partner as accurately as possible.

Remember, your reading goal is 85 Words Correct Per Minute (WCPM).

{ **ROLE OF THE LISTENER** }

As your partner reads, mark these errors with a strikethrough:

- mispronounced words
- skipped words
- changed words
- added words

## Excerpt from
# Tsunamis: The Ocean's Killer Waves

|  | Number of Words |
|---|---|
| The ocean appeared to shrink as water quickly pulled away from | 11 |
| the shoreline. It was as if someone had pulled a plug at the floor of | 26 |
| the ocean. The water looked like it was draining away. Boats tipped | 38 |
| over in the sand, and fish flopped around helplessly. Many people ran | 50 |
| to get a closer look. Some scooped up fish, while others took pictures | 63 |
| of the unusual sight. Nobody expected what came next. | 72 |
| A giant wave raced toward the beach. Some witnesses said it | 83 |
| sounded like a jet or a freight train. After the first wave crashed down | 97 |
| on the beach, waves as high as 50 feet continued to pound the shore. | 111 |
| Men were knocked from their boats. Water rushed through streets | 121 |
| and markets. Schools and businesses flooded. Entire towns along the | 131 |
| coast were engulfed by water. | 136 |
| As the waves reached inland, the water moved with great force. | 147 |
| Huge rocks were pushed and tossed like small stones. Trees were | 158 |
| ripped from the ground. Roads were destroyed, and cars were swept | 169 |
| away. Most homes were reduced to rubble. | 176 |
| People tried to get away. They ran for higher ground. Some | 187 |
| grabbed onto things that would float: a door, a log, a sign. | 199 |

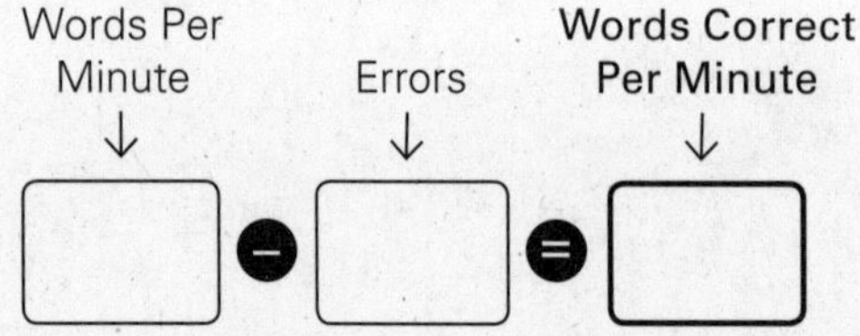

# High-Frequency Words

| pull | found | seen | wash | work | page | read | once |
|------|-------|------|------|------|------|------|------|
| why | every | sleep | table | ship | better | know | |

# Words of the Day

_______________     _______________     _______________

_______________     _______________

# Scrambled Letters

Use the scrambled letters below to spell the Words of the Day.

| done | wanted | hold | then | bring |
|------|--------|------|------|-------|

1. l  o  h  d  = _______

2. o  e  n  d  = _______

3. b  i  r  g  n  = _______

4. t  e  n  a  w  d  = _______

5. n  h  e  t  = _______

# Word Study Skill

Read the words in the box. Circle five words that belong to the *-ouch, -ought,* or *-old* word families.

| | | | | |
|---|---|---|---|---|
| **fought** | **couch** | **crawl** | **mold** | **sigh** |
| **caught** | **cold** | **crouch** | **cry** | **hat** |

# Phonics Practice

Circle the words that belong to the correct word family.

1. **–old**     rolled      gold      mauled      told
2. **–ought**   brought     hat       thought     caught
3. **–old**     behold      milled    held        scold
4. **–ouch**    pooch       grouch    pouch       house

# Apply It

Read the sentences below. In each sentence, there are two words that belong to the same word family. Circle them and write the ending they share on the line.

1. "Don't slouch, Tisha!" her mother called from the couch.  ________

2. After we sold the apartment, we packed up our household.  ________

3. Luis thought that if he bought a bike, it would be easier to get around.  ________

4. Officer Lewis fought the small fire with the hose he had brought.  ________

# Spell It

| Spelling Tip | Listen carefully to a word before you try to spell it. |

1. ___________________________________

2. ___________________________________

3. ___________________________________

4. ___________________________________

5. ___________________________________

# Tsunamis: The Ocean's Killer Waves

*by Karen Sandoval*

*Part 2 of 4*

Tsunami (Soo-NAH-mee) is a Japanese word. It means "harbor wave." A tsunami is actually a series of large waves. You may have heard the term *tidal wave*. Tsunamis are different from tidal waves because they have nothing to do with tides. Tsunamis are caused by natural disasters such as earthquakes, volcano eruptions, and underwater landslides.

When the earth moves and shifts as a result of one of these disasters, the ocean is disturbed. Waves travel in all directions from the source of the disturbance the same way ripples travel away from a rock that has been dropped into a puddle of water. The size and speed of these waves depend on the **severity** of the disturbance.

**severity** harshness or intensity

## Notes

1. What does the word tsunami mean in Japanese?

_______________________

_______________________

_______________________

_______________________

_______________________

2. Based on what you just read, predict the size and speed of the waves created by a small underwater landslide.

_______________________

_______________________

_______________________

_______________________

_______________________

_______________________

_______________________

_______________________

_______________________

Tsunami waves can move up to 500 miles per hour. Some travel across entire oceans. These waves are hard to see in the deep ocean. They may be only a few inches high. The waves get taller and more powerful as they reach the shore.

Before a tsunami hits, ocean water often pulls away from the shore. Water is sucked from harbors and beaches. That is because waves are made up of crests, or high points. Between the crests are troughs, or dips. When a trough hits land first, the water level drops greatly. Soon after, a big wave roars in. Usually another wave blasts ashore about 15 minutes later. More waves frequently follow. This cycle can continue for hours. ⏸

## Notes

3. When does the water level drop greatly?

_______________________________

_______________________________

_______________________________

_______________________________

4. Tsunamis are hard to see in the deep ocean. Predict what problems this might cause.

_______________________________

_______________________________

_______________________________

_______________________________

_______________________________

_______________________________

_______________________________

_______________________________

_______________________________

_______________________________

_______________________________

An earthquake called the Indian Ocean earthquake caused the tsunami that occurred on the coast of Thailand. Earth's crust is made up of sections called plates. The plates move and rub against one another all the time. The plates push one another up and down. The places where the plates meet are called fault lines.

On December 26, an underwater plate near Indonesia bent up. The fault line stretched hundreds of miles along the South Asian coastline. The ocean floor moved and stirred up a huge part of the sea. This set off one of the largest earthquakes in many years. It was at least a 9.0 on the Richter scale. ⓫

{ **What causes a tsunami?** }

## Notes

{ 5. What was the sequence of events that caused the December 26 tsunami? }

______________________________

______________________________

______________________________

______________________________

______________________________

______________________________

______________________________

{ 6. Recall your prediction from question 2. How would you modify or change your prediction if there was a large earthquake instead of a small underwater landslide? }

______________________________

______________________________

______________________________

______________________________

______________________________

______________________________

# Information Log

**Text:** _______________________________________________

{ Subject }                          { Notes }

On-the-Surface
*who, where, when, and what happened*

Under-the-Surface
*how, why, would, could, and should*

## Reflection

_______________________________________________

_______________________________________________

_______________________________________________

# Proper Adjectives

| About Proper Adjectives | • A proper adjective is a type of adjective that is formed from a proper noun. Example: *American* <br> • A proper adjective begins with a capital letter. |
| --- | --- |

## Find the Proper Adjective

Underline the proper adjectives in each sentence.

1. Mr. Wong is a Chinese citizen.

2. Nigeria is a powerful African nation.

3. Italian food consists of much more than pasta and tomato sauce.

4. The Japanese railway system is very reliable.

5. Did you know that Christopher Columbus was neither Spanish nor Portuguese?

6. Peru is a South American country.

7. Lisa's family is Indian, but they have lived in Trinidad for years.

8. The *euro* is a kind of money used in many European countries.

# Find It in Your Reading

Write three sentences from your reading that include proper adjectives.
Underline the proper adjectives. Write the proper noun from which the proper
adjective is formed at the end of the line.

1. _______________________________________________

_______________________________________________

2. _______________________________________________

_______________________________________________

3. _______________________________________________

_______________________________________________

# Put It in Your Writing

Write sentences to describe state and country flags you know about. Use as
many proper adjectives as you can in your sentences.

_______________________________________________

_______________________________________________

_______________________________________________

_______________________________________________

_______________________________________________

{DONE ✔}

### STEP **1** Making Connections

I will connect what I already know to the expository article "Living Through Katrina" by Eric Shocket and discuss how people in "Living Through Katrina" are affected by natural disasters.

### STEP **2** Developing Vocabulary

I will discuss the six vocabulary words: *frequent, survive, devastation, pasture, salvage,* and *turmoil.*

### STEP **3** Practicing Fluency

I will read aloud part of "Tsunamis: The Ocean's Killer Waves" with fluency by practicing phrasing and conveying emotion and meaning.

I will chart my fluency progress.

### STEP **4** Building Word Study Skills

I will learn five new high-frequency words.

I will practice recognizing and using words in the *–edge, –eigh,* and *–unch* word families.

I will understand the spelling homework assignment.

### STEP **5** Reading for Understanding

I will review the reading strategy of predicting.

I will review the reading skill of predicting for the main idea, supporting details, and problem/solution.

### STEP **6** Applying the Conventions of English

I will identify and correctly use commas and capitalization with dates and place names in my speaking, reading, and writing.

### STEP **7** Writing with Purpose

I will review the problem/solution prompts.

I will complete *Editor's Workshop* to edit for complete and correct declarative and interrogative sentences.

{Summarizing My Learning}

# Crossword Puzzle

Read the clues for each number. Write the correct vocabulary word on the puzzle.

## Across

1. means the same as *total ruin*
2. means the same as *often*
3. means the same as *keep living*

## Down

1. means the same as *to save from ruin*
2. means the same as *a grassy field*
3. means the same as *confused and out of order*

| Vocabulary | frequent | survive | devastation |
|---|---|---|---|
| | pasture | salvage | turmoil |

# Practice Reading Phrases

1. the severity of the disturbance

2. in the deep ocean

3. taller and more powerful

4. from harbors and beaches

5. drops greatly

# Practice Reading Sentences

1. The size and speed of these waves depend on the severity of the disturbance.

2. These waves are hard to see in the deep ocean.

3. The waves get taller and more powerful as they reach the shore.

4. Water is sucked from harbors and beaches.

5. When a trough hits land first, the water level drops greatly.

# Timed Reading

**{ ROLE OF THE READER }**

Read the passage to your partner as accurately as possible.

Remember, your reading goal is 85 Words Correct Per Minute (WCPM).

**{ ROLE OF THE LISTENER }**

As your partner reads, mark these errors with a strikethrough:

- mispronounced words
- skipped words
- changed words
- added words

## Excerpt from
# Tsunamis: The Ocean's Killer Waves

| | Number of Words |
|---|---|
| When the earth moves and shifts as a result of one of these | 13 |
| disasters, the ocean is disturbed. Waves travel in all directions from | 24 |
| the source of the disturbance the same way ripples travel away from | 36 |
| a rock that has been dropped into a puddle of water. The size and | 50 |
| speed of these waves depend on the severity of the disturbance. | 61 |
| Tsunami waves can move up to 500 miles per hour. Some travel | 73 |
| across entire oceans. These waves are hard to see in the deep ocean. | 86 |
| They may be only a few inches high. The waves get taller and more | 100 |
| powerful as they reach the shore. | 106 |
| Before a tsunami hits, ocean water often pulls away from the | 117 |
| shore. Water is sucked from harbors and beaches. That is because | 128 |
| waves are made up of crests, or high points. Between the crests are | 141 |
| troughs, or dips. When a trough hits land first, the water level drops | 154 |
| greatly. Soon after, a big wave roars in. Usually another wave blasts | 166 |
| ashore about 15 minutes later. More waves frequently follow. This | 176 |
| cycle can continue for hours. | 181 |

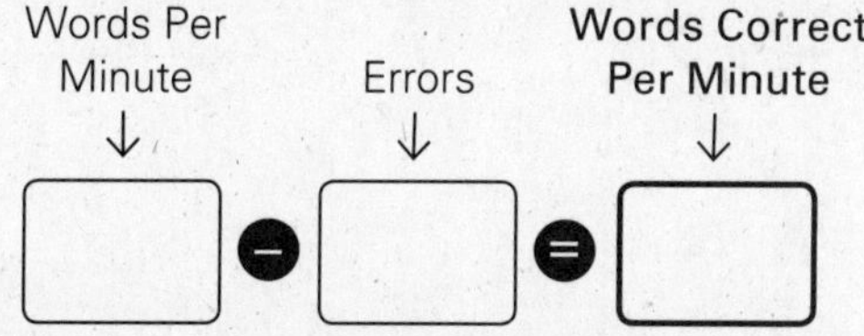

# High-Frequency Words

| | | | | | | |
|---|---|---|---|---|---|---|
| pull | done | sleep | table | ship | then | once |
| why | every | wanted | work | page | read | bring |
| found | seen | wash | hold | better | know | |

# Words of the Day

__ __ __ __ __ __ __ __ __ __

__ __ __ __ __ __ __ __ __

# Word Riddles

Answer the riddles below with the Words of the Day.

| used | far | were | hurt | light |
|---|---|---|---|---|

1. Which is the shortest word on the list?  __________

2. Which word tells what someone might
   have done with a stamp?  __________

3. Which word could complete this sentence?
   *Don't* _______ *yourself!*  __________

4. Which word tells what comes from a lamp?  __________

5. Which word rhymes with *fur*?  __________



Practice Book • Unit 2

## Word Study Skill

Read the words in the box. Circle five words that belong to the *-edge, -eigh,* or *-unch* word families.

| | | | | |
|---|---|---|---|---|
| **hedge** | **weigh** | **way** | **tray** | **bunch** |
| **herd** | **sleigh** | **hunch** | **pay** | **fun** |

## Phonics Practice

Circle the words that belong to the correct word family.

1. *–edge*       sledge       budge       fudge       ridge
2. *–eigh*       tray       feign       neigh       high
3. *–unch*       cinch       brunch       munch       bench
4. *–edge*       wedge       dredge       range       nudge

# Apply It

Read the sentences below. In each sentence, there are two words that belong to the same word family. Circle them and write the ending they share on the line.

1. Ms. Carlisle carefully trimmed the edge of the hedge with clippers. _________

2. I made a bunch of sandwiches for our lunch at the park. _________

3. Dara heard a crunch behind her, but it was a deer stopping to munch on plants. _________

4. The postal worker wanted to weigh the sleigh we were sending. _________

# Spell It

| Spelling Tip | Words may be spelled with different endings even if they rhyme. |
| --- | --- |

1. _______________________________

2. _______________________________

3. _______________________________

4. _______________________________

5. _______________________________

# Quick Write

What causes a tsunami?

# Prediction Log

**Text:** _______________________________________________

**Prediction #1:** _______________________________________

_______________________________________________

**Textual Evidence:** ____________________________________

_______________________________________________

**Summary:** ____________________________________________

_______________________________________________

_______________________________________________

_______________________________________________

**Prediction #2:** _______________________________________

_______________________________________________

**Textual Evidence:** ____________________________________

_______________________________________________

**Summary:** ____________________________________________

_______________________________________________

_______________________________________________

_______________________________________________

**Prediction #3:** _______________________________

_______________________________

**Textual Evidence:** _______________________________

_______________________________

**Summary:** _______________________________

_______________________________

_______________________________

_______________________________

## Summary

_______________________________

_______________________________

_______________________________

_______________________________

_______________________________

_______________________________

_______________________________

# Commas and Capitalization in Dates and Place Names

| Commas and Capitalization in Dates and Place Names | • The names of months are capitalized. When writing a complete date, use a comma between the day and the year. Example: _May 14, 2009_<br>• The names of cities and states are capitalized. When writing the name of a city and state together, use a comma between the city and state. Example: _Sacramento, California_ |
| --- | --- |

## Fix the Mistakes

Fix each date and place name to include commas and capital letters as needed.

1. las vegas nevada


2. august 28 1975


3. december 25 2010


4. sacramento california


5. northborough massachusetts


6. may 10 1809


7. brooklyn new york


8. golden gate bridge san francisco california

# Find It in a Paragraph

Read the paragraph below. Add commas where needed. Circle letters that should be capitalized.

On october 17 1989, an earthquake struck outside of santa cruz california. It only lasted about 15 seconds, but it caused great damage. One city that felt the quake was san francisco california. Houses fell, and part of a bridge between san francisco and oakland did, too. The quake happened right before the third game of the baseball World Series. Amazingly, the series was taking place that year between san francisco and oakland! People all over the country watched on TV as the ground shook and sports fans panicked during the quake. The game was postponed until october 27 1989.

# Put It in Your Writing

Write sentences telling about the birthday and birthplace of someone you know. Include the year and the city and state where that person was born. You may write about yourself if you wish. Make sure to use commas and capital letters where needed.

{ DONE ✔ }

## STEP **1** Making Connections

I will connect what I already know to a photograph and discuss the essential question, *How are people affected by natural disasters?*

## STEP **2** Developing Vocabulary

I will review and complete an assessment of six vocabulary words.

## STEP **3** Practicing Fluency

I will read aloud part of "Tsunamis: The Ocean's Killer Waves" with fluency by practicing phrasing and using punctuation to inform meaning.
I will chart fluency progress.

## STEP **4** Building Word Study Skills

I will learn five new high-frequency words.
I will review, practice, and spell words in the *–ouch, –ought, –old, –edge, –eigh,* and *–unch* word families. I will take a spelling test.

## STEP **5** Reading for Understanding

I will review the reading strategy of predicting.
I will review the reading skill of predicting for the main idea, supporting details and problem/ solution.

## STEP **6** Applying the Conventions of English

I will review my understanding of articles, proper adjectives, common and proper nouns, commas, and capitalization in dates and place names.
I will create complete sentences using the conventions learned in this chapter.

## STEP **7** Writing with Purpose

I will edit my letter for word choice and to correct spelling, capitalization, and punctuation errors.

{ Summarizing My Learning }

# Show What You Know

Read each question. Check the box beside the best answer.

1. If you **salvage** a broken toaster, you—

   ☐ throw it away.
   ☐ buy a new one.
   ☐ sell it.
   ☐ fix it.

2. Which event would create the greatest **turmoil** in a person's life?

   ☐ Losing a job
   ☐ Reading a magazine
   ☐ Buying a new car
   ☐ Getting a haircut

3. The rainstorm caused **devastation** to Greg's yard.

   Which word would work best as a substitution for the underlined word?

   ☐ growth
   ☐ ruin
   ☐ beauty
   ☐ improvement

4. If visits from your grandmother are **frequent**, they—

   ☐ happen a lot.
   ☐ are enjoyable.
   ☐ bother you.
   ☐ are rare.

5. Select the word that has the most similar meaning to **survive**.

   ☐ destroy
   ☐ confuse
   ☐ live
   ☐ listen

6. A **pasture** is a _______ area.

   ☐ grassy
   ☐ wet
   ☐ dry
   ☐ wooded

## Practice Reading Phrases

1. in the dirty water

2. Disease-carrying insects

3. People from several countries

4. to stop the spread of disease

5. landed on the beach

## Practice Reading Sentences

1. Because the weather was so hot, some people drank and bathed in the dirty water.

2. Disease-carrying insects laid eggs in these pools.

3. People from several countries sent money, food, clean water, and healthcare supplies.

4. Victims were treated and received shots to stop the spread of disease.

5. Special ships landed on the beach to deliver more supplies.

## Timed Reading

**{ ROLE OF THE READER }**

Read the passage to your partner as accurately as possible.

Remember, your reading goal is 85 Words Correct Per Minute (WCPM).

**{ ROLE OF THE LISTENER }**

As your partner reads, mark these errors with a strikethrough:

- mispronounced words
- skipped words
- changed words
- added words

Excerpt from
# Tsunamis: The Ocean's Killer Waves

| | Number of Words |
|---|---|
| The waves destroyed entire towns. People had no clothes, food, | 10 |
| or water. There was no power for lights. There were no phones or | 23 |
| bathrooms. The waves ruined the fresh water in wells and in rivers. | 35 |
| Because the weather was so hot, some people drank and bathed in | 47 |
| the dirty water. They got very sick. | 54 |
| The seawater also ruined the land. The crops and pastures people | 65 |
| had harvested were gone. Pools of water covered the muddy, rocky | 76 |
| ground. Disease-carrying insects laid eggs in these pools. Some | 85 |
| people were bitten by the insects and got sick. | 94 |
| News of the tsunami spread all over the world. People from | 105 |
| several countries sent money, food, clean water, and healthcare | 114 |
| supplies. Aid workers set up care centers in large tents. Victims were | 126 |
| treated and received shots to stop the spread of disease. Thousands | 137 |
| of doctors helped those in need. | 143 |
| It was hard to reach the victims in some places because so many | 156 |
| roads had been washed away. Many roads that weren't destroyed | 166 |
| were blocked by debris. Airstrips were submerged, so airplanes | 175 |
| dropped supplies from the air. Special ships landed on the beach to | 187 |
| deliver more supplies. Even elephants helped. People guided them to | 197 |
| clear trees from the roads. | 202 |

Words Per Minute ↓ — Errors ↓ = Words Correct Per Minute ↓

# High-Frequency Words

| | | | | | | |
|---|---|---|---|---|---|---|
| pull | used | wanted | work | page | read | light |
| why | every | far | hold | better | know | |
| found | seen | wash | were | then | once | |
| done | sleep | table | ship | hurt | bring | |

# Words of the Day

______ ______ ______    ______ ______ ______

______    ______ ______

# Alphabetical Order

List the Words of the Day in alphabetical order.

| carry | past | always | full | keep |
|---|---|---|---|---|

1. ______
2. ______
3. ______
4. ______
5. ______

# Word Study Skill

Read the words in the box. Circle five words that belong to the *-ouch, -old, -unch, -ought, -edge,* or *-eigh* word families.

| | | | | |
|---|---|---|---|---|
| brunch | crunch | book | fold | eight |
| write | sight | couch | loyal | lunch |

# Phonics Practice

Read the words in the box. Write each one next to the word below that belongs to the same word family.

| | | | |
|---|---|---|---|
| ledge | lunch | sought | blindfold |
| neigh | bold | crouch | hunch |

1. grouch _________________________

2. told _________________________

3. scrunch _________________________

4. fought _________________________

5. bunch _________________________

6. wedge _________________________

7. sold _________________________

8. sleigh _________________________

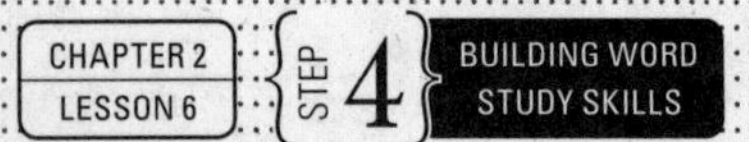

# Apply It

Read the sentences below. In each sentence, there are two words that belong to the same word family. Circle them and write the ending they share on the line.

1. There is a grouch on the couch. ___________________

2. I have wedge shoes and they have a design on the edge. ___________________

3. The shopkeeper sold a watch made of gold. ___________________

4. Aunt Louise sought out a new rug and bought it on sale. ___________________

5. The salesperson sold her a coat to keep out the cold. ___________________

6. We could go out to eat lunch today and brunch tomorrow. ___________________

7. I have a hunch there will be a bunch of people waiting to
   get into the restaurant. ___________________

8. As we piled into the sleigh, I heard a horse neigh. ___________________

# Spell It

| **Spelling Tip** | If you are not sure how to spell a word, think of another word that sounds like it. Ask yourself: "Are these words in the same word family?" If so, the endings will be spelled the same way. |
| --- | --- |

1. ___________________________________________

2. ___________________________________________

3. ___________________________________________

4. ___________________________________________

5. ___________________________________________

# Tsunamis: The Ocean's Killer Waves

*by Karen Sandoval*

○ ··· ○ ··· ○ ··· **4** ·································

*Part 4 of 4*

Warning systems are one way to detect tsunamis and save lives. There is a warning system in the Pacific Ocean. It has a network of **buoys.** The buoys float in the ocean. They record information about waves. They monitor events that might cause tsunamis. When signs of a tsunami are recorded, scientists track them. They put out a warning if a place is in danger.

The Indian Ocean did not have a warning system in 2004. This was mainly because it had not had a major tsunami since 1883. Now the **United Nations** is working on a warning system for the Indian Ocean. Many experts think we should create a system for the whole world. ⏸

**buoys**  floats that mark locations on the ocean
**United Nations**  a group including most of the countries in the world founded in 1945 to promote peace and prosperity

## Notes

1. What problem does a tsunami warning system solve?

_______________________________

_______________________________

_______________________________

_______________________________

_______________________________

2. What is the main reason that the Indian Ocean did not have a warning system in 2004?

_______________________________

_______________________________

_______________________________

_______________________________

_______________________________

_______________________________

_______________________________

_______________________________

_______________________________

There are other ways people can stay safe. It is important to know the signs of a tsunami. An earthquake is nature's warning system. On one Indonesian island, the people fled to the hills after feeling the earthquake. The island was one of the few coastal areas to **evacuate** before the big waves struck.

A fall in water level also often comes before a tsunami. Experts say this sign may give people as much as five minutes to escape the first wave. Even one person can make a difference. A ten-year-old girl, Tilly Smith, was on a beach in Thailand the day the tsunami hit. She watched the water foam and bubble. She saw it draw away from the beach. She knew from a book she'd read in school that these were bad signs. She helped warn others on the beach. All the people ran away from the shore. The tsunami hit minutes later. Almost everyone on that beach survived. ⏸

---

**evacuate** leave or escape



> ## Notes
>
> 3. What are two signs of a tsunami?
>
> _______________________
>
> _______________________
>
> _______________________
>
> _______________________
>
> _______________________
>
> 4. What do you predict would have happened if people on other islands knew that an earthquake warns of tsunamis?
>
> _______________________
>
> _______________________
>
> _______________________
>
> _______________________
>
> _______________________
>
> _______________________
>
> _______________________
>
> _______________________
>
> _______________________
>
> _______________________

Another fact to remember is that the first wave is not always the worst. The waves often continue crashing in for hours. It is important to stay far away from shore until the danger is truly over. In fact, it is important to stay away from all water that connects to the ocean. Tsunamis can travel up rivers and streams, too.

There is no way to stop these killer waves. We must pay attention to the signs and react quickly to make sure that a tragedy like the 2004 tsunami does not repeat itself. ⑪

{ **How are people affected by tsunamis?** }

## Notes

{ 5. Is there any way to completely solve the problem of tsunamis? Why or why not? }

______________________________

______________________________

______________________________

______________________________

{ 6. What do you predict will happen the next time a big tsunami hits? }

______________________________

______________________________

______________________________

______________________________

______________________________

______________________________

______________________________

______________________________

______________________________

______________________________

# Information Log

**Text:** _______________________________________________

{ **Subject** }                                           { **Notes** }

On-the-Surface
*who, where, when, and what happened*

Under-the-Surface
*how, why, would, could, and should*

## Reflection

# Conventions Review

## Review Articles

Circle the article that best completes each sentence. Then write the complete subject of the sentence at the end of the line.

1. (A, An) airplane landed in the field. ______________________

2. Tomorrow, (the, a) schools will close. ______________________

3. (A, An) firefighter arrived in minutes. ______________________

## Review Adjectives

Read the paragraph. Underline the adjectives.

Today, many neighborhood volunteers will gather to clean up San Ramo's parks. They will clear trash, fallen branches, and overturned tables left by the heavy storm that came through town yesterday. The storm brought little rain, but strong winds damaged many small and old trees.

## Review Common and Proper Nouns

Read each sentence below. Circle the common nouns. Underline the proper nouns.

1. How many mountains are there in California?

2. Mt. Shasta is in the northern part of the state.

3. Roberto wrote a report on the mountains near Santa Cruz.

## Review Proper Adjectives

Underline the proper adjectives in each sentence.

1. Have you ever tasted real Caribbean hot sauce?

2. Charleen's mother is Pakistani but her father is British.

3. Brazil is a large South American country.

## Review Commas and Capitalization in Dates and Place Names

Fix each date or place name. Include commas and capital letters where needed.

1. november 21 1997

3. san diego california

2. june 2 2091

4. baltimore maryland

## Put It in Your Writing

Write three declarative sentences to tell about a real or made-up natural disaster. Use as many of the conventions from this chapter as you can.

___________________________________________

___________________________________________

___________________________________________

___________________________________________

___________________________________________

**404**

**STEP 1  Developing Test-Taking Strategies**                    {DONE ✔}

I will read a test-taking manual.
I will learn strategies for taking multiple-choice tests.



**STEP 2  Assessing My Learning**

I will take a multiple-choice test on skills I learned in this chapter.

**STEP 3  Writing with Purpose**

I will publish the final draft of my problem/solution letter.

**STEP 4  Analyzing My Results**

I will identify which questions I answered correctly and which questions I answered
   incorrectly.

**STEP 5  Reinforcing My Learning**

I will reinforce my understanding of using sentence and word clues.
I will reinforce my understanding of how to develop a topic sentence and include supporting
   facts and details.

**STEP 6  Speaking with Purpose**

I will watch a video of a speech and evaluate the speaker's delivery skills.

{Summarizing My Learning}

_______________________________________________

_______________________________________________

_______________________________________________

# Test-Taking Manual
## Before the Test

### Be Prepared

- Know what you will be tested on and study.
- Get a full night's rest.
- Have all your materials (pencil, eraser, calculator, dictionary) at your desk.

### Be Comfortable but Alert

- Make sure you have enough room to work.
- Do not slouch in your chair.

### Stay Relaxed and Confident

- Remember that you are well prepared and can do well.
- Take deep breaths if you feel anxious.
- Do not talk about the test with the other students.

## During the Test

Follow these five steps for each question on the test.

**Step 1:** Determine what the question is asking you to do.

**Step 2:** Try to answer the question in your own words.

**Step 3:** Eliminate any answers you know are incorrect.

**Step 4:** Choose the best answer.

**Step 5:** If time allows, review your answers to each question.

## Example Question

1. **Which is the meaning of <u>allow</u> in this sentence?**

   I asked Dad if he would <u>allow</u> me to go to camp this summer.

   **A.** sleep

   **B.** let

   **C.** arrange

   **D.** pay

# Skills Assessment 5

**1. Which is the meaning of <u>gradually</u> in this sentence?**

> My coach said that I would <u>gradually</u> get better at soccer if I practiced every day.

A. nervously

B. slowly

C. smoothly

D. happily

**2. Which is the meaning of <u>companion</u> in this sentence?**

> My mother and her dog go everywhere together. I think he is her favorite <u>companion</u>.

A. pet

B. neighbor

C. animal

D. friend

**3. Which is the meaning of <u>bewildered</u> in this sentence?**

> That riddle was so difficult that it <u>bewildered</u> me.

A. confused

B. moved

C. tickled

D. scared

**4. Which is the meaning of <u>entire</u> in this sentence?**

> There is no more cake because my brother ate the <u>entire</u> thing.

A. huge

B. whole

C. biggest

D. best

*Go on to the next page* →

# Skills Assessment 5, continued

**5.** Which is the meaning of <u>hence</u> in this sentence?

My father's car broke down; <u>hence</u>, we are not going to the lake this weekend.

A. after all

B. yet

C. therefore

D. because

**6.** Which is the meaning of <u>vanish</u> in this sentence?

The duck seemed to <u>vanish</u> when the dog ran into the backyard. I couldn't find it anywhere.

A. crawl away

B. fly

C. cry out

D. disappear

*Go on to the next page* →

# Skills Assessment 5, continued

**Directions:** Read this draft of a letter, then answer the questions.

Dear Dr. Murai,

1    (1) Our school is putting on a science fair, and we need judges. (2) I am not very good at science, but my friends are. (3) Since you are a science teacher at the college, you would be an excellent judge. (4) My brother says that you are one of the best teachers in the school. (5) Since you are so good, we know you will make our fair a success.

2    (6) Some students made experiments that prove a science fact. (7) Others made things that work with batteries. (8) One group actually made a robot. (9) If you come to the fair, you will enjoy seeing all the projects. (10) You probably never went to a science fair before this. (11) Also, the students will know that if you say something is good, it is really good.

3    (12) I hope you decide to help us. (13) If you do, our science fair will be the best yet. (14) Please call our school if you are interested. (15) Call our principal, Mrs. Lee at 555-1234. (16) She is waiting to hear from you.

Thank you for your interest,
Lucinda Long

---

7. **Which sentence does not belong in paragraph 1?**

   A.  sentence 1
   B.  sentence 2
   C.  sentence 3
   D.  sentence 5

8. **Which is the BEST sentence to put after sentence 4?**

   > (4) My brother says that you are one of the best teachers in the school.

   A.  He says you make him want to be a science teacher some day.
   B.  He says he enjoys his college classes very much this year.
   C.  He says that he wishes his summer vacation was longer.
   D.  He says his history teacher is good, but the class is too hard.

*Go on to the next page →*

---

# Skills Assessment 5, continued

**9.** **Which is the BEST sentence to put at the beginning of paragraph 2?**

A. All of the students at our school have projects in the science fair.

B. We also have an art fair at the end of the school year.

C. My brother's school had a science fair during summer school.

D. I do not think that you have science fairs at the college.

**10.** **Which sentence does not belong in paragraph 2?**

A. sentence 6

B. sentence 7

C. sentence 10

D. sentence 11

**11.** **Which is the BEST sentence to put after sentence 8?**

> (8) One group actually made a robot.

A. I saw a movie about robots in my class.

B. There are a lot of group projects, too.

C. It walks and moves like a real person.

D. Toy robots are on sale at the Hobby Lane.

**12.** **Which is the BEST sentence to put after sentence 13?**

> (13) If you do, our science fair will be the best yet.

A. Science fairs are going to be popular at most schools.

B. Last year our science fair was really a lot of fun.

C. It will probably be fun even if you do not help us.

D. Your knowledge and love of science will help us all.

**End of test** ■

# Using Word and Sentence Clues

**Reminder:
Finding the
Meaning of an
Unknown Word**

- When you come to an unknown word, first look for word parts you recognize such as prefixes, root words, or suffixes.
- Look at the sentence and sentences nearby for clues. Picture what is happening in the sentence. Also substitute a different word for the word you are trying to figure out.

## Clarifying Log

Read the letter. Use the Clarifying Log to figure out the meanings of the underlined words.

Dear Uncle Lou and Aunt Marie,

How is everything? A lot has <u>occurred</u> since I saw you this summer. I joined my school's baseball team. I am still taking piano lessons, too. I have been very busy!

I had a lot of fun during our last visit. Dad said that I should ask if I could come for another visit during my spring break. I would love to go <u>hiking</u> again at the park by your house. It was so much fun to walk in the woods and see all the animals. Please write back to let me know what you think!

Love,

Sammy

| Words to Clarify ⟶ | occurred | hiking |
|---|---|---|
| 1. Make a quick prediction. | | |
| 2. Look for a word ending, prefix, suffix, or root word. | | |
| 3. Identify the part of speech. | | |
| 4. Look for clues in the words and sentences nearby. | | |

| | | |
|---|---|---|
| 5. Make a more informed prediction. | | |
| 6. Confirm the meaning of the word. | | |

# Identify the Meaning

Read each sentence, then find the choice that means the same as the underlined word.

**1. Which is the meaning of attend in this sentence?**

> Please let me know by Friday if you will attend my party.

A. come to

B. plan to

C. call

**2. Which is the meaning of deliver in this sentence?**

> Rachel promised to deliver my letter to the post office.

A. read

B. bring

C. open

**3. Which is the meaning of rarely in this sentence?**

> I have a great memory, so I rarely forget my homework.

A. very often

B. almost never

C. usually

**4. Which is the meaning of neglect in this sentence?**

> If you neglect to bring keys, you won't be able to get into the house!

A. remember

B. like

C. forget

## Choices & Challenges
On your own piece of paper…

**A.** Choose one of the underlined words above. Write another sentence that includes clues to the word's meaning.

**B.** Look at the word *reread*. Write to explain how you could use word parts to figure out its meaning.

**C.** Make a list of new words you have learned in this lesson by using word and sentence clues. Choose one and write its meaning.

# Developing a Topic Sentence with Supporting Facts and Details

Read the draft of the letter on page 409 of *Skills Assessment 5*. Then answer the following questions.

## Idea Workshop: Problem/Solution Letter

REVIEWER: _______________________________

Write the topic sentence of the first paragraph.

_______________________________________________

_______________________________________________

_______________________________________________

1. In one sentence, summarize the problem.

_______________________________________________

_______________________________________________

_______________________________________________

2. What solutions did the author offer?

_______________________________________________

_______________________________________________

_______________________________________________

3. What would you like to hear more about?

_______________________________________________

_______________________________________________

_______________________________________________

# Idea Workshop: Problem/Solution Letter

4. What could this student do to improve the letter?

## Which Revision?

Choose the best answer to each question.

**1. Which is the BEST sentence to put after sentence 1?**

> (1) Our school is putting on a science fair, and we need judges.

**A.** We are hoping for three judges to help choose the best projects.

**B.** Our school is over 50 years old.

**C.** When I get to high school, I plan to take advanced science classes.

**2. Which sentence does not belong in paragraph 3?**

**A.** sentence 12

**B.** sentence 14

**C.** sentence 16

## Choices & Challenges
On your own piece of paper...

**A.** Look back at a piece of writing you have done recently. Make notes about details you included that are unnecessary.

**B.** Write the topic sentence of the second paragraph in the sample letter. Then write to explain how you know it is the topic sentence.

**C.** Find another place in the passage above where the author might have added another detail. Write a sentence that he or she might have added.

## STEP **1** Making Connections

{ DONE ✔ }

I will connect what I already know to a photograph and discuss the essential question, *How are people affected by natural disasters?*

## STEP **2** Developing Vocabulary

I will discuss vocabulary words in a cumulative review.

## STEP **3** Practicing Fluency

I will read aloud part of "Tsunamis: The Ocean's Killer Waves" with fluency by reading in phrases and chart my fluency progress.

## STEP **4** Building Word Study Skills

I will learn five new high-frequency words.
I will understand, practice, and spell compound words.
I will understand the spelling homework assignment.

## STEP **5** Reading for Understanding

I will learn to use the reading strategy of questioning.

## STEP **6** Applying the Conventions of English

I will review my understanding of declarative sentences.
I will identify and use question words and punctuation of an interrogative sentence in my speaking, reading, and writing.

## STEP **7** Writing with Purpose

I will review stages of the writing process.
I will deconstruct the problem/solution prompt and scoring guide to understand features and evaluation.
I will begin prewriting about preparing for a natural disaster.

{ Summarizing My Learning }

# Practice Reading Phrases

1. for the whole world

2. the signs of a tsunami

3. On one Indonesian island

4. one of the few coastal areas

5. from a book she'd read

# Practice Reading Sentences

1. Many experts think we should create a system for the whole world.

2. It is important to know the signs of a tsunami.

3. On one Indonesian island, the people fled to the hills after feeling the earthquake.

4. The island was one of the few coastal areas to evacuate before the big waves struck.

5. She knew from a book she'd read in school that these were bad signs.

# Timed Reading

**{ ROLE OF THE READER }**

Read the passage to your partner as accurately as possible.

Remember, your reading goal is 85 Words Correct Per Minute (WCPM).

**{ ROLE OF THE LISTENER }**

As your partner reads, mark these errors with a strikethrough:

- mispronounced words
- skipped words
- changed words
- added words

Excerpt from
# Tsunamis: The Ocean's Killer Waves

|  | Number of Words |
|---|---|

The Indian Ocean did not have a warning system in 2004. This | 12
was mainly because it had not had a major tsunami since 1883. Now | 25
the United Nations is working on a warning system for the Indian | 37
Ocean. Many experts think we should create a system for the whole | 49
world. | 50

There are other ways people can stay safe. It is important to know | 63
the signs of a tsunami. An earthquake is nature's warning system. | 74
On one Indonesian island, the people fled to the hills after feeling the | 87
earthquake. The island was one of the few coastal areas to evacuate | 99
before the big waves struck. | 104

A fall in water level also often comes before a tsunami. Experts | 116
say this sign may give people as much as five minutes to escape the | 130
first wave. Even one person can make a difference. A ten-year-old | 141
girl, Tilly Smith, was on a beach in Thailand the day the tsunami hit. | 155
She watched the water foam and bubble. She saw it draw away from | 168
the beach. She knew from a book she'd read in school that these were | 182
bad signs. She helped warn others on the beach. All the people ran | 195
away from the shore. The tsunami hit minutes later. Almost everyone | 206
on that beach survived. | 210

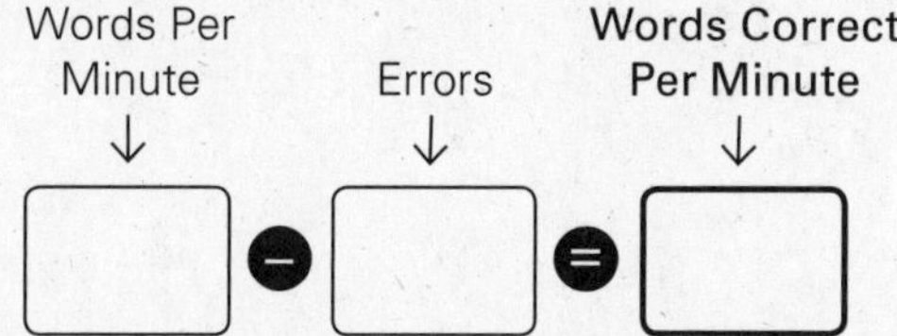

# Words of the Day

___ ___ ___ ___ ___ ___ ___ ___ ___ ___ ___

___ ___ ___ ___ ___ ___

# Alphabetical Order

List the Words of the Day in alphabetical order.

mind     clean     grow     kind     because

1. ___ ___ ___ ___ ___ ___ ___
2. ___ ___ ___ ___ ___
3. ___ ___ ___ ___
4. ___ ___ ___ ___
5. ___ ___ ___

# Word Study Skill

<table>
<tr><td>Morphographs and Compound Words</td><td>

- Morphographs are the smallest part of a word that has meaning.
- A compound word is a word made by combining two smaller words.
- Readers can break unfamiliar compound words into two smaller words that they recognize.

</td></tr>
</table>

# Compound Word Practice

Write the smaller words that make up each compound word. Then write the meaning of each compound word.

1.  bedroom = ______________ + ______________

    _______________________________________________

2.  downhill = ______________ + ______________

    _______________________________________________

3.  birdhouse = ______________ + ______________

    _______________________________________________

4.  doorbell = ______________ + ______________

    _______________________________________________

# Apply It

Read the paragraph below about a person's experience with an earthquake. As you read, look for compound words and circle them.

I remember waking up suddenly because I felt my bed shake. It was sunrise. There was just a hint of daylight coming through my bedroom window. At first I thought the rumbling was a thunderstorm. Then I realized I was feeling my first earthquake. I heard dishes falling in the kitchen and books falling out of my bookcase. I got down on the floor and crawled under my desk. In a matter of seconds the shaking had passed. I waited under my desk in case there were aftershocks. When it was all over, I felt lucky that my home wasn't badly damaged.

# Spell It

| Compound Word Spelling Rule | The spellings of the smaller words usually stay the same when they are joined to make a compound word. |
| --- | --- |

1. _______________________________

2. _______________________________

3. _______________________________

4. _______________________________

5. _______________________________

# Text Feature Search

**Text:** _______________________________

**Example**

How many?

Captions
_______________________________
_______________________________

How many?

Title, Subtitle
_______________________________
_______________________________

How many?

Boldface,
Italics
_______________________________
_______________________________

How many?

Visual Aids
(charts, maps,
graphs, etc.)
_______________________________
_______________________________

## Prediction

_______________________________
_______________________________
_______________________________

# Summary Tree

**Text:** _______________________________

1.

2.

3.

1.

2.

3.

1.

2.

3.

1.

2.

3.



**Summary**

# Question Log

**Text:** _______________________________________

| Question #1 | Question #2 | Question #3 |
|---|---|---|
|  |  |  |

## On-the-Surface
*who, where, when, and what happened*

## Under-the-Surface
*how, why, would, could, and should*

| Question #1 | Question #2 | Question #3 |
|---|---|---|
|  |  |  |

## Summary

_______________________________________

_______________________________________

_______________________________________

# Interrogative Sentences

**About Interrogative Sentences**

- An interrogative sentence asks a question.
- An interrogative sentence ends with a question mark.
- Many interrogative sentences begin with one of these question words: *who, how, what, when, where,* and *why.*

## Read and Answer Interrogative Sentences

Circle the question word in each interrogative sentence. Then write an answer to each one.

1. How would it feel to be in an earthquake?

____________________________

____________________________

2. Who could help people who get hurt during an earthquake?

____________________________

____________________________

3. Where are some places that often have earthquakes?

____________________________

____________________________

# Find It in a Passage

Underline the interrogative sentences. Circle the question words and the question marks.

When have you felt the ground shake and wondered if it was an earthquake? This happened to me one time. I found out that it wasn't really an earthquake, however.

What do you think it was? A sudden gust of wind came down my street and uprooted a large tree. The shaking I felt was the tree landing on the roof. What do you think happened then? A squirrel jumped out of the tree and ran into the house!

# Put It in Your Writing

Write at least three interrogative sentences about a time you felt the ground shake. Begin your interrogative sentences with question words such as *who, how, what, when, where,* or *why.*

1. _______________________________________________

_______________________________________________

2. _______________________________________________

_______________________________________________

3. _______________________________________________

_______________________________________________

AGENDA

{DONE ✔}

## STEP 1 Making Connections

I will connect what I already know to the memoir "Surviving the Quake" by Helen Garcia and discuss how the people in "Surviving the Quake" are affected by natural disasters.

## STEP 2 Developing Vocabulary

I will learn three new vocabulary words: *insist, crouch,* and *disconcerting.*

## STEP 3 Practicing Fluency

I will read aloud part of "Earthquake!" with fluency by practicing phrasing and conveying emotion and meaning and chart my fluency progress.

## STEP 4 Building Word Study Skills

I will learn five new high-frequency words.
I will review, practice, and spell compound words.
I will understand the spelling homework assignment.

## STEP 5 Reading for Understanding

I will review the reading strategy of questioning.
I will learn to use the reading skill of questioning for main idea and supporting details and problem and solution.

## STEP 6 Applying the Conventions of English

I will review my understanding of subjects and past tense verbs.
I will identify simple predicates and use irregular past tense verbs in my speaking, reading, and writing.

## STEP 7 Writing with Purpose

I will review the problem/solution prompt and scoring guide and complete the prewriting stage.

{Summarizing My Learning}

# Hidden Clues

Read the clues for each number. Write the correct vocabulary word under each clue. The letters in the boxes will complete the answer to the question at the bottom of the page.

1. My parents tell me that I must clean my room before friends come over.

___ [1] ___ ___ ___ [2] ___ ___

2. My brother and I used to bend down behind the couch and hide for fun.

___ ___ ___ ___ ___ [3]

3. At first I had a very strange feeling when I started classes at my new school.

___ ___ ___ ___ ___ [4] [5] ___ ___ ___ ___

4. Every year I make sure that the school bus leaves for the contest at 7 a.m. sharp!

___ ___ ___ [6] ___ ___

5. It was disturbing when I lost my gift card because I remember putting it in my pocket.

___ ___ ___ ___ ___ ___ [7] [8] ___ ___ ___

6. When I was little, I used to squat on the beach and build sand castles.

___ ___ ___ ___ [9]

## Why is the day of the earthquake special to Helen?

___ t ' ___ ___ ___ ___ b ___ ___ ___ d a y .
 1   2   3  4  5   6  7  8  9

| Vocabulary | insist | crouch | disconcerting |

## Practice Reading Phrases

1. the walls around them

2. the earthquake was over

3. piles of rubble

4. Workers finally arrived

5. from the rubble

## Practice Reading Sentences

1. School children hid together as the walls around them caved in.

2. By the time the earthquake was over, around 75,000 people were dead.

3. Buildings were reduced to piles of rubble.

4. Workers finally arrived to help the trapped and injured people.

5. When workers finally pulled Iqbal from the rubble, his heart stopped beating.

## Timed Reading

**{ ROLE OF THE READER }**

Read the passage to your partner as accurately as possible.

Remember, your reading goal is 85 Words Correct Per Minute (WCPM).

**{ ROLE OF THE LISTENER }**

As your partner reads, mark these errors with a strikethrough:

- mispronounced words
- skipped words
- changed words
- added words

Excerpt from
# Earthquake!

| | Number of Words |
|---|---|
| The ground rumbled and shook. It split apart. People on the | 11 |
| streets screamed and ran. Those in their homes looked for shelter. | 22 |
| School children hid together as the walls around them caved in. | 33 |
| Buildings fell, and the sounds of their falling echoed through the | 44 |
| streets. The air was thick with dust, smoke, and flames. By the time | 57 |
| the earthquake was over, around 75,000 people were dead. Many | 67 |
| more were hurt, homeless, or in need of rescue. | 76 |
| The earthquake that shook southern Asia on October 8, 2005 | 86 |
| wiped out entire towns and villages in northern Pakistan, where | 96 |
| the quake was centered. Buildings were reduced to piles of rubble. | 107 |
| Many people were trapped. The shelter they had looked for simply | 118 |
| collapsed on top of them. Workers finally arrived to help the trapped | 130 |
| and injured people. They also tried to save materials that would help | 142 |
| them rebuild the towns and villages. | 148 |
| In one village, people ran to the workers as they arrived. They led | 161 |
| the workers toward a pile of rubble. A man named Iqbal had been | 174 |
| trapped there for over a day. He was trapped between two pieces | 186 |
| of concrete. | 188 |
| When workers finally pulled Iqbal from the rubble, his heart | 198 |
| stopped beating. | 200 |

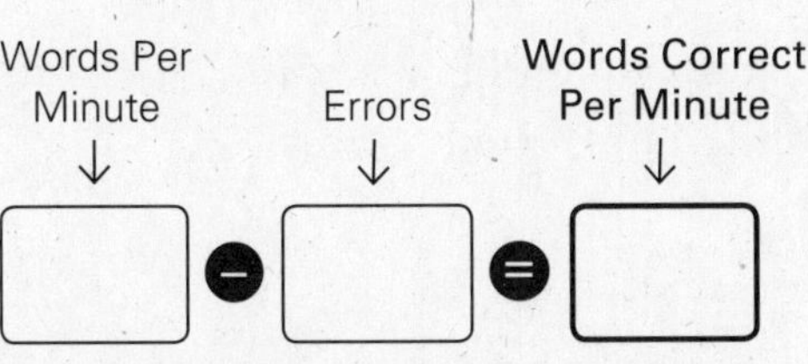

# High-Frequency Words

| mind | clean | grow | kind | because |

# Words of the Day

__ __ __ __ __ __ __ __ __ __ __ __ __ __ __ __ __

__ __ __ __ __ __ __ __ __ __

# Categorize

Write each Word of the Day under the correct category.

| place | time | myself | shall | been |

**End in *e***

1. ______________

2. ______________

**Have double letters**

3. ______________

4. ______________

**Two-syllable words**

5. ______________

# Word Study Skill

- Morphographs are the smallest part of a word that has meaning.
- A compound word is a word made by combining two smaller words.

# Compound Word Practice

Write the smaller words that make up each compound word. Then write the meaning of each compound word.

1. { **raincoat** = _______________ + _______________ }

2. { **blueberry** = _______________ + _______________ }

3. { **sidewalk** = _______________ + _______________ }

4. { **footprint** = _______________ + _______________ }

# Apply It

**Read the paragraph below about landslides. As you read, look for compound words and circle them.**

A landslide occurs when masses of rock and earth move down a slope. Some landslides move slowly and cause damage gradually. Others move so quickly that they can destroy property and take lives suddenly. Landslides are sometimes caused by earthquakes. The underground shaking can cause a sudden avalanche of rock and earth to crash down. In 1959, a famous landslide was triggered by an earthquake in Montana. The earthquake caused an entire mountainside to slide into the Madison River. It made a dam and formed a new lake! It is still there today. It is called Earthquake Lake.

# Spell It

| **Compound Word Spelling Rule** | The spellings of the smaller words usually stay the same when they are joined to make a compound word. |
| --- | --- |

1. _______________________________

2. _______________________________

3. _______________________________

4. _______________________________

5. _______________________________

## Earthquake! *by Gail Blasser Riley*

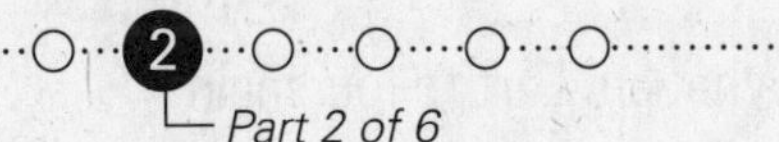

*— Part 2 of 6*

Earthquakes happen every day. Most earthquakes are small, and people don't feel them. However, the southern Asia earthquake measured 7.6 on the Richter scale. It caused damage over a large area.

Scientists now understand earthquakes much better than they did long ago. There was little known about earthquakes before the 1900s. In fact, some people insisted that earthquakes were caused when air was forced out of caves. We now know that this is not true. Scientists are learning more about earthquakes every day. ⏸

### Notes

{ 1. When do earthquakes happen? }

_______________________________

_______________________________

_______________________________

_______________________________

_______________________________

_______________________________

_______________________________

{ 2. What is the theme or underlying message of this section? }

_______________________________

_______________________________

_______________________________

_______________________________

_______________________________

_______________________________

_______________________________

_______________________________

_______________________________

Understanding Earth's different layers helps scientists understand earthquakes. Earth has four main layers. These layers are called the inner core, outer core, mantle, and crust. Some of Earth's layers are cooler than others. The inner core is under great pressure. It is solid. The outer core is very hot. The heat has turned it to liquid. The mantle is not as hot as the outer core. Still, some parts of the mantle are hot enough to be liquid.

The crust is the thinnest layer. Many compare the crust's thickness to the thickness of an apple peel. This is because the crust is very thin compared to Earth's other layers. The crust is not smooth like an apple peel, though. Instead, it is very rocky. The crust is the layer where people, animals, and plants live. This is the part of Earth that breaks apart in an earthquake. ⏸

## Notes

3. What are Earth's four main layers called?

4. If you dug far down into the soil by your home, what do you think you would find? Why?

Parts of Earth's crust are moving all the time. This is because the crust is made up of large pieces called *plates*. The plates move and drift atop the softer mantle beneath them. If you crouch down and touch the ground, you won't feel the plates moving. However, the ground you stand on is part of a very large, moving piece of Earth's crust. Right now, North America and Europe are moving apart. Other continents are also moving toward and away from one another. Many people find this fact disconcerting, but the movement is so slow that people can't feel it. However, this movement slowly changes Earth's landscape. Scientists have learned that this movement also causes earthquakes. ⏸

{ **What is the main idea of this part of the article?** }

## Notes

{ 5. What is Earth's crust made up of? }

____________________

____________________

____________________

____________________

____________________

____________________

____________________

{ 6. Why do you think many people find the idea of moving plates disconcerting? }

____________________

____________________

____________________

____________________

____________________

____________________

____________________

____________________

# Information Log

**Text:** _______________________________

| **{ Subject }** | **{ Notes }** |
|---|---|
| | |

**On-the-Surface**
*who, where, when, and what happened*

**Under-the-Surface**
*how, why, would, could, and should*

## Reflection

_______________________________
_______________________________
_______________________________

# Irregular Past Tense Verbs

**About Irregular Past Tense Verbs**

- A sentence always includes a subject and a verb. The predicate is the part of the sentence that tells something about the subject. The verb and all the words that describe the verb and complete its meaning make up what we call the complete predicate. The simple predicate is just the verb.
- Most past tense verbs are formed by adding *-ed*. Irregular past tense verbs do not form the past by adding *-ed*. Some common irregular past tense verbs are *went, bought, told, felt, thought, heard, hung, ate, slept, kept,* and *knew*.

## Write Irregular Past Tense Verbs

Write the past tense of the verbs in bold. Use words from the word bank.

| thought | said | told | found | bought | felt |
|---|---|---|---|---|---|

1. **find**   We _______________ ourselves in the middle of an earthquake on our trip to California.

2. **feel**   I _______________ it myself.

3. **think**   At first I _______________ I was imagining it.

4. **tell, say**   When I _______________ my father, he _______________ it was a small tremor.

5. **buy**   I _______________ a postcard that shows the San Andreas Fault.

# Find It in Your Reading

Write three sentences from your reading that include irregular past tense verbs. Circle the irregular past tense verbs.

1. _______________________________________________

_______________________________________________

2. _______________________________________________

_______________________________________________

3. _______________________________________________

_______________________________________________

# Put It in Your Writing

Write at least three sentences about a time you were surprised by something in nature. Try to include an irregular past tense verb in each sentence.

_______________________________________________

_______________________________________________

_______________________________________________

_______________________________________________

_______________________________________________

## STEP **1** Making Connections

{DONE ✔}

I will connect what I already know to the memoir "Surviving the Quake" by Helen Garcia and discuss how people in "Surviving the Quake" are affected by natural disasters.



## STEP **2** Developing Vocabulary

I will learn three new vocabulary words: *clench, reverberate,* and *urgent.*

## STEP **3** Practicing Fluency

I will read aloud part of "Earthquake!" with fluency by practicing phrasing and conveying emotion and meaning and chart my fluency progress.

## STEP **4** Building Word Study Skills

I will learn five new high-frequency words.
I will review, practice, and spell compound words.
I will understand the spelling homework assignment.

## STEP **5** Reading for Understanding

I will review the skill of questioning for main idea and supporting details and problem and solution.
I will review the reading strategy of questioning.

## STEP **6** Applying the Conventions of English

I will review my understanding of interrogative sentences.
I will identify and use subject-verb agreement in interrogative sentences using *do* and *did.*

## STEP **7** Writing with Purpose

I will review the *Evidence Organizer* and use a problem/solution frame to complete a first draft of a letter.

{Summarizing My Learning}

# Crossword Puzzle

Read the clues for each number. Write the correct vocabulary word on the puzzle.

**Across**

1. The falling rocks sound as if they shake the walls of the canyon.
2. Christina needs immediate help from the doctor.
3. My grandpa hugs me so hard that I feel like I can hardly breathe.

**Down**

1. When Victor saw his sister faint, he pulled out his cell phone and called 911.
2. The sound of the vase smashing echoed through the house.
3. Manny likes to squeeze a balloon until it pops!

| **Vocabulary** | clench | reverberate | urgent |

## Practice Reading Phrases

1. the thickness of an apple peel

2. breaks apart

3. Right now

4. moving toward and away

5. also causes earthquakes

## Practice Reading Sentences

1. Many compare the crust's thickness to the thickness of an apple peel.

2. This is the part of Earth that breaks apart in an earthquake.

3. Right now, North America and Europe are moving apart.

4. Other continents are also moving toward and away from one another.

5. Scientists have learned that this movement also causes earthquakes.

## Timed Reading

**{ ROLE OF THE READER }**

Read the passage to your partner as accurately as possible.

Remember, your reading goal is 85 Words Correct Per Minute (WCPM).

**{ ROLE OF THE LISTENER }**

As your partner reads, mark these errors with a strikethrough:

- mispronounced words
- skipped words
- changed words
- added words

Excerpt from
# Earthquake!

| | Number of Words |
|---|---|
| The crust is the thinnest layer. Many compare the crust's | 10 |
| thickness to the thickness of an apple peel. This is because the crust | 23 |
| is very thin compared to Earth's other layers. The crust is not smooth | 36 |
| like an apple peel, though. Instead, it is very rocky. The crust is the | 50 |
| layer where people, animals, and plants live. This is the part of Earth | 63 |
| that breaks apart in an earthquake. | 69 |

The crust is the thinnest layer. Many compare the crust's thickness to the thickness of an apple peel. This is because the crust is very thin compared to Earth's other layers. The crust is not smooth like an apple peel, though. Instead, it is very rocky. The crust is the layer where people, animals, and plants live. This is the part of Earth that breaks apart in an earthquake.

Parts of Earth's crust are moving all the time. This is because the crust is made up of large pieces called *plates*. The plates move and drift atop the softer mantle beneath them. If you crouch down and touch the ground, you won't feel the plates moving. However, the ground you stand on is part of a very large, moving piece of Earth's crust. Right now, North America and Europe are moving apart. Other continents are also moving toward and away from one another. Many people find this fact disconcerting, but the movement is so slow that people can't feel it. However, this movement slowly changes Earth's landscape. Scientists have learned that this movement also causes earthquakes.

| | |
|---|---|
| Parts of Earth's crust are moving all the time. This is because the | 82 |
| crust is made up of large pieces called *plates*. The plates move and | 95 |
| drift atop the softer mantle beneath them. If you crouch down and | 107 |
| touch the ground, you won't feel the plates moving. However, the | 118 |
| ground you stand on is part of a very large, moving piece of Earth's | 132 |
| crust. Right now, North America and Europe are moving apart. Other | 143 |
| continents are also moving toward and away from one another. Many | 154 |
| people find this fact disconcerting, but the movement is so slow that | 166 |
| people can't feel it. However, this movement slowly changes Earth's | 176 |
| landscape. Scientists have learned that this movement also causes | 185 |
| earthquakes. | 186 |

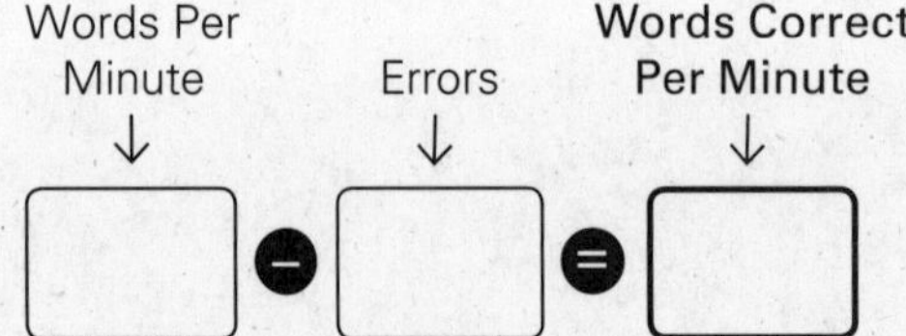

# High-Frequency Words

| mind | clean | grow | kind | because |
| --- | --- | --- | --- | --- |
| place | time | myself | shall | been |

# Words of the Day

______  ______

______  ______  ______

# Missing Letters

Write the missing letter or letters for each Word of the Day. Then write the complete word.

1. **tr**▢  ·····▶ _____ ·····▶ __________

2. **sh**▢▢  ·····▶ _____ ·····▶ __________

3. **b**▢▢**r**  ·····▶ _____ ·····▶ __________

4. **toge**▢▢**er**  ·····▶ _____ ·····▶ __________

5. **ne**▢▢**r**  ·····▶ _____ ·····▶ __________

# Compound Word Practice

Write the smaller words that make up each compound word. Then write the meaning of each compound word.

1. **wastebasket** = _________________ + _________________

2. **toothbrush** = _________________ + _________________

3. **lifeboat** = _________________ + _________________

4. **roommate** = _________________ + _________________

# Apply It

Read the paragraph below about how to prepare for an earthquake. As you read, look for compound words and circle them.

Having a disaster plan can be a lifesaver. The first step in earthquake safety is to prepare in advance. Make a safety kit for your home. Include first aid supplies, canned food and an opener, bottled water, a battery-operated radio, and a flashlight. Choose a safe place in every room where you can hide. It is best to get under sturdy things that can protect you from falling objects. If you live in an earthquake-prone area, bolt bookcases and other tall furniture to the wall. Install latches to cupboards so that items don't come crashing out.

# Spell It

| Compound Word Spelling Rule | The spellings of the smaller words usually stay the same when they are joined to make a compound word. |
| --- | --- |

1. _______________________________

2. _______________________________

3. _______________________________

4. _______________________________

5. _______________________________

# Quick Write

{ What is the main idea of this part of the article? }

# Summary Tree

**Text:** ___________________________________________

1.

2.

3.

---

1.

2.

3.

---

1.

2.

3.

---

1.

2.

3.

Where

When

Who

What Happened

**Summary**

_______________________________________________
_______________________________________________
_______________________________________________
_______________________________________________

# Question Log

**Text:** _______________________________

| Question #1 | Question #2 | Question #3 |
|---|---|---|
| | | |

**On-the-Surface**
*who, where, when, and what happened*

**Under-the-Surface**
*how, why, would, could, and should*

| Question #1 | Question #2 | Question #3 |
|---|---|---|
| | | |

## Summary

_______________________________

_______________________________

_______________________________

# Interrogative Sentences

| **About Interrogative Sentences** | • Many interrogative sentences begin with question words such as *who, how, what, when, where,* or *why.* Many questions also begin with *do.*<br>• Often, part of the verb comes before the subject in an interrogative sentence. Example: *Do you like loud music?*<br>• *Did* is the past tense of *do. Did* can be used as a helping verb to form a past tense interrogative sentence. Example: <u>Did</u> *he do his homework?*<br>• Use the base form of the main verb to complete the interrogative past tense sentence. Use the present tense of the verb. Example: *Did she* <u>go</u> *with you?* |
| --- | --- |

## Choose the Correct Verb in Interrogative Sentences

Circle the correct verb to complete each interrogative sentence.

1. Did I leave/left my book here?

2. Does he has/have a brother?

3. Did you eat/ate your dinner?

4. Did she catch/caught the bus?

5. Does Eric likes/ like to travel?

6. Did you visit/visited your aunt?

7. Did they had/have a good trip?

8. Did we have/had math homework yesterday?

9. Does that picture remind/reminds you of anyone?

10. Did it rained/rain yesterday?

# Find It in a Passage

Underline the interrogative sentences. Circle the simple predicate (the verb) in each one.

Dear Fiona,

Did you get my last e-mail? I did not hear back from you. Did your brother tell you I called after the rain storm?

Did you do anything fun over the weekend? Do you want to come over after school? We can swim at my neighborhood pool.

Write back soon.

Tonya

# Put It in Your Writing

Write at least three questions you want to ask your favorite artist or musician.

___________________________________________

___________________________________________

___________________________________________

___________________________________________

___________________________________________

AGENDA

## STEP **1** Making Connections

{ DONE ✔ }

I will connect what I already know to the journal "An Earthquake That Changed America" by Shelley Tanaka and discuss how the people in "An Earthquake That Changed America" are affected by natural disasters.

## STEP **2** Developing Vocabulary

I will discuss six vocabulary words: *insist*, *crouch*, *disconcerting*, *clench*, *reverberate*, and *urgent*.

## STEP **3** Practicing Fluency

I will read aloud part of "Earthquake!" with fluency by practicing phrasing and using punctuation to inform meaning and chart my fluency progress.

## STEP **4** Building Word Study Skills

I will learn five new high-frequency words.
I will practice and spell contractions.
I will understand the spelling homework assignment.

## STEP **5** Reading for Understanding

I will review the skill of questioning for main idea and supporting details and problem and solution.
I will review the reading strategy of questioning.

## STEP **6** Applying the Conventions of English

I will review my understanding of singular and plural nouns.
I will identify simple predicates and use future tense verbs in my speaking, reading, and writing.

## STEP **7** Writing with Purpose

I will review stages of the writing process, review the first draft of my letter, and complete an *Idea Workshop* to revise for ideas.

{ Summarizing My Learning }

_______________________________________________

_______________________________________________

# Hidden Clues

Read the clues for each number. Write the correct vocabulary word under each clue. The letters in the boxes will complete the answer to the question at the bottom of the page.

1. His mother will demand that Preston clean his room.

___ _1_ ___ ___ ___ ___

2. It was strange to see my teacher at the mall.

___ ___ ___ ___ ___ _2_ ___ ___ ___ ___ ___

3. The school nurse saw Alana fall and immediately called her dad at work.

___ _3_ ___ ___ _4_

4. Sometimes my jaw hurts because I squeeze my teeth too tightly together at night.

___ ___ ___ ___ _5_

5. Rudy, did you bend down to look at that bug through your magnifying glass?

___ ___ _6_ ___

6. I remember the sound of my falling books echoing all the way down the hall.

___ ___ ___ ___ ___ _7_ ___ _8_ ___ ___

## What natural disaster destroyed the narrator's apartment?

a _ a _ _ q _ k _
1  2  3  4  5  6  7  8

| **Vocabulary** | insist | crouch | disconcerting |
| --- | --- | --- | --- |
| | clench | reverberate | urgent |

## Practice Reading Phrases

1. continues to build
2. becomes too great
3. causes many changes
4. all this damage
5. always be in motion

## Practice Reading Sentences

1. The pressure continues to build until a strong movement or slip occurs along the fault line.
2. When the pressure becomes too great, the twig will break.
3. When the plates shift, the movement in Earth's crust causes many changes.
4. A few seconds of shaking can cause all this damage!
5. Scientists know that Earth's plates will always be in motion.

## Timed Reading

{ ROLE OF THE READER }

Read the passage to your partner as accurately as possible.

Remember, your reading goal is 85 Words Correct Per Minute (WCPM).

{ ROLE OF THE LISTENER }

As your partner reads, mark these errors with a strikethrough:

- mispronounced words
- skipped words
- changed words
- added words

Excerpt from
# Earthquake!

| | Number of Words |
|---|---|
| The pressure continues to build until a strong movement or slip | 11 |
| occurs along the fault line. When this happens, Earth's crust may | 22 |
| break apart. The plates may also rise and fall. This is what causes an | 36 |
| earthquake. | 37 |
| To better understand how this happens, you can imagine bending | 47 |
| a small twig between your fingers. The harder the twig is clenched, | 59 |
| the more pressure it must bear at its center. When the pressure | 71 |
| becomes too great, the twig will break. This is like the pressure along | 84 |
| a fault line. Eventually the pressure between the plates becomes too | 95 |
| great, and they must shift. | 100 |
| When the plates shift, the movement in Earth's crust causes | 110 |
| many changes. The soil may move or break apart. Trees may sway | 122 |
| or be torn in two. Buildings may shake and fall. Bridges, roads, and | 135 |
| power lines may also be destroyed. Sounds of destruction reverberate | 145 |
| throughout the affected area. A few seconds of shaking can cause | 156 |
| all this damage! Over many years, earthquakes have shaped Earth's | 166 |
| landscape. They have also caused great destruction. Scientists | 174 |
| know that Earth's plates will always be in motion. Because of this, | 186 |
| earthquakes will continue to change Earth's landscape. | 193 |

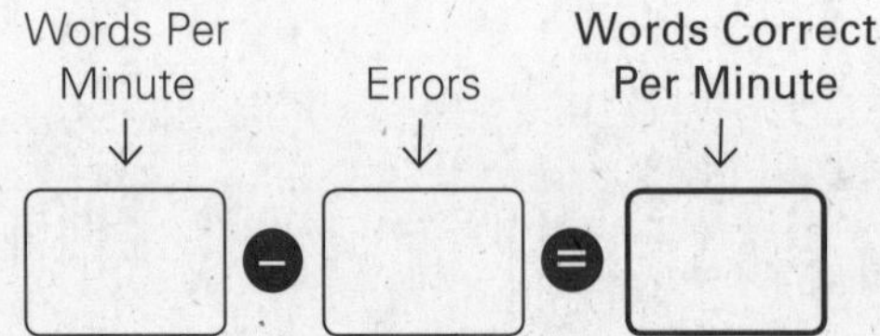

# High-Frequency Words

| | | | | |
|---|---|---|---|---|
| mind | clean | grow | kind | because |
| place | time | myself | shall | been |
| together | never | show | try | bear |

# Words of the Day

# Scrambled Letters

Use the scrambled letters below to spell the Words of the Day.

| that's | only | would | warm | sick |
|---|---|---|---|---|

1. d  u  o  w  l  = __________

2. n  l  y  o  = __________

3. k  i  c  s  = __________

4. h  a  's  t  t  = __________

5. m  a  r  w  = __________

# Word Study Skill

<table>
<tr><td>Morphographs and Contractions</td><td>

- Morphographs are the smallest part of a word that has meaning.
- A contraction is a short way of writing two words as one. The words are combined and an apostrophe (') replaces one or more of the letters.
- Readers can break contractions into two words that they recognize when they know how contractions are formed.

</td></tr>
</table>

# Contraction Practice

Write the two words that make up each contraction. Then write which letter or letters were replaced by the apostrophe (').

1. doesn't = ______ + ______

   ______

2. they'll = ______ + ______

   ______

3. don't = ______ + ______

   ______

4. he'll = ______ + ______

   ______

# Apply It

Read the paragraph below about animals and earthquakes. As you read, look for contractions made with *not* and *will* and circle them.

Do animals know when an earthquake is coming? Some people think so. Imagine an earthquake were to strike tomorrow. In the minutes before, you'll hear wolves howling. Then deer will start to panic. They'll run as if afraid for their lives. Then the earthquake strikes! You might think that animals predicted the quake. Some scientists say this doesn't prove anything, however. They say that animals act strangely for many reasons. They argue that it isn't easy to study animals' behavior before an earthquake. This is because even if animals do know a quake is coming, people who study them usually don't!

# Spell It

| **Contraction Spelling Rule** | For contractions made with *not*, the *n* comes before the apostrophe ('), and the apostrophe (') replaces the *o*. For contractions made with *will*, the apostrophe (') replaces the *wi*. |
| --- | --- |

1. _______________________________

2. _______________________________

3. _______________________________

4. _______________________________

5. _______________________________

## Earthquake! *by Gail Blasser Riley*

*Part 4 of 6*

There are different kinds of earthquakes. A different type of movement causes each one. Each can also happen on a different type of fault. Tight stretching or pulling of Earth's crust causes an earthquake that occurs on a normal fault. An earthquake caused by a thrust fault happens when rock is pressed or squeezed. An earthquake caused by a strike-slip fault happens because of stretching, pulling, pressing, or squeezing. Scientists closely study the movement between different types of faults. They hope to one day predict where and when an earthquake will happen. If scientists can do this, they will save many lives.

### Notes

{ 1. What happens when an earthquake is caused by a thrust fault? }

{ 2. What is the theme or underlying message of this section? }

The San Andreas Fault in California is a strike-slip fault. This fault runs up and down near the coast of California. Movement along this fault caused a huge earthquake in 1906. The earthquake destroyed most of San Francisco. Buildings fell where the ground was soft. Fires started through the city. The fires burned for days and damaged many homes, and the need for help was urgent. There is a lot of movement in the San Andreas Fault. As a result, California will likely experience many more earthquakes.

Earthquakes do not happen only on land. They can also happen on the ocean floor. When an earthquake happens on the ocean floor, the water around the earthquake is pushed outward. When this happens, two natural disasters occur at the same time! As the water pushed by the earthquake travels toward land, it forms waves called tsunamis. ◐

## Notes

3. If a huge earthquake happened again in a California city, what do you think might happen?

_______________________

_______________________

_______________________

_______________________

_______________________

_______________________

4. What other disaster can an underwater earthquake cause?

_______________________

_______________________

_______________________

_______________________

_______________________

_______________________

_______________________

_______________________

_______________________

All earthquakes, above and below water, happen after a break in a fault. The spot where the break reaches Earth's surface is called the epicenter. The epicenter is the place of greatest damage. It is the place where the most energy is released by the earthquake. Special types of waves, known as P-waves, move away from the epicenter. P-waves travel very quickly through Earth's body. As these waves travel they cause damage to Earth's surface. The further from the epicenter they travel, the less damage P-waves cause. The waves lose energy as they move. ⓘ

{ **What are different kinds of earthquakes?** }

## Notes

5. When do all earthquakes happen?

6. Where do you think an earthquake would cause more damage, 10 miles from the epicenter or 100 miles from the epicenter? Why?

# Information Log

**Text:** _______________________________________________

{ **Subject** }  { **Notes** }

On-the-Surface
*who, where, when, and what happened*

Under-the-Surface
*how, why, would, could, and should*

## Reflection

_______________________________________________
_______________________________________________
_______________________________________________

# Future Tense Verbs

<table>
<tr><td>About Future Tense Verbs</td><td>

- A future tense verb is a verb indicating the time of action existing or happening in the future.
- Many future tense verbs are formed by using the helping verb *will* with the main verb. The main verb stays in the base form of the present tense verb. The main verb does not change to agree with singular or plural subjects when it is used with the helping verb *will*.
  **Future:** They <u>will play</u> ball. She <u>will play</u> ball.
- Sometimes another word may come between the helping verb and the main verb.
  **Example:** They <u>will</u> sometimes <u>play</u> ball before school.
</td></tr>
</table>

## Choose Future Tense Verbs

Circle the correct verb to complete each sentence.

1. Delbert will help/helps at a car wash.

2. I will study/studies for the test tonight.

3. Jack will remain/remains home until his chores are done.

4. She will drives/drive when she is sixteen.

5. The cat will stay/stays out all night.

6. He will recites/recite a poem from memory.

7. Lorna will competes/compete in a race on Saturday.

8. Angus and Carlos will take/takes a first aid class.

# Find It in Your Reading

Write three sentences from your reading that include future tense verbs. Circle the future tense verbs.

1. ________________________________________________

________________________________________________

2. ________________________________________________

________________________________________________

3. ________________________________________________

________________________________________________

# Put It in Your Writing

Write at least three sentences about something you plan to do next weekend. Be sure to include at least one future tense verb in each sentence.

________________________________________________

________________________________________________

________________________________________________

________________________________________________

________________________________________________

{ DONE ✔ }

## STEP 1 Making Connections

I will connect what I already know to the journal "An Earthquake That Changed America" by Shelley Tanaka and discuss how the people in "An Earthquake That Changed America" are affected by natural disasters.

## STEP 2 Developing Vocabulary

I will discuss six vocabulary words: *insist, crouch, disconcerting, clench, reverberate,* and *urgent.*

## STEP 3 Practicing Fluency

I will read aloud part of "Earthquake!" with fluency by practicing phrasing and using punctuation to inform meaning and chart my fluency progress.

## STEP 4 Building Word Study Skills

I will learn five new high-frequency words.
I will learn, practice, and spell contractions.
I will understand the spelling homework assignment.

## STEP 5 Reading for Understanding

I will review the skill of questioning for main idea and supporting details and problem and solution.
I will review the reading strategy of questioning.

## STEP 6 Applying the Conventions of English

I will identify and correct double negatives in speaking and reading.
I will write my own sentences using negative words correctly in declarative sentences.

## STEP 7 Writing with Purpose

I will review the problem/solution prompt, *Idea Workshop,* and my first draft and edit my letter for subject-verb agreement.

{ Summarizing My Learning }

# Crossword Puzzle

Read the clues for each number. Write the correct vocabulary word on the puzzle.

**Across**

1. The dog breeder will _______ that you walk a new puppy at least 5 times a day.
2. My dad has a bad knee and can't _______ when we play games.
3. Police sirens _______ through the thin walls of my apartment.

**Down**

1. Sometimes, I _______ my pencil so hard that I hurt my hand.
2. It is _______ that I find my missing homework!
3. My little brother finds it _______ to sleep in a different bed.

| **Vocabulary** | insist | crouch | disconcerting |
| | clench | reverberate | urgent |

## Practice Reading Phrases

1. caused by a strike-slip fault
2. runs up and down
3. a huge earthquake
4. burned for days
5. occur at the same time

## Practice Reading Sentences

1. An earthquake caused by a strike-slip fault happens because of stretching, pulling, pressing, or squeezing.
2. This fault runs up and down near the coast of California.
3. Movement along this fault caused a huge earthquake in 1906.
4. The fires burned for days and damaged many homes, and the need for help was urgent.
5. When this happens, two natural disasters occur at the same time!

## Timed Reading

**ROLE OF THE READER**

Read the passage to your partner as accurately as possible.

Remember, your reading goal is 85 Words Correct Per Minute (WCPM).

**ROLE OF THE LISTENER**

As your partner reads, mark these errors with a strikethrough:

- mispronounced words
- skipped words
- changed words
- added words

# Excerpt from Earthquake!

Number of Words

An earthquake caused by a strike-slip fault happens because of | 10
stretching, pulling, pressing, or squeezing. Scientists closely study the | 19
movement between different types of faults. They hope to one day | 30
predict where and when an earthquake will happen. If scientists can | 41
do this, they will save many lives. | 48

The San Andreas Fault in California is a strike-slip fault. This fault | 60
runs up and down near the coast of California. Movement along this | 72
fault caused a huge earthquake in 1906. The earthquake destroyed | 82
most of San Francisco. Buildings fell where the ground was soft. Fires | 94
started through the city. The fires burned for days and damaged | 105
many homes, and the need for help was urgent. There is a lot of | 119
movement in the San Andreas Fault. As a result, California will likely | 131
experience many more earthquakes. | 135

Earthquakes do not happen only on land. They can also happen | 146
on the ocean floor. When an earthquake happens on the ocean floor, | 158
the water around the earthquake is pushed outward. When this | 168
happens, two natural disasters occur at the same time! As the water | 180
pushed by the earthquake travels toward land, it forms waves called | 191
tsunamis. | 192

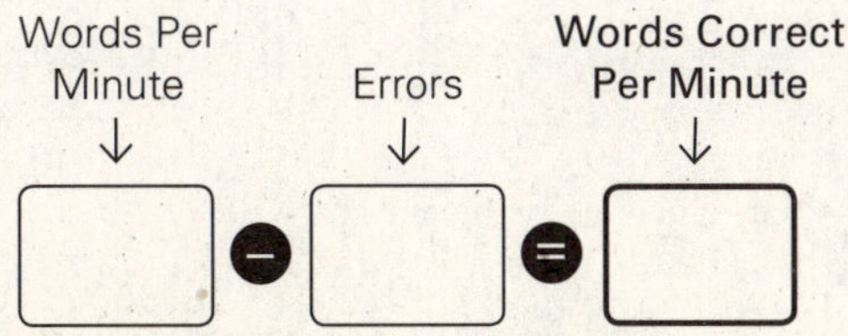

# High-Frequency Words

| | | | | | | |
|---|---|---|---|---|---|---|
| mind | that's | never | myself | kind | warm | bear |
| place | clean | only | show | shall | because | sick |
| together | time | grow | would | try | been | |

# Words of the Day

____________  ____________  ____________

____________  ____________

# Word Riddles

Answer the riddles below with the Words of the Day.

| bread | own | ready | turned | their |
|---|---|---|---|---|

1. Which word could complete this sentence?   I'm __________ to go!

2. Which word is something you eat?   __________

3. Which word rhymes with *hair*?   __________

4. Which word has the same 3 letters as the word *won*?   __________

5. Which word has 2 vowels and 4 consonants?   __________

# Word Study Skill

- Morphographs are the smallest part of a word that has meaning.
- A contraction is a short way of writing two words as one. The words are combined and an apostrophe (') replaces one or more of the letters.

# Contraction Practice

Write the two words that make up each contraction. Then write which letter or letters were replaced by the apostrophe (').

1. { she's = _________ + _________ }

   _________

2. { we're = _________ + _________ }

   _________

3. { he's = _________ + _________ }

   _________

4. { you're = _________ + _________ }

   _________

# Apply It

Read the paragraph below about what to do during an earthquake. As you read, look for contractions made with *are* and *is* and circle them.

Earthquakes are very powerful. They're also frightening. But we're all more likely to stay safe in an earthquake if we follow some simple rules. First, it's important to: Drop! Cover! Hold On! If you're inside, stay there. Keep away from windows. Look for something sturdy, such as a table, and get under it. This will protect you from falling objects. If you're outside, find a place away from buildings, trees, and power lines. Then, drop to the ground and wait until the shaking stops.

# Spell It

| Contraction Spelling Rule | For contractions made with *are,* the apostrophe (') replaces the *a*. For contractions made with *is*, the apostrophe (') replaces the *i*. |
|---|---|

1. _______________________________

2. _______________________________

3. _______________________________

4. _______________________________

5. _______________________________

# Quick Write

What are different kinds of earthquakes?

# Question Log

**Text:** _______________________________________________

<table>
<tr><td>Question #1</td><td>Question #2</td><td>Question #3</td></tr>
</table>

**On-the-Surface**
*who, where, when, and what happened*

**Under-the-Surface**
*how, why, would, could, and should*

<table>
<tr><td>Question #1</td><td>Question #2</td><td>Question #3</td></tr>
</table>

# Summary

_______________________________________________

_______________________________________________

# Double Negatives

| **About Double Negatives** | • Negative words can change the meaning of a statement to mean its opposite. Some negative words are *no, nothing, never, no one, none, nobody, not,* and *nowhere*. |
| --- | --- |
| | • Using two negative words in a sentence changes the meaning again. Do not use a double negative, or two negative words in a sentence, to express a negative idea.<br>**Correct use of negative:** We have no homework tonight.<br>**Double negative:** We don't have no homework tonight. |
| | • Avoid using negative contractions such as *don't, can't,* and *won't* along with a negative word such as *never* or *nobody*. These words can create a double negative. |

## Avoiding Double Negatives

Read each sentence. Use a word from the word box to rewrite each one and make it negative. Be sure you do not create a double negative.

| no | never | none | not |
| --- | --- | --- | --- |
| nothing | no one | nobody | nowhere |

1. There was an earthquake in Japan.

_________________________________________________

2. My father studied earthquakes.

_________________________________________________

3. Earthquakes are all alike.

_________________________________________________

# Find It in a Passage

Read the passage below. Underline each sentence that contains a double negative. Rewrite the sentence correctly on the numbered lines below the passage.

Scientists use the Richter scale to compare earthquakes. This scale measures earthquakes from 1 to 10. An earthquake that measures 5.0 isn't nowhere nearly as strong as one that measures 6.0.

Although earthquakes are common, most people don't never feel them. People don't usually feel earthquakes that measure less than 3.5 on the Richter scale.

1. ______________________________________________

______________________________________________

2. ______________________________________________

______________________________________________

# Put It in Your Writing

Would you like to be an earthquake scientist when you grow up? Write three sentences telling what you think. Include some negative words but be careful not to use double negatives in your writing.

1. ______________________________________________

______________________________________________

2. ______________________________________________

______________________________________________

3. ______________________________________________

______________________________________________

{DONE ✔}



## STEP 1 Making Connections

I will connect what I already know to a photograph and discuss the essential question, *How are people affected by natural disasters?*

## STEP 2 Developing Vocabulary

I will review and complete an assessment of six vocabulary words.

## STEP 3 Practicing Fluency

I will read aloud part of "Earthquake!" with fluency by reading in phrases and chart my fluency progress.

## STEP 4 Building Word Study Skills

I will learn five new high-frequency words.
I will review, practice, and spell contractions.
I will take a spelling test.

## STEP 5 Reading for Understanding

I will review the reading strategy of questioning.
I will review the skill of questioning for main idea and supporting details and problem and solution.

## STEP 6 Applying the Conventions of English

I will review my understanding of declarative and interrogative sentences.
I will create complete sentences using the conventions learned in this chapter.

## STEP 7 Writing with Purpose

I will edit my letter for word choice and verb tense and to correct spelling and punctuation errors.

{Summarizing My Learning}

# Show What You Know

Read each question. Check the box beside the best answer.

1. If you **clench** your fist, you—

   ☐ wash it thoroughly.

   ☐ squeeze it tightly.

   ☐ open it wide.

   ☐ bandage it carefully.

2. Which event would most likely **reverberate** through your school?

   ☐ a new student starting classes

   ☐ a school bus running out of gas

   ☐ a thunderstorm overhead

   ☐ classes letting out for the day

3. It is **disconcerting** to lose your keys.

   Which word would work best as a substitution for the underlined word?

   ☐ funny

   ☐ disturbing

   ☐ common

   ☐ sad

4. If you think that doing laundry is **urgent**, then you will—

   ☐ wash clothes right now.

   ☐ have someone do it for you.

   ☐ do laundry every week.

   ☐ learn how to do it.

5. Select the word that has the most similar meaning to **crouch**.

   ☐ bend

   ☐ stretch

   ☐ squeeze

   ☐ shake

6. To **insist** is to _________.

   ☐ echo and shake a place.

   ☐ bend down low to the ground.

   ☐ squeeze something tightly.

   ☐ say something must be done.

## Practice Reading Phrases

1. to compare earthquakes
2. An earthquake that measures
3. is ten times stronger
4. in hopes of learning
5. to know exactly

## Practice Reading Sentences

1. Scientists use the Richter scale to compare earthquakes.
2. An earthquake that measures 6 or above is very strong.
3. Each number on the scale is ten times stronger than the number before it.
4. Scientists continue to study earthquakes in hopes of learning how to predict them.
5. It is not yet possible to know exactly when and where an earthquake will strike.

## Timed Reading

**{ ROLE OF THE READER }**

Read the passage to your partner as accurately as possible.

Remember, your reading goal is 85 Words Correct Per Minute (WCPM).

**{ ROLE OF THE LISTENER }**

As your partner reads, mark these errors with a strikethrough:

- mispronounced words
- skipped words
- changed words
- added words

Excerpt from
# Earthquake!

Number
of Words

Scientists use the Richter scale to compare earthquakes. This | 9

scale measures earthquakes from 1 to 10. An earthquake that | 19

measures 1 on the Richter scale is the weakest. Though these | 30

earthquakes are common, people don't feel them. People don't usually | 40

feel earthquakes that measure less than 3.5 on the Richter scale. An | 52

earthquake that measures 6 or above is very strong. The South Asia | 64

earthquake in 2005 was a 7.6 quake! | 71

One might guess that an earthquake that measures a 6 on the | 83

Richter scale is not much more powerful than an earthquake that | 94

measures a 5. The fact is that an earthquake measuring 6 is *ten times* | 108

stronger than an earthquake measuring 5. Each number on the scale | 119

is ten times stronger than the number before it. | 128

Scientists have learned a lot about earthquakes. However, they | 137

still have a long way to go. Scientists continue to study earthquakes | 149

in hopes of learning how to predict them. If scientists could predict | 161

the location and strength of an earthquake, many lives could be | 172

saved. It is not yet possible to know exactly when and where an | 185

earthquake will strike. | 188

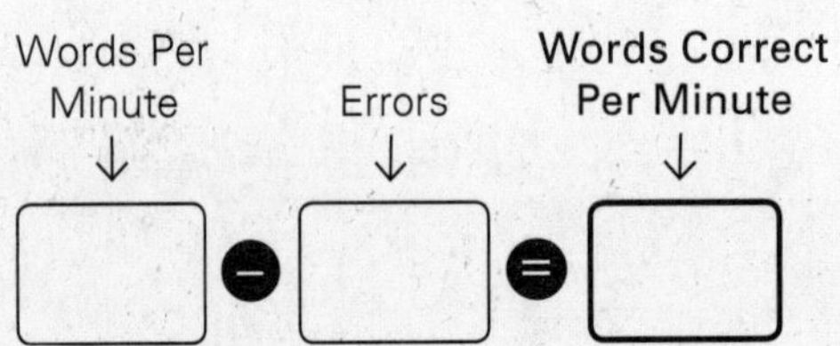

# High-Frequency Words

| | | | | | | |
|---|---|---|---|---|---|---|
| mind | bread | only | show | shall | because | their |
| place | clean | own | would | try | been | |
| together | time | grow | ready | warm | bear | |
| that's | never | myself | kind | turned | sick | |

# Words of the Day

# Alphabetical Order

List the Words of the Day in alphabetical order.

| slow | brother | lady | start | easy |
|---|---|---|---|---|

1.
2.
3.
4.
5.

# Contraction Practice

Write the two words that make up each contraction. Then write which letter or letters were replaced by the apostrophe (').

1. they're = __________ + __________

   __________

2. it's = __________ + __________

   __________

3. you'll = __________ + __________

   __________

4. isn't = __________ + __________

   __________

# Apply It

Read the paragraph below about a class that prepares people for earthquakes. As you read, look for contractions with *not*, *will*, *are*, and *is* and circle them.

It's Thursday night at a San Francisco police station. A group of people waits to begin class. They're part of a special program called Neighborhood Emergency Response Training. These aren't police officers, though. These are ordinary men and women. They are here to help their communities prepare for an earthquake. They'll learn how to prepare for a disaster and how to save lives after an earthquake, too. After ten classes, the students will graduate. Then they'll share what they know with neighborhood families.

# Spell It

| **Contraction Spelling Rule** | For contractions made with *not*, the *n* in *not* comes before the apostrophe ('). For contractions made with *is*, *will*, and *are*, the remainder of the second word comes after the apostrophe ('). |
| --- | --- |

1. _______________________________

2. _______________________________

3. _______________________________

4. _______________________________

5. _______________________________

## Earthquake! *by Gail Blasser Riley*

*Part 6 of 6*

Scientists can predict some things about earthquakes. They can tell how many may happen over a long period of time. They do this by measuring how much stress has built up along fault lines. They can tell when stress is building, and they know how much stress Earth can take. However, they cannot tell exactly when the earthquake will happen. They know only that an earthquake will happen at some point after stress builds.

Scientists can also predict how many aftershocks will happen after an earthquake. Aftershocks are a series of earthquakes that occur after the first quake. An aftershock can be more dangerous than the first earthquake. That is because it affects an already damaged landscape. It is important to predict aftershocks. Doing so helps scientists know how many police officers, firefighters, and rescuers will be needed after a big earthquake.

## Notes

1. What is an aftershock?

_______________________

_______________________

_______________________

_______________________

_______________________

2. What is the theme or underlying message of this section?

_______________________

_______________________

_______________________

_______________________

_______________________

_______________________

_______________________

_______________________

_______________________

_______________________

_______________________

_______________________

Although scientists cannot predict exactly when an earthquake will happen, they do know which regions of the United States are most likely to have earthquakes. For example, they know that more earthquakes are likely to occur in California than in any other state in the U.S. The San Andreas Fault in California moves very slowly. It moves about as fast as a person's fingernails grow. The motion is from east to west. However, there are many pressure points along the San Andreas Fault. Because of the pressure along the fault, California will have many earthquakes in the future. Scientists would like to be able to predict how big these quakes will be. ⏸

## Notes

3. Based on the information in this paragraph, what do you think leaders in California should do about earthquakes?

4. What is the main idea of this paragraph?

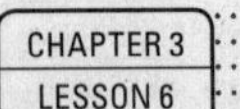

Scientists hope to better understand the pressure that builds along fault lines. They want to know exactly when the pressure along a fault line will become too much. That way they will be able to predict when and where an earthquake will occur. Scientists hope to achieve this understanding not only so they can warn people, but also so they can describe the potential effects of an earthquake. If scientists can one day do this, people will be able to ready themselves and prepare for the changes earthquakes bring. ⏸

**How are people affected by earthquakes?**

## Notes

5. What are two reasons that scientists want to be able to predict when and where an earthquake will occur?

6. What would you do if you knew an earthquake was coming soon?

# Information Log

**Text:** _______________________________________________

| { **Subject** } | { **Notes** } |
| --- | --- |
|  |  |

**Under-the-Surface**
*how, why, would, could, and should*

**On-the-Surface**
*who, where, when, and what happened*

## Reflection

_______________________________________________
_______________________________________________
_______________________________________________

# Conventions Review

## Review Interrogative Sentences

Circle the question word in the interrogative sentence. Then write a sentence to answer the question.

1. Where did you learn about earthquakes?

______________________________________________________

## Review Irregular Past Tense Verbs

Write the irregular past tense of the verb in bold.

1. **lose/get**    We _______________ our way once it _______________ dark.

2. **buy/break**    He _______________ a box of eggs, but they all _______________.

## Review Verbs in Interrogative Sentences

Circle the correct verb to complete each interrogative sentence.

1. Did I leave/left my book here?

2. Did the dog scared/scare you?

3. Does this music bother/bothers you?

## Review Future Tense Verbs

Circle the correct verb to complete each sentence.

1. Rhonda will earn/earns some money babysitting.

2. Luis will travels/travel around the world some day.

3. Tammy will teach/teaches me how to do some jump rope stunts.

## Review Avoiding Double Negatives

Read each sentence. Rewrite each as a negative sentence. Be sure you do not create a double negative.

1. We did hear a loud noise.

_______________________________________________

2. It was important.

_______________________________________________

## Put It In Your Writing

Write three sentences to tell about an earthquake or another event you might hear about on the news. Include at least one interrogative sentence. Use as many of the conventions from this chapter as possible in your writing.

_______________________________________________

_______________________________________________

_______________________________________________

_______________________________________________

{ DONE ✔ }

## STEP 1 Developing Test-Taking Strategies

I will read a test-taking manual.
I will learn strategies for taking multiple-choice tests.

## STEP 2 Assessing My Learning

I will take a multiple-choice test on skills I learned in this chapter.

## STEP 3 Writing with Purpose

I will publish the final draft of my letter.

## STEP 4 Analyzing My Results

I will identify which questions I answered correctly and which questions I answered
   incorrectly.

## STEP 5 Reinforcing My Learning

I will reinforce my understanding of predicting.
I will reinforce my understanding of main idea and supporting details.

## STEP 6 Speaking with Purpose

I will watch a video of a speech and analyze its organizational structure.
I will create an outline for my speech.

{ Summarizing My Learning }

# Test-Taking Manual
## Before the Test

### Be Prepared

- Know what you will be tested on and study.
- Get a full night's rest.
- Have all your materials (pencil, eraser, calculator, dictionary) at your desk.

### Be Comfortable but Alert

- Make sure you have enough room to work.
- Do not slouch in your chair.

### Stay Relaxed and Confident

- Remember that you are well prepared and can do well.
- Take deep breaths if you feel anxious.
- Do not talk about the test with the other students.

## During the Test

Follow these five steps for each question on the test.

**Step 1:** Determine what the question is asking you to do.

**Step 2:** Try to answer the question in your own words.

**Step 3:** Eliminate any answers you know are incorrect.

**Step 4:** Choose the best answer.

**Step 5:** If time allows, review your answers to each question.

## Example Question

**1. Read the title of the article.**

Sewing Made Easy

**You can tell by the title of this article that the author is *probably* going to**

- **A.** tell stories about the inventor of the sewing machine.
- **B.** give simple tips on how to sew.
- **C.** explain why sewing is an important craft.
- **D.** discuss why sewing is difficult.

# Skills Assessment 6

**Read this article, and then answer the questions.**

## Gold Fever

1.  On January 28, 1848, James Marshall discovered gold in California. He was building a sawmill at the American River, when he saw something sparkling in the water. He reached into the water, and pulled out a piece of gold. It was smaller than a bean, but he was sure there was more gold. He was right.

2.  Soon, people everywhere were talking about Marshall's discovery. They thought that life in California had to be better than where they were. If they came to California, they might find gold. It was free. All you had to do was take it. They would no longer be poor. They would be rich! Gold was the answer! People got "gold fever."

3.  By 1849, people from all over the world were hurrying to California to find gold. Some had to travel across the country. Some people had to travel across the sea. They came from as far away as China, Mexico and Chile. This was the beginning of the California Gold Rush.

4.  People who came to find gold were called miners. Most of the miners were men. Some men found a lot of gold, but most men did not. In fact, many of them did not find any gold at all.

5.  Mining for gold was hard work. The miners worked long hours searching for gold. They needed food and supplies to keep working. Some people had the idea to sell food and supplies to the miners. They charged a lot of money. A miner might pay as much as $25 for a meal! That was a lot for people who usually paid less than a dollar for a meal. So, some people got rich from the Gold Rush even though they did not mine gold.

6.  The Gold Rush did not make many people rich. It did change California. Many moved to California looking for gold, but found different jobs instead.  Many moved to cities, like San Francisco. They started new businesses. Many stayed in the country and started new farms. If it were not for "gold fever," California would not be the same today.

*Go on to the next page →*

# Skills Assessment 6, continued

1. **Most of the people who moved to California wanted to**
   A. become farmers.
   B. cook for the miners.
   C. get rich quickly.
   D. move to San Francisco.

2. **Which sentence from the article supports the idea that mining was hard work?**
   A. "People who came to find gold were called miners."
   B. "The miners worked long hours searching for gold."
   C. "They needed food and supplies to keep working."
   D. "The Gold Rush did not make many people rich."

3. **A theme of paragraph 2 is that**
   A. gold can make you sick with fever.
   B. James Marshall discovered gold.
   C. people liked to talk a lot about gold.
   D. people wanted to have a better life.

4. **People were willing to leave their homes because they**
   A. thought life would be better in California.
   B. wanted to start a new business.
   C. had friends living in California.
   D. knew how to be farmers in California.

5. **Which sentence from the article supports the statement that people came from all over the world?**
   A. Some people had to travel across the sea.
   B. This was the beginning of the California Gold Rush.
   C. People who came to find gold were called miners.
   D. Many moved to cities, like San Francisco.

6. **People solved the problem of not finding gold by**
   A. listening to stories about gold.
   B. moving to California with family.
   C. making their own meals.
   D. farming or working in a new business.

7. **Which is a theme of the article?**
   A. Gold is easy to mine when you are near a river.
   B. The discovery of gold changed California.
   C. People should travel to California to mine gold.
   D. James Marshall worked for a sawmill in California.

*Go on to the next page* →

# Skills Assessment 6, continued

**Read this article, and then answer the questions.**

## Panning for Gold

Today, many people still try to find gold. They do this by panning for it. It is called "panning" because to do it, they use a pan. The pan looks like a metal pie pan. To find gold this way, one needs to follow these steps.

1.  Put about four handfuls of sand or gravel from the river into the pan.

2.  Dip the pan into the river to add some water to the sand and gravel. Lift the pan out of the water.

3.  Shake the pan back and forth. The gold will sink to the bottom of the pan.

4.  Pick out the big rocks. Do not take out a shiny rock. It might be gold.

5.  Tilt the pan so that the sand and water will slowly pour out of the pan. Do not tilt it too much or the gold might fall out.

6.  Add more water to the pan. Gently move the pan in a circular motion to help the gold sink to the bottom.

7.  Pour out the last bit of sand and water. Do this slowly and carefully, so the gold does not pour out, too.

8.  Put your gold in a glass container.

*Go on to the next page* →

# Skills Assessment 6, continued

8. **When you pour the sand and gravel out of the pan, you should**
   A. dip the gold into the river.
   B. move the pan in a circular motion.
   C. be careful not to let the gold out.
   D. put it into a glass container.

9. **Which detail supports the idea that it takes time to get the last bit of sand out of the pan?**
   A. "Put about four handfuls of sand or gravel from the river into the pan."
   B. "Do not take out a shiny rock. It might be gold."
   C. "Gently move the pan in a circular motion to help the gold sink to the bottom."
   D. "Do this slowly and carefully, so the gold does not pour out, too."

10. **Based on this article, one could predict that gold will sink to the bottom of the pan because**
    A. gold is shinier than gravel.
    B. gold is heavier than water.
    C. the water cleans the gold.
    D. the pan is shaped like a pie pan.

11. **Based on the article, people will learn that**
    A. you do not need many special tools to pan for gold.
    B. there is more gold in creeks than in rivers.
    C. gold can be found in many places in California.
    D. it is easy to get sand and gravel out of water.

12. **Which is a theme of the article?**
    A. It is still possible to pan for gold.
    B. There are many different types of pans.
    C. Panning is the only way to find gold.
    D. Gold can be found almost anywhere.

**End of test** ■

# Predicting

| Reminder:<br>Predicting | • To predict is to guess what will happen next based on evidence in the text.<br>• Evidence is facts and details that support or confirm an idea, conclusion, or opinion. |
| --- | --- |

## Prediction Log

The title of the text you will read is "The Grizzly: One Interesting Bear." Make a prediction about what you will read. Record your prediction in the prediction log. Then read the passage on page 495. After you read the text, return to this page. Write your evidence summary and then draw a picture of the summary.

**Prediction #1:** What will happen next? _______________

_______________

**Textual Evidence:** What's your proof? _______________

_______________

**Summary:** _______________

_______________

_______________

_______________

### Choices & Challenges
On your own piece of paper…

**A.** Use what you know about why animals may be endangered and write about why you think the grizzly bear is threatened.

**B.** Predict what may happen if laws do not protect the grizzly. Write about your prediction and give evidence for it.

**C.** Write a story about the first year of a grizzly cub's life. What do you predict might happen to it?

# The Grizzly: One Interesting Bear

1     The grizzly bear is a powerful bear that lives in western North America. It is also the bear you see on the state flag of California. Many grizzlies once lived in that state. The grizzly is a symbol of power. Learning about the grizzly bear is very interesting.

2     Grizzly bears are enormous animals. They weigh from 400 to 1,500 pounds. When standing on their hind legs, they may be up to eight feet tall. Male grizzlies are about twice as heavy as females. In spite of their size, grizzlies can run at speeds up to 35 miles per hour.

3     Grizzly bears are part of the brown bear family. Their fur color ranges from blond to deep brown. The color range is a result of differences in their food and the climate where they live.

4     Grizzly bears eat nearly everything. They hunt large animals, such as moose and sheep, and catch many kinds of fish. They may also dine on roots, grasses, nuts, berries, and small animals. Garbage dumps are also favorite grizzly dining sites. People have found grizzlies at their campsites and in their garbage cans.

5     Most grizzlies spend their winters in their dens. Most dens are small caves dug into the soil. Usually grizzlies enter their dens after the first severe winter weather. They come out in spring. All winter long the bears sleep without eating.

6     The mother grizzly has her cubs in winter while she is still in her den. Newborn cubs are tiny and weigh little more than one pound. When they come out of the den three months later, the cubs have gained about 30 pounds. Bear cubs stay with their mother for at least a year. Their mother keeps them safe. She also teaches her cubs. The cubs learn to hunt, recognize enemies, and find good dens.

7     Grizzly bears are considered threatened. About 200 years ago many grizzlies lived throughout western North America. But by 1870, grizzly bears were hard to find. Today laws protect them from people who may want to harm them. Some groups are working to reintroduce grizzlies to places where they once lived. Hopefully these steps will help the grizzly bear survive.

# Main Idea and Supporting Details

| Reminder:<br>Main Idea and<br>Supporting Details | • The main idea is the most important point, opinion, or message in a text.<br><br>• Supporting details are the facts that support or confirm an idea, conclusion, or opinion. |
| --- | --- |

## Information Log

Look back at "The Grizzly: One Interesting Bear." Then read each main idea in the *Subject* column below. In the *Notes* column write two or three details that support each main idea in the *Subject* column.

| { Subject } | { Notes } |
| --- | --- |
| Grizzly bears are enormous animals. | |
| Grizzly bears eat nearly everything. | |
| The mother grizzly has her cubs in winter while she is still in her den. | |
| Grizzly bears are considered threatened. | |

On-the-Surface
*who, where, when, and what happened*

Under-the-Surface
*how, why, would, could and should*

## Reflection

# Identify the Main Idea and Supporting Details

Turn back to page 495 and reread the article "The Grizzly: One Interesting Bear." Then answer these questions.

1. **All of the following support the idea that grizzly bears eat nearly everything *except***

   A. They hunt large animals, such as moose and sheep, and catch many kinds of fish.

   B. Garbage dumps are also favorite grizzly dining sites.

   C. The color range is a result of differences in their food and the climate where they live.

2. **Which sentence *best* summarizes the main idea of paragraph 6?**

   A. Grizzly cubs grow a lot during their first year of life.

   B. It is amazing that tiny newborn cubs survive.

   C. The mother grizzly bear takes good care of her cubs.

3. **Which sentence from the article supports the statement that grizzly bears are enormous animals?**

   A. They weigh from 400 to 1,500 pounds.

   B. Male grizzlies are about twice as heavy as females.

   C. In spite of their size, grizzlies can run at speeds up to 35 miles per hour.

4. **From reading "The Grizzly: One Interesting Bear," we can tell all of the following *except***

   A. what it eats.

   B. why it is endangered.

   C. what it looks like.

## Choices & Challenges
On your own piece of paper...

A. Write the who, where, when, and what happened for "The Grizzly: One Interesting Bear." Then use these facts to write a summary.

B. Write about another interesting animal you know something about. Tell what it looks like, what it eats, and other details.

C. Use the information from this article to write a story about the life of a grizzly bear.

## STEP 1 Assessing My Learning

{DONE ✓}

I will take a multiple-choice test on skills I learned in this unit.

## STEP 2 Speaking with Purpose

I will practice giving my speech with my partner.
I will get and give feedback to my partner about the speeches.

## STEP 3 Discussing the Essential Question

I will review all the texts from the unit.
I will discuss the texts and the unit's essential question with my partner.
I will write a reflection about the essential question.

{Summarizing My Learning}

# Discussing the Essential Question

Think about each theme question and how it helps you answer the essential question. Discuss each theme question with your partner. Write down your thoughts.

How do fire and water disasters affect people? Give some examples from the texts.

How do tsunamis affect people? Give some examples from the texts.

How do earthquakes affect people? Give some examples from the texts.

# Reflect on the Essential Question

Think about this unit's essential question. Using your prior knowledge from all texts and activities you have read and done, write everything you know about this question.

> How are people affected by natural disasters? Give some examples from the texts.

## STEP **1** Writing on Demand

{DONE ✓}

I will use a writing prompt to independently write and publish a final draft.

## STEP **2** Speaking with Purpose

I will present my speech to the class.
I will get and give feedback to my partner about the speeches.

{Summarizing My Learning}

___________________________________________

___________________________________________

___________________________________________

On-Demand Writing: On-demand writing is your opportunity to practice all five stages of the writing process independently. No one can help you, but you can use everything you have learned about the writing process to help you be successful. Use the checklist below to help you write an effective response to the prompt:

**PREWRITING**

- ☐ Read the prompt carefully.
- ☐ Deconstruct the prompt by circling the verbs, underlining what the verbs tell you to do, and numbering each feature.
- ☐ Identify different prewriting strategies you could use for this prompt:
  - Topic Toss
  - Problem/Solution Organizer
  - Evidence Organizer. Problem/Solution Letter
- ☐ On scratch paper, create and complete your own copy of one of the graphic organizers.

**WRITING**

- ☐ Write your first draft neatly in the space provided: Remember, even if your ideas are good, if the person reading your response can't read your writing you will not receive a high score.

**REVISING**

- ☐ Reread the deconstructed prompt and draw a check or circle next to each feature. For any missing features, go back to your draft and decide where you can make this revision.
- ☐ Read your draft carefully to make sure you said what you meant to say.
  - Add details that are missing.
  - Delete details that aren't relevant.
  - Reorganize any details that are not in a logical sequence.

**EDITING**

- ☐ Edit your draft carefully. Use proofreader's marks to edit for:
  - word choice
  - spelling
  - grammar
  - punctuation

**PUBLISHING**

- ☐ When you are sure that you have written an effective response to the prompt, you are ready to turn in your draft.

# Fluency Progress Chart: Unit 1

For each lesson, graph the number of words correct per minute by shading to the nearest number. Try to reach the **GOAL** of 80 WCPM. Remember, WCPM only measures accuracy and pacing. Intonation and expression are also important to reading with fluency.

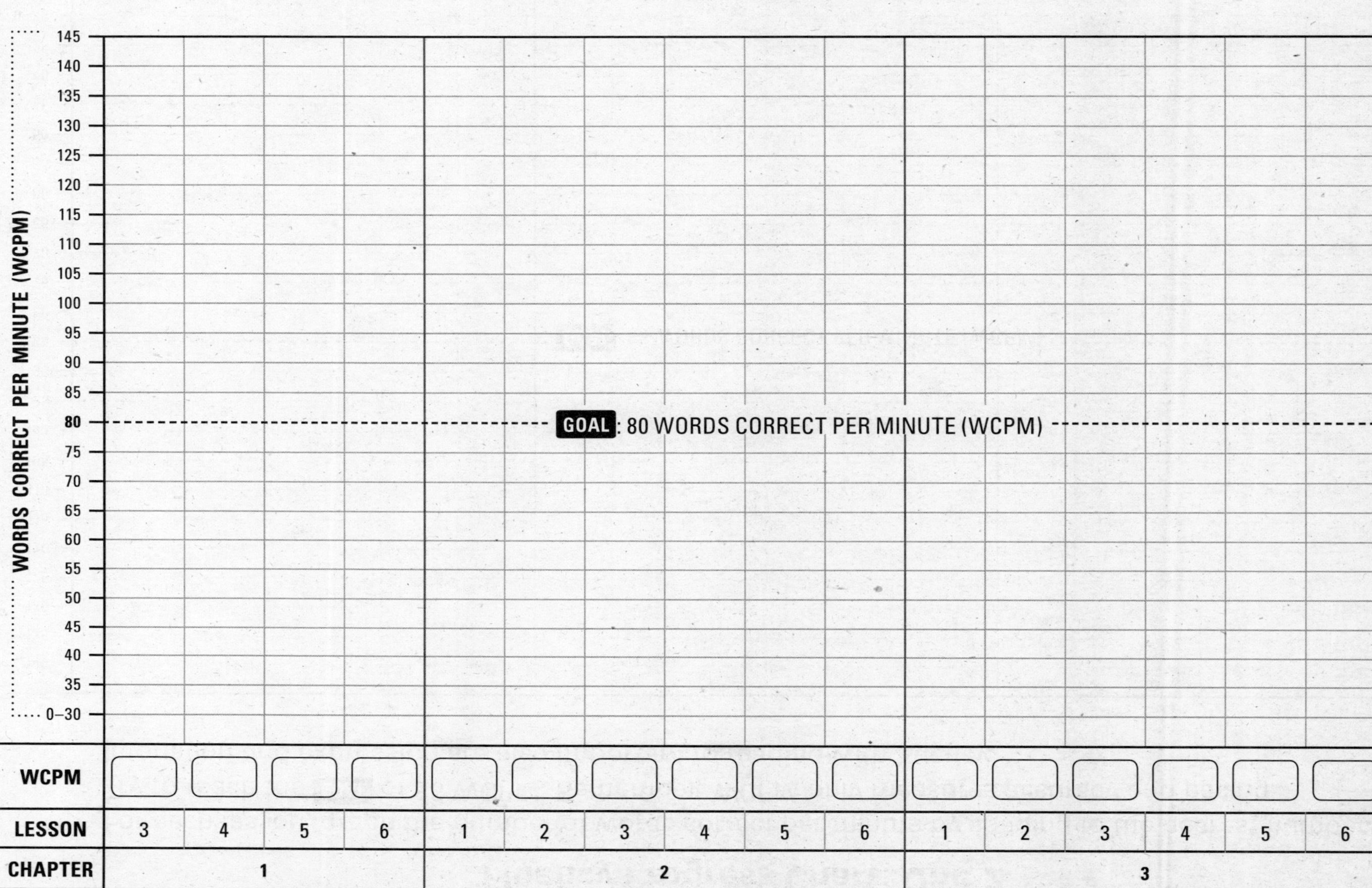



| WCPM | | | | | | | | | | | | | | | | |
|---|---|---|---|---|---|---|---|---|---|---|---|---|---|---|---|---|
| **LESSON** | 3 | 4 | 5 | 6 | 1 | 2 | 3 | 4 | 5 | 6 | 1 | 2 | 3 | 4 | 5 | 6 |
| **CHAPTER** | 1 | | | | 2 | | | | | | 3 | | | | | |

# Fluency Progress Chart: Unit 2

For each lesson, graph the number of words correct per minute by shading to the nearest number. Try to reach the **GOAL** of 85 WCPM. Remember, WCPM only measures accuracy and pacing. Intonation and expression are also important to reading with fluency.

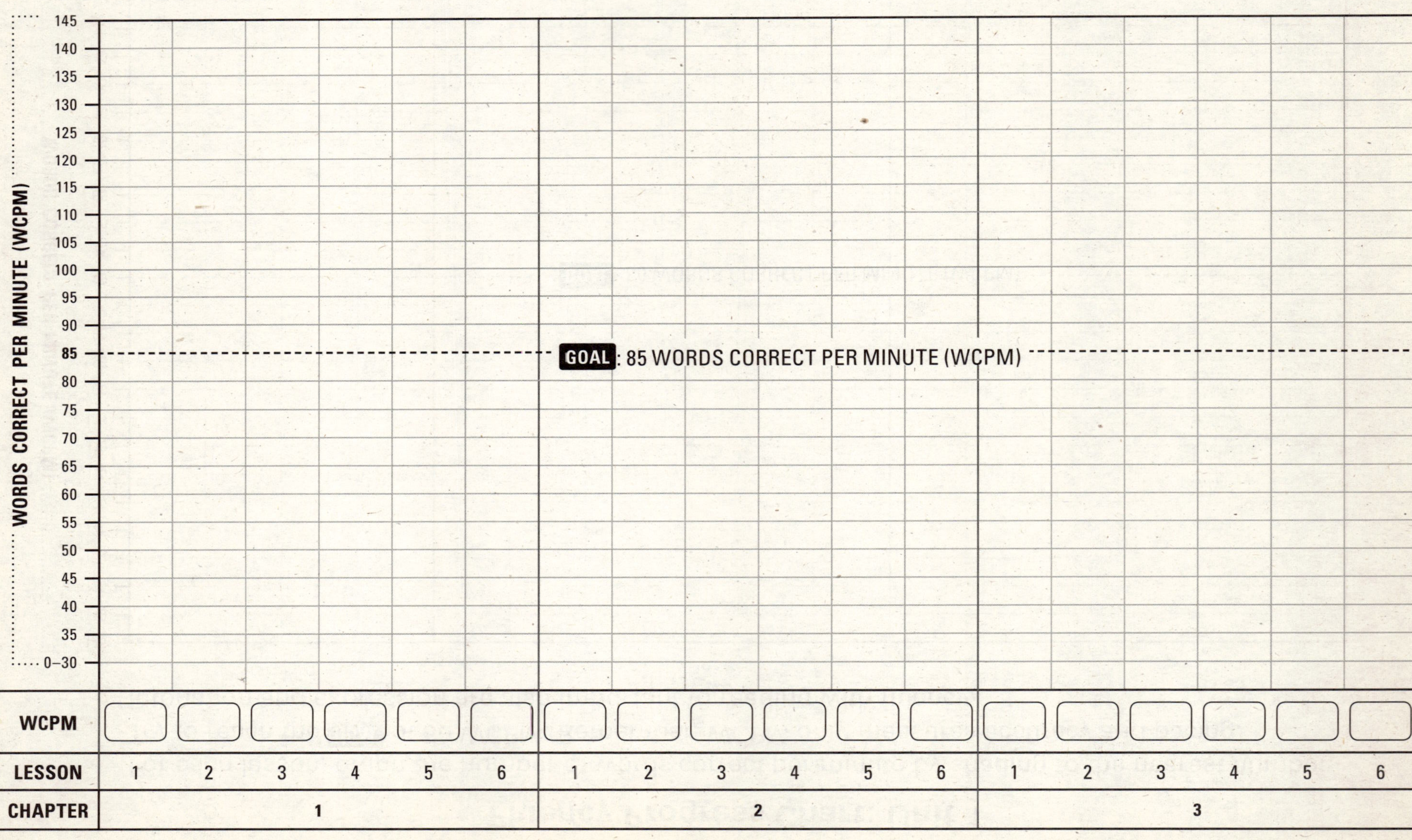


| WCPM | | | | | | | | | | | | | | | | | | |
|---|---|---|---|---|---|---|---|---|---|---|---|---|---|---|---|---|---|---|
| **LESSON** | 1 | 2 | 3 | 4 | 5 | 6 | 1 | 2 | 3 | 4 | 5 | 6 | 1 | 2 | 3 | 4 | 5 | 6 |
| **CHAPTER** | | | 1 | | | | | | 2 | | | | | | 3 | | | |

## {a}

**accuracy**
reading words, phrases, and passages correctly

## {b}

**boldface type**
special type used to emphasize or highlight a word or words

## {c}

**caption**
a line of text that explains what is shown in a picture or illustration

**character**
a person or an animal in a story

**clarify**
to determine meaning of unknown vocabulary or unclear ideas

**coherence**
the arrangement and connection of details in a text so that they make sense to the reader

**compare and contrast**
compare: to look at how two or more things are similar; contrast: to look at how two or more things are different

## conventions
rules that support the correct spelling and grammar of a language

## {e}

**edit**
to correct spelling, grammar, and punctuation errors

**evidence**
facts and details that support an idea, conclusion, or opinion

**expository text**
a text that informs the reader and includes facts and details

**expression and intonation**
reading in a way that sounds like natural speech

## {f}

**fluency**
reading aloud correctly with understanding, and at a speed, expression, and intonation that sounds like natural speech

## {g}

**genre**
the different types of written expression

$\{i\}$

**italics**
special type used to emphasize or
highlight a word or words

$\{m\}$

**main idea**
the most important point, opinion, or
message in a text

$\{n\}$

**narrative**
a story that has characters, setting,
and plot

**narrator**
a person or character who tells the story

$\{p\}$

**pacing**
reading at a speed that is right for the text
type

**plot**
the main events of a story that include a
beginning, middle, and end

**poetry**
writing that expresses the writer's
thoughts, often with rhythm or rhyme

**predict**
to guess what will happen next based on
evidence in the text

**preread**
to discuss texts before reading

**prewrite**
to develop ideas about a topic before
writing

**problem and solution**
the part of a narrative plot that states the
issue (the problem) and the resolution of
that issue (the solution)

**proofread**
to read and mark corrections in a text

**publish**
to make a piece of writing available to the
public

$\{q\}$

**question**
to explore information by making
thoughtful inquiries

$\{r\}$

**revise**
to improve ideas and organization by
adding, deleting, and rearranging text

{s}

**sentence**
a group of words that contains a subject and a verb and expresses a complete thought

**setting**
the place and time of a story

**subtitle**
a secondary title that tells more about the text

**summarize**
to restate the main idea by including only the important details

**supporting facts and details**
pieces of evidence that support an idea, conclusion, or opinion

{t}

**theme**
what the story reveals about life

**title**
the main heading used to identify a text

**topic sentence**
a sentence in a paragraph that points to a single main idea

{v}

**visual aids**
graphic features such as maps, charts, tables, and illustrations used to help the reader picture something described in the text

{w}

**write**
to create a first draft